Tunnel of Light

Published by
William & Warren
1200 Paint Rock Rd.
Kingston, TN 37763

ISBN: 0-9652007-1-X

Printed in the United States.

Text and cover design: Debbie Patrick

About the Author

Richard Dew has published a widely acclaimed book of poetry, *Rachel's Cry.* He has written and lectured extensively on coping with grief and loss. *Tunnel of Light* is his first novel. Dr. Dew received his medical degree in 1965 from the University of Tennessee. He has been in family practice for 35 years in East Tennessee, where he makes his home with his wife, Jean.

To Ron
Richard A Dew

Acknowledgements

I am deeply indebted to many people who helped me bring Tunnel of Light *to print: First and foremost to Jude Martin who critiqued, cajoled, prodded and proofread throughout the entire project and remained supportive even while disagreeing with several points; to Carolyn Dipboye who helped with spiritual concepts and suggested critical changes in focus; to June Gibbs and Phyllis Finlay who edited tons of typos and grammatical errors; to Debbie Patrick for her help in the final touches for publication; and last, but by no means least, to my many friends in The Compassionate Friends who have walked with me as we personally experienced many of the major themes of this book.*

to Jean

Chapter 1

"They didn't have heart attacks just to spite me," he muttered, but this rationalization didn't help. The fact remained, Dave DeMarco was late. Again. You idiot, he silently berated himself. You just had to be Super Doc. Three months ago he promised Kelli he'd chaperone the prom. A colleague even offered to see his patients for him, but, as usual, he had declined and hoped for the best. When the second coronary patient hit the emergency room, he knew he'd blown it.

Come on, come on. His fingers drummed on the steering wheel as he paused for three cars in the gymnasium parking lot. Grabbing the first available space, he jumped from the car and loped past couples in technicolored tuxes and billowing gowns. Dave headed for a large cluster of students on the lawn beside the curving drive.

He leaped back as a dark station wagon roared past. "Hey, watch out!" he shouted, but it was too late. Never swerving, the car catapulted the curb and hurtled toward the milling mass of students who scattered—all but the one who apparently never saw it coming. Her pale green chiffon gown fluttered as she bounced from the bumper into the windshield and over the car. She landed heap, twitched twice and then was still.

Dave vaulted a low hedge and sprinted to where the girl lay face down in a circle of light from a nearby street lamp. Her right leg jutted out at an odd angle. The back of her head was flattened and bits of skull protruded through the bloody tangle of hair.

"Someone call 911," he yelled. Several bystanders scampered toward the gym. Placing his coat under the girl's head to stabilize her neck, he gently rolled her onto her back. The blank, dilated eyes of his daughter stared up at him. Kelli. Oh, God no. She wasn't breathing. Frantically he felt for a pulse in her neck and, finding none, he began mouth-to-mouth respiration.

"What do you want me to do?" It was Don Morgan the football coach.

"No pulse," Dave gasped. "You breathe her. I'll pump."

Each time he paused for Don to breathe, Dave prayed silently. "Oh, God, help her, don't let her die. Come on, Kelli, breathe, please."

A lifetime later, Dave watched as the EMTs continued CPR, and loaded her into the ambulance.

Above the roar of the departing ambulance someone yelled, "Mrs. DeMarco, don't go over there." Betty ran to him.

"What happened?" she asked.

He stared at the retreating ambulance.

"Dave, what happened?...Dave!"she jerked his lapel.

"It's...it's Kelli."

"Oh, no! What happened? Is she hurt? How is she? Dave?"

He struggled to comprehend the situation.

"Dave, how is she?"

"She...I...It doesn't look good."

She grabbed his hand and tugged. "We've got to get to the hospital. Where's the car?" He gestured in the general direction of the driveway. As Betty dragged him across the lawn, Sarah Maxwell, her best friend, intercepted them.

"Come with me; my car's right here. You shouldn't be driving anyway."

On the way to the hospital Dave gave a fragmented account of what had happened. As soon as they stopped at the emergency entrance, Betty burst from the car and dashed into the ER.

"Go with her." Sarah shoved Dave out the door. "I'll park the car and be right in."

Dave found two nurses barring Betty from the trauma room.

"I'm her mother. I'm a nurse. Let me go in!" Betty shouted.

Dave took her hand. "Wait here just a minute. I'll check on her."

Jodie, the head ER nurse, stepped between him and the door.

"Dr. DeMarco, you know neither of you should be in there; you'll just get in the way." They both strained to see into the room, but she took his hand, put her other arm around Betty and pulled them back. "Come on, let's go to the Quiet Room. You can't stay here, and the waiting room's starting to fill up with students." Jodie half dragged, half guided them out of the treatment area. Their eyes remained riveted on the small window in the entrance to the trauma room until the swinging doors shut. She led them to a door with a stained glass panel, ushered them into a small, dimly lit room, and assumed her position outside. "Thank goodness," she said when she recognized Sarah charging headlong down the hall. "Mrs. Maxwell, could you stay with them? Dr. Maxwell's working on their daughter."

"Of course." Sarah paused before entering. "How is she?" she whispered.

Jodie's chin quivered. She shook her head then turned and vanished through the double doors.

Dave hunched forward on a sagging ottoman, clenching and unclenching his fists. Why didn't I just take the afternoon off like Betty asked?

Betty paced back and forth in the small room, her breath coming in shallow gasps . Pausing for a moment she said, "What are they doing? What's taking so long? Why don't they tell us something?" then resumed her pacing.

Dave sprang to his feet and grasped Betty's hand when the door opened and Bob stepped in. His eyes were red.

"Bob?...Bob?" Betty's voice rose in pitch with each word.

He put his arms around them both. "I'm so sorry. There was nothing we could do."

ॐ

"I don't think this is a good idea," Dave said with growing apprehension. "Just let Tom do it. Come on, Betty, please."

Betty didn't look up but remained intent on the hissing steam iron as she pressed the pleats in the yellow and black plaid skirt for the third time.

He sighed and leaned against the doorframe of the laundry room. He was dead tired, but his mind raced, skipping from one jumbled recollection to another, the nightmare of the last twenty-four hours reduced to a horrific blur. At the same time insignificant, disjointed objects grabbed his attention with crystal clarity, but just for a moment—the box of Tide on the shelf, his work shoes by the door, the ant crawling up the Christmas cactus in the window.

The iron spat as Betty set it aside. She ran her fingers gently across the fabric. Holding up the skirt for one final inspection, she picked off an invisible bit of lint, then clipped it to a hanger and hung it on the back of the door. Her eyes were swollen and red but set with a steely resolve.

"I was the first person to dress her, and I'll dress her now." She took a long-sleeved white blouse from the counter and spread it. "I won't allow some strange men to put clothes on her. She wouldn't have it." She returned her attention to the blouse.

The only sounds were the creak of the ironing board, the wheeze of the iron and the smooth swish as it slid over the slick fabric. Dave started to speak, then, feeling somehow chastened, turned and walked down the hallway to the sunroom where Bob and Sarah Maxwell, their best friends, sat. A suffocating fog of sadness filled the house, stifling breath and muffling speech.

"Sarah, can you talk some sense into her?"

"Dave, this is something she feels compelled to do; it's important to her. In her position, I might do the same."

He rubbed his temples. "It's unnatural; it's macabre. I think she's losing it; maybe we both are."

"Just let her do what she must. You might just be driven to do something that seems weird yourself."

His jaw clenched. "Yeah, like getting the creep that did this. I'd like to kill him."

Bob and Sarah exchanged worried glances as Dave pace around the room smacking a clenched fist into his open palm.

They looked up when Betty entered the room carrying the skirt, blouse and a small tote bag. Her movements were deliberate, almost mechanical, as if she had to consciously remember how to walk and move. Her listless eyes gazed through them, fixed somewhere in the distance.

"It's time. Could you carry that box with her shoes?" she said in a monotone to no one in particular.

"Mrs. DeMarco, are you sure you want to do this?" Tom Wells, the stocky funeral director in a black suit, was backed against the double doors as if guarding them from an unwanted assault. His somber expression was giving way to near panic. "We can do it for you, and then you can make any adjustments you want."

"Thank you, no, I'm going to do this myself. Now would you please let me in?" She took a step forward, almost bumping him.

"Yes, yes, of course." From the tone in her voice, he knew better than to argue.

Betty looked at Dave.

"I can't, I just can't, I'm sorry," he faltered. "I haven't seen her naked since she was a baby. It would be like violating her."

She nodded and opened the door. Sarah took the shoebox from Dave and followed.

"I'll be right here." The door closed, cutting off his plaintive reassurance.

"Oh." The sound was somewhere between a whimper and a moan. Betty drew back, hesitant to go farther.

Tom had described everything in detail in an attempt to prepare them, but it didn't help, and he'd forgotten to mention the acrid aroma of formaldehyde which stung their noses and eyes despite the two cans of air-freshener he'd used. This, combined with the sweet scent of past and present sprays of flowers that seemed to have seeped into the pores of the entire building, was almost nauseating. The room was dark except for the bright light in the center. Kelli, covered from the neck down by a sheet, lay on a stainless steel table beneath the light.

Sarah grasped Betty's hand.

Betty took a deep breath. "I'm okay," she said, her jaw set.

Sarah fumbled with the switch beside the door, and more lights flickered on, making the room less foreboding.

Betty laid the clothes on a metal folding chair that Sarah retrieved from against the wall then stood looking down at Kelli. She appeared to be sleeping; her lips looked almost ready to smile. Betty stiffened as she caressed her cheek. The embalmed flesh was cold and hard, almost like a statue. Her fingers trembled as she folded the sheet down, but only to the waist, in an irrational attempt to keep her warm. Kelli appeared unmarked because most of her injuries had been to her back. Tom had taken care to cover any scrapes and bruises with makeup, matching the near perfection of her re-styled hair.

Uncertain of where to start, they hesitated then began the rite tainted by modern fears and funeral practice but as old as human existence. Though numbed by grief, Betty still sensed an air of awe and reverence as they dressed her. They handled her gently as if the use of any force might cause a stiffened limb to just snap off. After Betty smoothed the skirt and blouse, they stepped back and stood in silence for several minutes.

"This was her favorite outfit. We got it at Macy's in Atlanta. She wouldn't have wanted to wear some frilly party dress." Betty fumbled for a tissue and blew her nose. "I'll bet she'd rather have worn her basketball uniform."

Sarah began to cry softly when Betty made minute adjustments to Kelli's hair and then took a small pair of scissors from her pocket, snipped a lock from the back, tied it with a pink ribbon, and placed it in a small jewelry box.

"Would you like to be alone?" Sarah asked.

Betty bit her lip and nodded.

After the door closed, Betty slumped, steadied herself on the edge of the table and stared in disbelief at the unmoving form which twenty-four hours before had been swirling around the living room—a gay, diaphanous blur.

She stooped, lifted the tote bag into the chair and retrieved a small bottle of Kelli's favorite perfume. The aroma accentuated the visions of last evening as she dabbed it behind Kelli's ears and in the hollow of her throat.

Returning to the bag she withdrew a linen handkerchief which was tied in a dainty bundle. Fumbling because of her blurred vision, she fought with the knot, almost spilling the linen's contents when it loosened. She spread the cloth on Kelli's skirt. The worn silver ring had been passed from mother to daughter on her wedding day for four generations. Betty's hands trembled as she slipped it onto

Kelli's finger. She raised the last item and held it at arm's length under the light. The delicate butterfly dangling from the fragile gold chain shimmered and almost seemed ready to take flight. Dave had given it to Kelli on her sixteenth birthday. "Fly away with my baby," Betty whispered as she fastened it on her neck.

Stepping back Betty tried to absorb the immensity of what had happened. She looked down at the silent form, then began to gently stroke Kelli's hair and kiss her cheeks and lips, taking care to prevent her tears from mussing the makeup. She wrapped her arms around the cold, rigid body, laid her head on her daughter's breast, and began to croon her favorite lullaby; "Where are you going, my little one, little one? Where are you going my darling, my life? Turn around and you're two, turn around and you're four, turn around and you're a young girl going out of the door..." singing her to sleep one last time.

"Do you think I should go get her?" Dave asked. "It's been over an hour."

"Let's just wait," Sarah said. "She needs this time alone with her."

Five minutes later the door swung open and Betty rushed out and pressed her face against Dave's chest. Her body shook with her hoarse sobs. For once Dave didn't try to make it okay but let her cry herself into exhaustion and become quiet.

"I'm ready to go home," she said, her monotone returning.

"I'd like to stay a while. Will you be okay?" Dave asked.

She looked deep into his eyes. Her chin began to quiver, and she kissed him quickly on the cheek.

"I'll be fine."

After the others had left, Dave turned to Tom.

"There's no need for you to stay. Just lock up; I'll let myself out."

"It's no bother. I'll wait," Tom said.

"I'd rather be alone."

Tom nodded. "I understand."

Yeah, sure you do.

Tom stood at the door for a while after Dave went in. At first there was no sound, then he heard deep guttural sobs and finally a long, moaning wail, almost a howl, began echoing from the room. Tom shook his head and shuddered. He locked the door, rushed to his car and didn't look back.

Dave was sitting in the chair beside Kelli when Tom returned the next morning.

ℬ

Dave watched as the last of the crowd trickled down the hill leaving him, Betty, Bob and Sarah and John Rankin, their pastor, in the small canvas pavilion. Two laborers slouched by their backhoe parked up the slope from the grave. The last two days had been like a surreal movie that Dave felt he'd viewed from somewhere outside of himself, just a numb bystander. The visitation, friends coming and going, the memorial service all were jumbled events remembered only as disconnected flash frames of activity. If asked to piece together some semblance of a chronology, he could not.

Dozens of long-stemmed roses dropped by friends and classmates lay on and around the casket, while strategically placed sprays of flowers hid the mound of dirt beneath a green indoor-outdoor carpet. Betty clasped his hand and stared with dull, sunken eyes at the shiny steel box. She hadn't eaten or slept in two days.

John came to them, followed by Sarah and Bob.

"I wish there was something I could say or do. I can't imagine how you must feel." The DeMarcos said nothing. "If you need me for anything, please call."

"Thank you," Dave said gazing somewhere over the pastor's head. "Could you take Betty home?" Dave asked Sarah. "I want to stay a while."

"Why don't you come on with us?" Bob asked.

"I need to stay."

He kissed Betty on the cheek. Bob kept looking back at him as they made their way to the car and drove away.

Dave sat in the hard folding chair staring at the casket for almost an hour. Finally, the two men shuffled down the hill. They wore coveralls and boots, and neither appeared to have shaved in several days. The taller man shifted his chew of tobacco, spit and walked under the pavilion.

"I'm sorry," he said—not unkind, very business-like—"but we have to start cleaning up if we're going to get done by dark."

Dave nodded, picked up his chair, stepped back a few yards and sat down again.

When they realized that Dave wasn't leaving, they began to disassemble the pavilion. Intimidated by Dave's presence, they worked in silence throwing furtive glances at him as they lowered the casket while he just sat and stared. When they'd removed the flowers and the carpet from the mound of dirt, Dave rose, walked to them, and took the shovel from the shorter man.

"I'd like to take over from here."

"You can't do that. We'll get fired," the tall man protested.

"I've talked with the caretaker. He said it's okay."

"I can't let you do that."

"Look," Dave said, his voice now flat and hard, "I'm going to do this. You'll be paid. Here," he opened his wallet and took out a fifty, "if I'm not done by dark, this will cover your trouble for coming back in the morning and arranging the flowers."

The tall man hesitated a moment longer and looked at the other one, who shrugged.

"All right, but if you get hurt, it's on your head. Understand?" he said grabbing the bill.

"Understood."

Their animated conversation faded as they hustled down the hill, got into a battered blue pickup and drove off.

Dave laid his coat on the chair and rolled up his sleeves. No way I'm going to have Kelli ushered from this earth by two unshaven, tobacco-chewing rednecks. No, it's more than that. Maybe this is penance for not going to the prom, for letting Kelli down, for not keeping it from happening. I'm her father. A father's supposed to protect his child, and she's dead. Some father.

He stamped the shovel into the soft mound and hoisted a heavy load of soil. As he shoveled scoop after scoop into the grave, the clods of dirt pounded on the casket lid like muffled drums in a cortege. Soon the casket lid disappeared, and the only sounds were his heavy breathing and the now dull clump of dirt in the diminishing hole. His shirt was soaked with sweat, but he refused to slow down. The sun was settling behind the ridge when he finished. He leaned on the shovel, panting and gasping. Mud caked his shoes and smeared his pants. Dropping the shovel, he fell to his knees onto the rounded pile of earth and very gently smoothed any irregularities. The musty smell of fresh loam rose around him, and from a nearby dogwood, a mockingbird trilled. Clutching two handfuls of dirt to his breast, Dave raised his face skyward.

"Why?" His long, piercing scream reverberated through the darkened hills and hollows, and each fading echo returned unanswered.

Chapter 2

Dave had been raised by three sets of foster families and had no memory of his parents . Because he was by nature pleasant and eager to please, there were never any major conflicts, so they accepted and, to a degree, loved him. For reasons he could never fathom, no tight bonds ever developed, and, after his departures, the few short-lived efforts at maintaining contact left no scars or ill will—just an acceptance of the way things were.

He was exceptionally bright, though not brilliant, and physically attractive, but not strikingly handsome with dark hair and soft brown eyes.

Around age eleven, he had decided to become a doctor, a decision from which he never wavered and later never fully understood, since he'd enjoyed good health and seldom saw a physician professionally or socially. With the logic and practicality that became characteristic, he realized this career choice would require financial assistance, so he forsook sports for studying. He did well in school and received a full scholarship to Eastern Kentucky University where he graduated with honors, then financed medical school with part-time jobs and student loans. His friendly demeanor and good sense of humor caused him to be well-liked by most, but he had few confidants or close friends, and never became truly close to anyone except Betty, Kelli, and Bob. Despite being a loner, buoyed by an inherent positive temperament, he'd never been depressed and was seldom moody for more than a few hours. Antithetically, however, he was seldom very happy.

His great good fortune—as he saw it—came one day early in his internship when he took a shortcut through the third floor pediatric ward on the way to the laboratory. Brushing past visitors, he hustled from the elevator toward the back stairway only to come to a screeching halt just short of the nurses' station.

She was the most stunning girl he'd ever seen. Lustrous auburn hair, worn in a pageboy, gleamed in contrast to a fair complexion and deep blue eyes. She was petite, but well proportioned, with full breasts and hips and great legs. At that moment, she was laughing, and, to him, her smile lit the entire area, her persona seeming to radiate joy and life. As if aware of his gaze, she turned and looked in his direction. Averting his eyes, he rushed to the safety of the stairs but after that, he took the third floor route as often as possible, and he selected pediatrics for each of his elective rotations. He never understood why a woman like Betty would marry him, but chalked this up to his further good luck.

As with many good marriages, each of their strengths complemented the other's weaknesses. He was logical and practical; she was carefree and romantic. He was emotionally even; she was mercurial, yet most of their likes and dislikes coincided. They both loved the outdoors, medicine, and simple home life, and they both wanted to have a large family which physiology unfortunately seemed to prevent. Most important of all, they loved each other without reservation. With very few exceptions, theirs was an idyllic life...until Kelli died.

℘

Two months after Kelli's death, Dave's world had become a succession of dull days draped in drab tones of black and gray. In times past he had marveled at glowing sunsets and how quickly night fell in the Cumberlands. On a day like today, when a front had just passed through and the haze of summer was burnt away, the sky was crystal clear. The huge, deep orange sun paused just for a moment above a ridge-line bristling with oaks and poplars—black silhouettes framed against a brilliant coral and gray sky—before being sucked into the next valley.

Today, Dave watched the flaming display with vacant eyes. "Big deal," he said. The evening air shrilled with the rattle of tree frogs counter-pointed by the mellow, pulsating call of a whippoorwill and the drone of an occasional car passing on the road below. Fireflies began to flicker on and off, and across the valley lights started to dapple the hillside. Glancing around, he noticed that the other regular visitors had gone home, leaving him alone in the gathering darkness. What a schmuck! Grand and glorious physician having a pity party in the graveyard.

He slumped on a curved concrete bench surrounded by tombstones and hundreds of faded plastic flowers. Just below, barely visible in the fading light, stood Jesus and the woman at the well. One of her hands was gone and Jesus' right index and third fingers were missing. Dave had intended to bring some lopping shears and cut a scraggy locust sapling that sprouted from the well, but he never remembered. He wasn't sure why he even came here because he felt foolish talking alone, and he was never comforted. In fact, he usually felt worse afterwards. There had been no mystical communications with the dead as some people reported, no sense of nearness, just emptiness and loneliness. Perhaps he came out of some perverse sense of duty, or obligation, or compulsion, but for whatever reason, from time to time the need grew, so he came.

His joints cracked as he stood and walked to a nearby headstone. A vase with fresh-cut lilacs and baby's breath, a small teddy bear, and a miniature basketball lay at its base.

KELLI ELIZABETH DEMARCO
June 7, 1969-May 16, 1987
The joy she brought can never die.

His throat tightened. Oh, yes it can. All it takes is one snot-nosed drunk. He knelt to lay a single rose on the grave. "Kelli, I miss you so." Fumbling for his handkerchief, he blew his nose, then strode quickly to the car and drove away.

Betty sat in the living room, idly leafing through one of the seven picture albums on the coffee table. All were full of photos of Kelli: as a newborn, on her tricycle, in her Brownie uniform, with her basketball team, in her prom dress. Daily review of the albums had become almost an obsession, as if studying them over and over again would sear them into her brain so that she couldn't possibly forget her.

Tonight she'd selected an older one and now smiled wistfully at the vibrant young couple in the photos. Her starched white dress and her nursing school's distinctive cap made her look antiquated, but she'd continued wearing them until she retired when Kelli was born, long after the other nurses had discarded their caps and donned brightly colored slacks and blouses. Dave, slender, and at six-two, ten inches taller than she, stood by her side. He was the only person she'd ever known who could look fashionable in the dorky intern's pants and jacket. He'd been wearing them the first time they met.

"Hello, I'm Dave DeMarco. Someone paged me."

She looked up from her charting, and there he stood smiling at her.

"Oh…yes…I ...I'm Betty McCarter," she stammered and silently scolded herself for being flustered. She was the one who usually kept the know-it-all interns in line and tried to minimize the damage they did, even those like this one whom she'd seen hanging around and had heard was good with patients. "We have a new admission with pneumonia in room 221," she said, regaining her composure. "You may need some help. She's scared to death, probably from having blood drawn in the ER."

"What's her name?"

Betty was surprised. She couldn't recall an intern ever asking a patient's name. Usually they were in such a hurry they just rushed in, did their work and left. Taking the chart from her, his brown eyes twinkled and a smile tugged at the corners of his mouth as he read aloud, "Arbella Mayellen Cifers. Where do they get these names? What would they call her?"

She smiled back at him. "Ellie."

He took the chart and strode toward the room. Betty followed more out of curiosity than to assist.

As they entered the room, the little girl dropped her teddy bear and ran shrieking to her mother, grabbing her leg in a vise grip. Mrs. Cifers was a gaunt woman, probably in her early twenties. She wore scuffed K-Mart shoes and an ill-fitting faded yard-sale dress. She snuffed out her cigarette, and smiled a weak apology, screening her stained teeth with her hand.

"Hello, Mrs. Cifers, I'm Dr. DeMarco. I'd like to see if we can get Ellie feeling better."

She avoided making eye contact. "They say she got pneumonia. Is it serious?" As she spoke, she tried to peel Ellie from her leg and drag her toward the bed.

"I don't think so." Noting their frantic struggle, he said, "That's okay, just let her sit in your lap." He pulled up a chair but sat far enough away not to appear threatening.

Ellie scrambled onto her mother's lap and hung on, trembling and eyeing him over her shoulder. Her huge brown eyes brimmed with tears. She was pale and scrawny and appeared to be about four years old, although the chart said she was six. Dave kept his distance, but he leaned down to be nearer her eye level.

"Hi, Ellie, I'm Dr. Dave." She stared back. "We won't be doing anything here that hurts, I promise." She continued to cling, but her grip loosened.

He turned to her mother and in a quiet voice took Ellie's history. Mrs. Cifers was twenty-two and said that Ellie was the oldest of four children, had always been small for her age and was a picky eater. Over the last month she'd lost weight and developed a hacking cough. As they talked, whenever he caught Ellie peeking at him, Dave smiled and winked at her. At first, this caused her to burrow back into her mother's bosom, but as they continued, she began to sit up and watch him, once almost smiling in response to a wink. When he had finished questioning Mrs. Cifers, he straightened up. Ellie cringed as he took out his stethoscope. Bending over he picked the tattered teddy bear off the floor.

"This is a very nice bear. Is he yours?" A slight nod. "Does he have a name?" Another nod. "What is it?"

Barely audible, "Bo."

Dave smiled at her. "I had a friend named Bo. He looked a lot like your bear." A slight smile. "May I give Bo a check-up?" Another nod.

Betty watched with interest. Interns seldom impressed her except by their ineptitude, but this one was different.

Ellie leaned forward, her eyes riveted on Dave and Bo, as he solemnly listened to the bear's chest, mashed on its belly and looked in its ears. "Very good." He handed Bo to Ellie. "Bo's in excellent health. You've done a good job of taking care of him."

"Now," Dave said, moving his chair closer, "I need to check your mom and you to see if you're both healthy." Ellie tensed as he leaned forward, but he bypassed her to look into her mother's ear.

"Here, look in mine," he invited. Ellie hesitated for a moment, then peered into the otoscope. "Do I look okay?" She smiled and nodded. "Now, let me look in your ears." She stiffened but didn't protest. "Very good."

Setting the otoscope aside, he put his stethoscope in his ears and pressed it first against Mrs. Cifer's chest, then Ellie's leg and then her arm. "Okay," he said softly, pulling up the hospital gown, "Now, let me listen to your chest." She didn't move as he listened to her. Straightening up, he took off the stethoscope. "Would you like to hear?" She nodded. He put the ear-pieces in her ears and held the diaphragm against her chest over her heart. Her eyes widened, and she smiled as she heard the throbbing noises.

"Is that me?" she asked.

Dave returned the smile and nodded.

Sliding his chair back he spoke to the mother. "Mrs. Cifers, Ellie has pneumonia, but the lab work is a little odd. I think the pneumonia's due to worms she has in her intestines. Does she wash her hands before meals?"

"She's supposed to," the mother said, looking at the floor. "I don't have time to check all of 'em."

Dave rose to leave. "We'll be giving Ellie some pills to make her better. She'll need to be on a healthy diet and take vitamins. You can probably take her home in a day or two." He smiled and winked at Ellie, "You're going to be as healthy as Bo."

As they left the room, a small voice wafted through the open door, "Bye, Dr. Dave."

He smiled and turned to Betty. "Try to give them a crash course in basic hygiene and proper diet. Watch her stools. I'll bet a nickel they'll be loaded with round worms."

"You handle children very well," Betty said. "Where did you learn, brothers and sisters?"

He laughed. "No siblings, I grew up here and there. I guess it's mainly instinct, but I like kids. Even they know if you care about them and will respond if you're nice to them."

He sat down to write orders in the chart and then dictated Ellie's history. When he was finished, he returned to the nurse's station where Betty was busy charting. She looked up and saw him staring across the counter at her. He fumbled with his pen and shifted from one foot to the other.

"Could I help you with anything?"

"No, no, I mean… I was just thinking, if you're not busy…I mean if you don't have any other plans…" He blushed. "Well, it's about noon. Would you like to have lunch with me?"

Her gaze locked on his. "I'd like that very much."

They were married six months later.

❧

The slam of the car door interrupted Betty's reverie. She closed the album and, without thinking, went to the mirror, straightened her dress and brushed her auburn hair from her forehead. She was trim and firm for fifty-two, only five pounds heavier than in the photo album. Taking a deep breath, she walked to the foyer.

Early in their marriage, greeting him at the door had become a family ritual in which each tried to surprise the other. It might be a limp bouquet of daisies he'd picked on the roadside or a dinner invitation he'd wheedled from a drug sales representative. At times she'd been more inventive, once opening the door wearing a filmy negligee, and another time she left a trail of discarded clothing leading to the bedroom. The greeting always ended with a passionate kiss, or more.

The ritual became less imaginative and less passionate when Kelli was born. Very early she recognized that this was a special time and threw herself into it. For Dave, every day was highlighted by coming home and letting the two most important people in his life know how much he loved them, and their letting him know that he was indeed special. Since Kelli's death, they continued out of habit or some unspoken superstition that, if they stopped, something else bad might happen.

He shut the door and hung his coat in the closet. "Hi, Honey," he said, just like always.

"Hi."

She hugged him, and he gave her the automatic peck on the forehead.

From his drawn features and red eyes, she knew he'd been to the cemetery, which always made him more tense and testy than usual. She'd have to be careful even though she despised having to walk on eggshells. They had always been open and frank with each other, seldom arguing, and quick to make up when they did. Disagreements arose but never the fights that the marriage books said you were supposed to have. They didn't fight now, but just snapped at each other or, worse, gritted their teeth and said nothing.

"Why don't you sit down and relax while I get dinner ready?"

"Okay, but I'm not that hungry"

In the living room he sighed, rolled his eyes, and moved the albums so he could prop his feet on the table. After clicking on the end of the seven o'clock news wrap up, he immediately saw the picture of Kelli on top of the TV. Swearing under his breath, he moved it back to the mantle where he couldn't see it. He started to say something, then just bit his lip, retreated to the kitchen and set the table.

Dinner had been the transition from the workday to family time, their sharing time. They had held hands and rotated saying grace. Then each would tell about their day: funny things that happened at the office, perplexing cases, adventures Betty and Kelli had, boyfriend problems, the progress of the girl's basketball team. Now dinner consisted of superficial, brief questions and answers.

"How was your day?"

"Fine, and yours?"

"Okay."

There was no handholding and no grace; they just ate. Tonight was no different. Afterwards he helped clear the table.

"That was good."

"Thank you."

He picked up the evening paper and returned to the living room, followed closely by Betty. Oh, God, he groaned silently, knowing she wanted to talk. She glanced at the new location of the picture but made no comment or move to change it, then sat down.

"Sarah called today. She and Bob would like to take us to that new restaurant down on the lake sometime soon. They say it's very good."

"That might be fun. I don't see much of Bob since they got the cath lab at the hospital. He's really busy. I know you see Sarah a lot, but I haven't seen her since...since..."

"Since you jumped all over her for talking about their kids."

"Yeah," he said, "I'm really sorry about that."

"Have you told her you're sorry?" No answer. "Dave, I know you hurt. I know you miss Kelli, but this is destroying us, and it frightens me. You were the kindest, gentlest person I'd ever known, but now you have such a hard edge. You always seem so bitter and angry, and sometimes you're downright mean. I've heard you cut the nurses down when they call you at night. You never did that." She hesitated. "Sarah mentioned a support group awhile back. Maybe we could—"

"Just stop right there," he cut her off. "You're darn right I'm angry. That worthless piece of garbage got drunk and splattered her all over the schoolyard in her prom dress. And what does he get? A stern speech and a slap on the wrist. Probation! If he'd been two months older, he'd be in jail, but instead, his record is sealed as if nothing ever happened. Now he's off to college where she ought to be, and she's in a damned hole in the ground. I'd love to have him alone for just five minutes. Yeah, I'm mad, but I'm doing the only thing I know to do to keep going. If I stay busy all the time, then once in a while, for a few minutes, I don't think about her."

"I just thought..." her voice trailed off.

"I won't go spilling my guts to a bunch of strangers. I won't sit all day reading books about dead kids and their parents. I won't spend hours and hours poring over pictures trying to recapture something that's gone and not coming back. You do that if you want to, but I won't do it. My daughter's dead. Don't you understand? My daughter is dead."

Betty drew back, frightened. Then her chin began to quiver and tears ran down her cheeks. She staggered to her feet and glared at him, her blue eyes boring into his soul. "Yes, I understand; I understand better than you think. You're so wrapped up in your loss and your anger and your grief that maybe you've forgotten. "*Our* daughter has died." She turned and ran from the room. Wisely he didn't follow.

Dave, you jerk. What's happening to me? He was floundering and had no idea how to right himself. He'd never sworn before, and now it had become a second language. Head in hands, he sat for over an hour. In times past he would have prayed, but he seldom tried that anymore. Finally, he rose and went to the sunroom where he knew she'd be and found her balled up in the tall rattan chair crying softly. When he knelt and put his hand on her shoulder, she pulled away.

Taking a deep breath, he said, "Darling, I apologize, I didn't mean that. I'm frightened. I feel so helpless. This is something I've never experienced before. I'm a doctor. I'm supposed to be in control, and I can't even control myself. I'm supposed to help ease people's pain, and I keep hurting the one person left who's important to me. I know that I'm doing it, but I just can't seem to stop. A father is supposed to protect his family, but I let our daughter be killed."

He paused for a long time then, gritting his teeth, he said what he'd never been able to say before. "I think I'm most angry at myself. If I'd only chaperoned the prom like you wanted and not tried to be Super Doc, then Kelli wouldn't have gotten run over." His face contorted, and his voice began to break. "I'm responsible, me. If it weren't for me, Kelli would still be alive. I know it, you know it, and you must hate me for it." He lay against her and began to sob. Betty gathered him in her arms, and they clung to each other and wept, certain that if they turned loose, they would drift apart and disappear.

After going to bed Betty heard him in the shower. Later he slid under the covers, leaned over and gently kissed her on the shoulder. She pretended to be asleep.

Betty was still sleeping when he awoke, and he quietly slipped out. Following the morning routine of years, he fixed coffee, poured a cup and went into the sunroom to watch the daybreak. This had been his favorite time of day, his time, before the demands of patients, family and business began tugging him in different directions. Time to think, to meditate, read poetry, his Bible or something inspirational, to pray or just to enjoy the sunrise. On rare occasions he'd been overwhelmed by the beauty of the world around him. Pragmatic and task oriented by nature and somewhat rigid in his thinking, this was the nearest he ever came to introspection or mysticism—but that was then. Now he couldn't concentrate to think or meditate, and he'd given up on prayer. His rather traditional religion—right was right, wrong was wrong, good was rewarded and evil punished—had been the cornerstone of his values and ethics, but was no comfort now. He still read poetry but only if it was sufficiently gloomy.

The bird feeder at the window stood empty, not filled in weeks. Picking up the bird identification book on the sill, he began to leaf through it, and without warning, the familiar sickening feeling grew in him as he saw the wobbly circles around the ones he and Kelli had identified together. When he got to the circled cardinal with the block-lettered scrawl, MY FAVORIT, he dropped the book, his trembling hands clenching and unclenching. The velvet sky beyond the ridge blushed a faint pink. In the gathering light, the silhouette of the saltlick stood starkly at the edge of the woods, and to one side was Kelli, sitting motionless watching a deer eat the corn she'd placed on the tray for it. Shaken, he refocused and saw only the saltlick and a small shrub.

This obsessive fixation on her was intensifying. With conscious effort he could keep himself centered in reality, but something like the book or the saltlick would wrench him back into his private gloom-filled world. It was as if he were viewing everything through glasses tinted dark with grief. His entire world had gone colorless, ash gray, and everywhere he looked, he saw Kelli, not in focus but through that dusky pall. The only time he saw her clearly was in an almost nightly nightmare. He would see Kelli in the distance, but when he ran to her she would be staring at him with the same blank, dilated eyes he had seen in the schoolyard. He always woke drenched in sweat. This had prompted him to schedule a session with Fred Michaelson, the staff psychiatrist. After some Freudian double-talk, Fred had told him to write a letter to Kelli telling her good-bye and then to "let go." Yeah, sure. After only two months, it was time to let go. He'd said nothing, but wondered if punching a shrink's face in would be considered a felony or a misdemeanor. There were no further sessions.

☙

The clatter of dishes told him Betty was up. She turned and forced a smile as he came into the kitchen.

"Honey, about last night—" but before he could finish, she put her finger to his lips, kissed him and, holding his hand, led him to the breakfast table where they sat down.

"Please hear me out," she said. "For the first time since I've known you, we're faced with something we can't overcome together. We're like two people who are drowning, each pulling the other under as they go down for the second time. I need to talk about Kelli. I need to ventilate and remember and replay my mind's tapes of her, but it kills you to listen, and I resent that."

"But—" Again she put her finger to his lips before he could protest or explain.

"I finally realized last night that maybe we can't help each other very much, if at all. It hurts you as much to listen as it hurts me to keep quiet. You're a doctor and a father, a fixer, but you can't fix Kelli, you can't fix me, and I think you have doubts that you can fix yourself. We just grieve differently."

She paused and sipped her coffee then continued, "That I can talk about her doesn't mean that I love her more; that you can't doesn't mean you love her less. We'll help each other as much as we can, but most of this we'll have to do alone. I'll support you as much as I can, but I don't know how much that will be. I don't understand why things happened as they did, and I'm hurt and angry that they did."

Her jaw tightened, and her eyes blazed into his. In a voice with more steel and determination than he'd ever heard from her she said, "But one thing I do know. I won't let this destroy me or our marriage. I owe this to Kelli and to us." She threw her arms around him for a moment. "Please don't say anything, or I'll go to pieces. I love you." With that, she dashed from the room.

He sat for several minutes mulling what she had said. While he had garnered the status and prestige that falls to a physician, he knew that she'd been the strength and emotional backbone of their marriage. She'd supported him financially through the lean years of his training, and, until Kelli was born, staffed and ran his office as they struggled to establish his practice. She never complained about the long hours and the repeated interruptions of their life, and through it all, she'd always greeted him in the foyer.

He ached for what had been, but was no more, for what should have been, but would never be. He envied her strength and determination. Uncertain what he should do next, he left without kissing her good-bye for the first time he could remember.

Chapter 3

Hillsdale   pop. 34,146
Home of the 1987 Girl's State Basketball Champions
A Good Place to Live

Dave hated that sign even though he'd been instrumental in erecting it right after the basketball tournament. He had loved it from March until May 16. There was a picture in one of the albums of Kelli standing beside it in her basketball uniform. Several times he'd considered spray painting it or knocking it over. There were no reasonable alternate routes in this place of hills and hollows, so at least twice a day, on the way to and from town, he passed the sign and the cemetery, and, however he might be feeling, he felt worse.

He'd gone to medical school determined to be a family doctor in a small town, but he wasn't sure why, since he'd grown up in Louisville and had never visited anyplace smaller. Perhaps his romantic idea of small-town living held a promise of the stability he'd never felt as he bounced from one foster home to the next.

During his residency, he and Betty had felt obliged to look at several towns, but there'd been little doubt that they would settle in Hillsdale, her hometown. Roots were important to her, and her family had lived there for three generations. After her parents were killed in an automobile accident when she was twenty-two, she'd rented out the old house until she and Dave moved back. For his part, his only regret was that he hadn't grown up there and met Betty sooner.

"Good morning, Dr. DeMarco," Mary Bolton, the charge nurse, greeted him. Very proper, very professional, but her eyes said, "Please be like you used to be." For twenty years he'd been the one with the funny story or the practical joke, the one who, despite himself, got too close to nurses and patients. She had the same off-center, warped sense of humor as he, and they delighted in making puns on patients' names or medical conditions. They had both started to work in the hospital about the same time and soon became close friends. Her husband, Mike, was a captain in the local police department, and they often went out as a foursome.

"Good morning, Mary, " he said a little too loud, a little too enthusiastic, smiling just as before, but his eyes were dead. He reviewed his charts, asked Mary clinical questions, saw the patients, and made notations. As they neared the end of the hall, Mary pulled out a chart.

"Mr. Blakely hasn't had a bowel movement in three days."

"Have you checked his rectum?"

Mary beamed, knowing she had him. "Wrecked 'um, I darn near killed him."

Involuntarily, Dave laughed, then choked up. Putting his arm around her shoulder he hugged her. "Thanks, Mary, I needed that," he said and turned to leave.

She caught his hand. "We all love you, Dave; we're here for you."

He nodded, gave a weak smile, and left. On his way out, he realized that this was the first time he could recall a spontaneous laugh since Kelli had…died. Thinking that word was still painful, much less saying it aloud. It encouraged him that he could still laugh, but at the same time he felt guilty that he'd done it. Laughing, even briefly, didn't seem appropriate, but when would it be appropriate?

He swallowed hard and opened the door to the pediatric ward. He'd always loved kids, but now he felt uncomfortable seeing anyone under forty and found it difficult to remain objective with younger patients. Thank goodness he had only one in the hospital.

He scanned the chart: Tamika Peterson, admitted through the emergency room during the night because of weakness and vomiting. "Has she vomited any more?" The nurse shook her head.

When he entered the room, an over-weight African-American woman of indeterminate age heaved up from a small rollaway bed by the window and smoothed her clothes.

"I'm Dr. DeMarco."

"Rosa Peterson. This is my daughter, Tamika." Tamika, a slender girl almost six feet tall, struggled to sit up.

"That's all right, just lie there." He towered above the girl, not bothering to sit down. "What seems to be the problem?"

She looked at her mother.

"Go on, honey, talk to the doctor," Mrs. Peterson said.

"I don't know exactly. I have this funny taste in my mouth, and I just started vomiting last night and couldn't stop."

"Did your stomach hurt?"

"No, sir."

"How did you feel until last night?"

"I don't know. I'm just tired all the time."

"Anything else?"

"My hands feel funny, and I sleep a lot."

"Your blood tests show a little anemia. Are your periods normal?"

She blushed and looked away. "I guess so," she mumbled.

He sighed. This is going nowhere. He listened to her chest and pressed on her abdomen, then, still standing, he began to write and talk at the same time. "I think she just has a touch of intestinal flu. She was a little dehydrated, but the IV's have fixed that and the vomiting has stopped. Here's a prescription for some stomach medicine and some vitamins with iron for the anemia. If she's not feeling better in a month or so, I need to see her again."

The mother frowned as he turned to leave. "Doctor, I don't mean to be no trouble, but there's something wrong with that child, and it ain't no flu." She drew back as he flushed and spun around.

"Look, we've X-rayed her, run blood tests on her, and except for a little anemia there's nothing wrong. The medicine will settle her stomach, and the iron will build up her blood."

"But, doctor." She took a deep breath, hunched her shoulders. "She won't eat, and she drops things and gets her feet tangled up. She's so clumsy she even had to quit the basketball team. Her grades are falling, and that just ain't like her. Something's wrong, bad wrong. A couple of other children have the same thing, just not so bad."

He forced a smile and patted her on the shoulder. "Now don't worry, Mrs. Peterson, I'm sure it's just a little bug that's going around." Before she could say anything else, he turned and darted out. The nurse handed him the chart as they walked down the hall, and he jotted a hurried note. "You just can't make some people happy," he said to no one in particular and disappeared down the stairwell.

His breath whooshed out as something heavy slammed into his back. "Hey, Davy, how's it going?" Bob Maxwell's deep baritone boomed. Bob was six feet-five and weighed at least two hundred fifty. He was Dave's best friend. They'd met on the first day of medical school and roomed together in one side of a dilapidated duplex until Dave and Betty got married. Bob simply moved into the other side and mooched meals as often as possible. He was a big teddy bear, and Dave and Betty loved him. Betty had introduced him to Sarah, who had also grown up in Hillsdale and gone to college with her. They married a year later, and, after only ten months, began having children. They had four before Kelli was born and two more afterwards. Bob often embarrassed Sarah by proclaiming at parties that if he took off his shorts in the same room with her, she conceived. They had come to Hillsdale when he finished his cardiology fellowship, two years after Dave and Betty.

"Bob, are you trying to stir up more business?" Dave gasped.

"No, man. I've got more than I can handle. Cath 'em and stretch 'em. Cath 'em and stretch 'em. I've got plenty to do without your flinty heart. So how are you doing?"

"I'm OK," Dave said.

Bob grabbed his arm and towed him into the doctor's lounge, which for once was empty. "You're running early," he said pouring two black coffees. "Sit down and don't blow smoke at me. Tell me how you're really doing."

Dave sipped his coffee and considered his question. Bob was the only person who dared ask how he was and want an answer. A few inquired, "How's Betty?" but most didn't say anything. He wanted to go, but knew he needed to talk.

"I feel rotten," he blurted. "I'm not very friendly. I dump on my patients. I can't concentrate, and I know it's only a matter of time until I screw up and kill someone." The floodgates were open. "I almost never laugh, but if I slip up and do, I feel guilty. I can't talk to Betty without hurting her or making her angry. I sleep about four hours a night and that's broken into two or three sessions. I'm celibate and didn't even get to take a vow. I'm angry at God, and I'm not sure I believe anything anymore. I sit for hours in the cemetery, and I think I'm going nuts."

He paused to sip his coffee. "What do you know about sleep?"

Bob looked puzzled. "Not much, just the little they taught us in physiology."

Dave continued as if he hadn't heard, "They've done studies and found that people who are deprived of REM sleep don't dream, and if they're deprived long enough, they either go insane or die. That's what I feel is happening to me. My dreams died with Kelli, and now my spirit is slowly dying, too." Then with a weak smile, "But other than that, I'm doing okay. Thanks for asking."

Bob ran his finger through his unruly red hair and stared at him, wide-eyed. "That bad, huh?"

"Yeah, that bad. But you know what? It feels good just getting it out and being able to take off my smiley face for a few minutes. Ask me again sometime."

"Preventative medicine, my man, preventative medicine. I just saved you a C & S."

"A what?"

"A C&S. A cath and stretch, a heart cath and an angioplasty done by the master." They sipped their coffee in silence. "You and Betty want to come over to our place for Labor Day? Lots of food, lots of booze."

"I don't know if we're ready for holidays yet; even the beginning of school isn't going to be much fun."

"Yeah, I understand."

You don't have a clue, he thought. "But Betty said we're going to get together out at The Embers. I hear the food is great."

"Great food, great food. Sarah said she and Betty are having lunch today. I'm sure they'll work out the particulars and coordinate our call schedules. Looking forward to it." He grasped Dave's shoulder. "Hang in there, buddy." Despite his bluster, Bob cared and did the best he could without leaving himself too vulnerable.

"I will," Dave said. At the door he turned back. "Thanks, Bob, you've got guts. I don't know what I'd do without you." The door closed before Bob could answer.

A while after hearing the car leave, Betty came back into the kitchen. A prescription pad lay in plain view on the counter.

I wish I had your strength. I'm doing the best I can. I love you and I need you even if I don't always show it.
Love,
Dave

Her throat tightened as she read his note, and the irony of the prescription pad wasn't lost on her. Oh, Dave, I wish I could help. Maybe just communicating through notes for a while would eliminate a lot of emotional booby traps.

Cursing her sloppiness, she shuffled through the jumbled litter on her desk looking for her list, then began to pick up books, papers and magazines and slam them down. Dave often called her "The Organization Woman" because she was so neat and well ordered . Now she couldn't even remember where she'd put her list that was supposed to keep her from forgetting. Feeling foolish, she looked in the refrigerator where she'd found it last week. "Betty, you doofus," she said, slapping her forehead. There it was on the table beside the door where she'd put it—so she wouldn't forget. She scanned it quickly.

8:30 Beauty shop
Grocery
12:30 Lunch with Sarah

The kitchen clock read ten after eight. Loosening her robe, she rushed to their room. She'd always been an early riser, preparing for the day while Dave did his meditation thing. Now she slept until he woke her getting ready for work, or when he kissed her good-bye. Even then she'd often go back to sleep, dragging out of bed in late morning feeling hung over and guilty. Throwing on her clothes and makeup, she cleared the door at eight-twenty, jumped into the car, slammed the car door and reached for her keys.

"Betty, you idiot!" Her fist pounded the steering wheel and tears of frustration flooded her eyes. Out of the car, back up the walk. Fumbling behind the mailbox, she found the spare key and let herself in where in plain sight on the counter were her keys. She snatched them, and, gritting her teeth, stomped to the car, got in and again slammed the door. She took several deep breaths until she stopped shaking. After blotting her eyes, she started the car and roared down the drive not bothering to fasten her seat belt or look in either direction as she flew onto the highway.

When Betty burst through the door, Paula, the hair stylist, stopped filing her nails and glanced at the clock. The chatter in the boutique ceased.

"I'm sorry, I just couldn't get it together this morning."

"That's OK," Paula said in a sincere, syrupy voice.

Betty settled into the chair. Why can't she be sarcastic like always? I'm not terminally ill. Or am I? As she closed her eyes and lay back for the shampoo, hushed conversations resumed, but not the usual bawdy laughter.

"This is the hottest summer that I can remember," Paula rattled. "If it weren't for air conditioning, I'd just die." Betty nodded, trying to concentrate on the usually soothing scalp massage and the warm water flooding her skin. For the next hour Paula chattered about safe, dull topics, no juicy gossip or racy jokes, as was her custom. Betty let her mind wander, murmuring a polite "Uh huh" from time to time.

Kelli may be dead, she wanted to scream, but you all knew her. Why can't any of you even say her name? Death's not catching.

"There," Paula gushed, "all done and looking good."

"Thank you." Betty paid and hurried out, taking all of the tension in the room with her.

She pulled into the space farthest from Kroger's door and sat debating whether to go in or not. She felt she'd accomplished something positive by talking to Dave, but things had deteriorated steadily since then. Finally, she got out and went into the store, realizing too late that she'd left her shopping list in the car. Taking a cart, she automatically started down the dairy product aisle on the left. Out of habit she put eggs and milk into the cart. She picked up a carton of butter and put it down three times before moving on without it. Not realizing how she got there, she found herself staring trance-like at the meat display.

"Betty. Betty DeMarco, how are you?" Donna Winton's high-pitched nasal voice snapped her back into reality.

Donna went to her church but seldom said much, perhaps self-conscious about her grating voice. She had sent brief notes on the sixteenth of June and July, somewhat easing those painful markers. She'd even collected all of the newspaper articles concerning Kelli and brought them to their home along with a lemon pound cake.

"Oh, I'm fine," Betty replied brightly.

Donna touched her arm. "I'm glad; I've been so worried about you. Let's get together sometime."

"I'd like that," Betty replied, her voice a little husky. They chatted about the weather and the fall church bazaar.

"Well, I've got to run," Donna said. "Please call when you're ready. Bye."

"I will," Betty lied. "See you." Superficial as it was, her visit had buoyed Betty's spirits. At least Donna had the gumption to risk a conversation. With no hesitation, Betty grabbed a chicken and tossed it into the cart, then moved along, avoiding the pitfalls of the cereals and candy aisles. Sugar Pops and Gummy Bears had blind-sided her before, and she wasn't going to chance it again.

Turning toward the detergents, she made brief eye contact with Joyce Adams, her next door neighbor. Joyce whirled around, pretending not to have seen her, and disappeared behind a tall stack of Tide. Betty's cart ground to a halt. She stared at the empty space where Joyce had been. Oh, well, you haven't been over since Kelli died; why should I expect you to speak now? Slumping, she plodded on, all sense of accomplishment in having selected the chicken gone. Absent mindedly, she wandered along and pitched a few last items into the basket. Stopping, she looked around to reorient herself, then pushed on. Rounding a pyramid of Campbell's soups, she slammed to a stop. No, oh, no. Before her stood a tower of Cheetos. Her head spun. They're not supposed to be here. Cheetos are on the potato chip aisle. I skipped it. I always skip it. I always got her Cheetos, but she's dead. She can't eat Cheetos anymore. Why are the Cheetos here?

Tears coursed down her cheeks. Grabbing her purse, she ran, leaving the cart in the center of the aisle. The automatic doors barely had time to open as she dashed through them and into the parking lot. She continued running to the car, jumped in, and roared out of the lot. Her vision blurred by tears, she sped home, barely touching the brakes until she careened into her drive. She leapt from the car, staggered to the door and fumbled with the lock, slammed the door behind her, ran straight to Kelli's room, and threw herself onto the bed. "Kelli, Kelli, Kelli," she shouted. Then she began to scream—high pitched, keening screams that went on and on.

The jangling of the phone jerked Betty upright. She'd cried herself to sleep and for a second was disoriented. She fumbled with the receiver, dropped it to the floor, then pulled it up hand-over-hand by the cord like a bucket from a well. "Hello. Hello. Hello," echoed from the receiver held in the vicinity of her mouth. Clumsily she turned it around.

"Hello."

"Betty, Sarah. Are you all right?"

"What time is it?"

"A little after one"

"Oh, Sarah, I'm sorry. I've had a horrible day; I must've gone to sleep. I'm so sorry," she repeated, her voice starting to tremble.

"That's OK," Sarah said, "I'm at Chuck's Deli getting sandwiches and chips. It's awfully crowded here, but I'll be there in twenty minutes."

"You're sure it's OK?"

"No problem. I'm on my way."

Betty went to the bathroom, splashed cold water in her face and looked in the mirror. What a mess. She exchanged her rumpled clothes for a fresh blouse and slacks, then repaired her hair as best she could. Finally, awake and alert she went to the kitchen, put a kettle of water on the front eye but turned on the back one. The kitchen was a shambles. Last night's and this morning's dishes were still in the sink, but she made no attempt to straighten it up. Outside the sunroom a lone chickadee searched the feeder for a stray morsel, throwing out a few empty hulls and then looking at Betty in the window. "OK, you win," she sighed. She retrieved a large scoop of sunflower seeds from the storage shed, filled the feeder and scattered the remaining seeds around on the ground beneath it.

"Oh, there you are," Sarah said. "I rang the doorbell and you didn't answer, so I just let myself in." Sarah was almost six feet tall. Her slender figure gave no hint she had borne six children. As usual, she wore her dark hair in a ponytail.

"I just became an honorary member of the Audubon Society."

"Go sit down while I fix tea and get some dishes. Tuna salad on pita bread okay with you?"

"Sounds great," Betty said with false enthusiasm. "There's water boiling for tea."

Sarah said nothing and moved the kettle to the glowing eye in the back. She took as long as possible to get out the sandwiches, pour the chips on their plates and lay napkins on their trays. Finally the kettle whistled.

"This should pep you up." Sarah set the trays with a steaming cup of tea before her. "I couldn't resist," she said, pointing to two large chocolate chip cookies.

"I'm really not hungry."

"Had anything to eat today?"

"Well, no."

"You might as well get started. I don't have to pick up Julie until three-thirty, and I'm not leaving until you clean your plate. Chow down."

"Yes, ma'am." Betty smiled at Sarah, the big sister she'd never had. She nibbled at the edge of the sandwich and sipped the tea.

"Bad day?" Betty nodded. Sarah said nothing. They didn't talk. The only sound was the soft slurp of tea and the crunch of chips. "Want to talk about it?"

Betty put her near pristine sandwich down. "I'm so frustrated. I gave this big, brave talk to Dave this morning, and two hours later I lost it in the middle of Kroger's. I completely lost it. I lay on Kelli's bed screaming for I don't know how long. I think I'm going crazy."

She twisted the napkin around her finger. "I know I'm overly sensitive, but people do avoid me. Maybe I'm so gloomy I drive them away. Some try to help, but even that irritates me. The next person who says, 'I know just how you feel' or 'you need to get on with your life' or 'you're not your old self' or 'it was God's will' is going to get smacked."

Sarah sipped her tea and said nothing.

"Dave and I can't talk. We used to share everything, but now he gets angry if I talk about Kelli, but I need to talk about her. You're the only person who'll say her name. He stays late at the office. I know he's uncomfortable there, but he's more uncomfortable with me, and he doesn't have anywhere else to go. And he's so angry. He's obsessed with Matt Williams and with the legal system, but the trial's over and done with. Dave's like a dog with a bone; he just won't turn it loose. The district attorney won't even answer his calls any more. Dave used to be so sweet and gentle, but now sometimes he frightens me. I'd never heard him use foul language before, but now he curses and swears constantly, sometimes even at me. I'm not sure who he is anymore. It's tearing me apart."

She began to tear bits of tissue from the napkin. "To make matters worse, Matt and his parents came over to apologize. They were broken hearted. I know Matt was wrong, but I can't live my life hating him, and his parents certainly aren't to blame. I'm afraid to even mention it to Dave. They asked to come back when he was home, but I know he'd just go crazy."

She rambled on for another half-hour, sometimes contradicting herself, often saying the same thing two or three times. She talked about Kelli: when she was small, their shopping trips, the talks they had in the kitchen. "You know, I think that's what I miss most. Kelli and I were always talking, and now the house is silent as a…tomb." She slumped back, her chin quivering.

Tears ran down Sarah's cheeks. She put her arms around Betty and hugged her. "Oh, Betty, I'm so sorry. I just wish I could help."

Betty buried her face in Sarah's breast and sobbed. Sarah rocked her back and forth and let her cry. Finally, Betty became quiet. She sat up, grabbed a fresh tissue, dabbed the damp spot on Sarah's blouse, then blotted her eyes and blew her nose.

"What a mess. I hope I didn't soak the sandwiches, too. Let's eat."

Sarah laughed and re-warmed the tea.

Emotionally emptied for the moment, Betty laughed at Sarah's silly quips, and they talked lightheartedly. They compared schedules and finally settled on the Saturday night before Labor Day for the couples to have dinner together.

"I didn't realize how hungry I was," Betty said, popping the last piece of cookie into her mouth. "This has been good, thank you. I don't know what I'd do without you. You're the only one who'll just listen and not judge me or give advice. However, right now I need some advice, or at least some information."

"What's that?"

"I don't remember just when, but several weeks ago you mentioned knowing someone who went to a support group in Lexington."

"Yes, The Compassionate Friends. Her name's Carolyn Sanders. She works at the bank. Her son, Billy, was in Cub Scouts with Jack and drowned at the lake about six years ago."

"I remember reading about it." A strange look came to Betty's face. "You know, it didn't even make an impression at the time. Could you get her phone number for me? I'm not doing very well at pulling myself up by my bootstraps. I'll take help from wherever I can get it."

"I may still have it," Sarah said rummaging through her purse. It was right where she knew it was in the zip pocket where she'd put it in hopes that Betty would ask sooner or later. "Here."

Betty took it. "What've I got to lose?"

"I've got to run," said Sarah, pulling on her coat. She hugged Betty and kissed her on the cheek. "You're going to be okay."

After she left, Betty washed the sink full of dishes, then vacuumed and tidied the kitchen and sunroom. Satisfied with her accomplishment, she stood at the window and smiled. The bird feeder was alive with juncos, titmice, chickadees, and one brilliant cardinal.

Dave sat at his desk sipping a Coke. Except for the obvious dissatisfaction of Mrs. Peterson at the hospital that morning, it had been a good day. After completing rounds he'd worked straight through lunch until 6 P.M., and now he was nearly hidden behind three stacks of charts—thirty-eight were dictations on patients he had seen that day, eighteen more were for phone calls he had just completed. While he was a near perfectionist in his charting and patient care, his office showed no such perfection. Piles of drug samples teetered precariously on shelves and in corners. A stack of unfinished insurance forms with corresponding charts formed a growing replica of the tower of Pisa beside his desk. His diplomas and licenses hung on the wall between two bookcases, unimpressive amid the litter. The only tidy area in the entire room was a shelf connecting the two bookcases. A Hummel figurine of a boy dressed as a doctor contemplating a broken doll, a gift from Betty when he had opened his office, stood on one side. Three pictures filled the rest of the shelf: Betty smiled radiantly from the one on the left, on the right was Kelli in her basketball uniform . In the center picture Betty and Kelli stood arm-in-arm by their tent in the Smokies. Kelli was six inches taller than her mother, but their resemblance was uncanny—auburn hair, deep blue eyes, the same flashing smile. To their delight, strangers often had mistaken them for sisters. He sighed, remembering that trip.

A soft rap on the door brought him back. "Dr. DeMarco."

"Come on in Millie. I'm okay," he said as she entered. "I forgot and closed the door." When he'd returned to work after the funeral, he'd made it clear that if his door was shut, he wasn't to be bothered for anything. He couldn't stand to expose his emotions to anyone, and the first few weeks he'd lose his composure and retreat to his sanctuary several times a day. That didn't occur nearly so often anymore. "I'll try to remember to leave it open in the future."

Millie Langston had been his office manager for sixteen years. She was fiftyish with prematurely gray hair, the self-educated daughter of a dirt-poor coal-miner. Her sweet, motherly face belied the shrewd businesswoman and manager she was. She knew Medicare and health insurance forward and backward, had a sixth sense about who would and wouldn't fit in as an employee, and had become skilled with computers at the local community college. Thanks to her, theirs was the first medical office in the area to become computerized. Had she been born twenty years later and given a minimum of opportunity she'd have gone far up the corporate ladder, maybe to the very top. He often said that he hoped he retired before she did because he knew his practice would surely go belly-up if she should leave. He was right.

"Is there anything else I can do?"

"No, thank you, Millie."

She was unable to hide the concern in her eyes. "All right, I'll see you tomorrow."

He switched the light off, then back on, picked up the phone and punched the speed dial.

"Hello." He smiled. Even now her voice sounded sultry when she answered the phone. It embarrassed her when he told her this, and she always retorted that no one else seemed to think so. Still, to him, she sounded sultry.

"Honey, I've just finished up. I'm going to drive around the long way. Would you like me to pick up something to eat? …Hey, that sounds good. What's the use of living in Kentucky if you don't eat fried chicken? See you in an hour, I love you, bye."

Emerging from the KFC just down the street from his office, he pitched the box of chicken in the passenger seat, started the car and turned onto Main Street. Three blocks down he made a right onto Boone and followed it along the river until Valley Street veered off around the back of the ridge.

Hillsdale was laid out like a capital letter H with Boone Street forming the connector. The center of town lay in a large flat gap where the Beaver River cut through White Oak Ridge. The ridge was about fifty miles long running roughly northeast to southwest and had been formed when a glacier from the last ice age had gouged out Buffalo Valley to the west and Apple Valley to the east. Apple Valley, referred to by locals as Affluent Valley, was fairly broad and relatively flat. In either direction from the center of town spread neat residential areas with well tended lawns, parks, schools, golf courses, the country club, and the cemetery. He and Betty lived about two miles beyond the city limits in the upper valley atop the ridge on what had been her parents' home place. Originally it consisted of about fifty acres, but they had bought a farm behind their house to prevent development too close to them. They now had about two hundred fifty acres stretching from the river to the road across which a new golf course with upscale condominiums was being built.

On nights like tonight, when Dave needed some time to himself, or just couldn't bring himself to drive by the cemetery, he drove home the roundabout way up Buffalo Valley and crossed over the ridge at Indian Gap about a mile above their home.

A small airport was located to the south. The zoning commission had placed all dirty industry and what little heavy industry there was in Buffalo Valley. Although only scattered lights were visible, he could visualize the valley as if it were daylight. The western flank was a red clay moonscape of abandoned strip mines where a few die-hards still scrambled to scratch a living from twelve-inch seams. When he'd first moved here, the road was a steady stream of trucks, brimming with coal, but now he almost never saw one . He wondered how they made a living. When the wind was right, you could hear the occasional boom of dynamite charges all the way to downtown. Housing on this side of the ridge consisted of deteriorating company houses clinging to the hillsides or an assortment of double-wides and house trailers of indeterminate vintage set on small plots along the road. Cars of all makes, in advanced stages of disintegration, sat in the yards—rusting hulks of once modest dreams, much like many of the lives in the dilapidated houses.

The houses became more widely separated as he went further up the valley until he reached a small cluster of neat clapboard dwellings. He had never heard this area referred to as anything but Boogertown. Ten or twelve African-American families lived here, the only blacks in Grainger County. Local folklore had it that they were the descendents of runaway slaves, but more likely they had come as laborers with the railroads around the turn of the century. While most had moved to Lexington or Louisville, these remained.

The majority worked at the chemical plant. This isolated pocket of people was not discriminated against, just ignored.

A mile above Boogertown stood International Chemicals, the largest employer in the county. The huge plant sat in splendid isolation on a plateau at the head of the valley. The play of light and shadows on the rounded tanks and towering cylinders interconnected by miles of serpentine pipes made for a surreal science fiction appearance. The bright lights reflected from the settling ponds terraced below the plant. As he passed the main gate, armed guards in bulletproof kiosks were clearly visible. Although International Chemicals manufactured primarily insecticides, there were rumors of chemical warfare research. These rumors were never publicly confirmed, but there was a large, heavily guarded area of the plant that no one could enter without high security clearance.

He continued driving along the shore of the lake formed by the dammed north branch of the Beaver River, which provided water and electricity for the plant. There were very few house lights as he started up the winding road to Indian Gap. He stopped at the overlook atop the gap. Looking down Apple Valley he could see almost to the main part of town.

I can't believe last night. Betty didn't deserve that. What a jerk. "Dave, you've got to get hold of yourself," he said aloud. "I just don't know how."

After stewing a few minutes longer, the aroma of the fried chicken brought him back to the present. He put the car in gear and started down.

The light in the foyer came on as he strode up the walk. When he opened the door, Betty stood in the foyer, just like always. He put his arms around her and kissed her, and to his surprise, she kissed him back. He held her for a moment. "Hi," he whispered in her ear. "Hi," she responded, smiling. Hand-in-hand they walked to the sunroom and sat down.

"How'd it go today?" he asked.

"It has been a roller coaster, really high and really low, but I ended up on an upper," she said. For once he didn't go straight to the TV but just sat and waited. She gave him a blow-by-blow account of the day's events ending with a sweeping gesture to the now spotless kitchen and sunroom.

"That's great. You needed a boost."

"Everything okay with you?"

"It was a good day. I was really busy." He didn't mention the near confrontation on the pediatric ward. He held up the box of chicken. "Hungry?"

"I'm starved." She led him into the dining room. Their best china gleamed in the candlelight and a bottle of chilled wine stood open on the table. "The perfect setting for a gourmet dinner."

They spoke formally as they parodied dining in a four-star restaurant. Finally Dave banged down his knife and fork. "Forget decorum! Fried chicken wasn't meant to be eaten with sterling silver; it spoils the taste." He picked up a large piece with his fingers and took a big bite. "Delicious," he said, licking his fingers. "The Colonel would be proud."

Betty giggled at his antics, then hiccuped, spurring more giggles. She fanned her face with her hand. "Wine always makes me silly."

"I know, won't you have some more?" This elicited more giggles.

When they'd finished, nothing was left but a stack of bones. Betty surveyed the stack. "My gosh, did we eat all of that?" She began clearing the table. He started to help, but she pushed him back into his chair. "Just sit still. You haven't seen my surprise." She returned with coffee and a carton of Rocky Road ice cream. "The perfect end to a high class dinner." They laughed and talked until they'd finished the whole box. Betty always insisted on doing the china and silver by hand, so Dave washed and she dried as had been their practice before they could afford a dishwasher. She flipped his apron. "You look good in that. You ought to wear it more often."

"Sorry. That's woman's work," he said, dodging the dishcloth she flung at him.

"All right, Mr. Chauvinist Pig, you go read your paper. I'm going to take a long hot bath."

He picked up the morning paper and went into the sunroom. Without thinking, he put a Dave Brubeck album in the tape deck. As the mellow tones spilled out, it hit him that this was the first time he'd played any music since Kelli died. He laid the paper aside, leaned back, closed his eyes and let the music roll over him. This had been a good day. A rustling noise roused him.

Betty was standing in the archway. "I thought you were asleep."

"No, just relaxing." She wore her fluffy terry cloth bathrobe and oversized furry, pink slippers.

He walked to her, took her in his arms and kissed her long and hard, and she responded in kind. She tensed as he untied the belt of her bathrobe then slid it from her shoulders and dropped it to the floor. "Dave, I don't know," she said.

"I love to look at you."

She forced a smile and pressed against him. He kissed her again, and arm-in-arm they went into the bedroom. She felt tense and uncomfortable as he gently drew her to him. She pretended to respond. Hurry up. Just get it over with. Afterwards as they lay cuddled like two spoons, she struggled not to cry, but despite her efforts tears trickled down her cheek. She tried to blot them on the pillow before he could see them. He nuzzled the hair on the back of her neck and gently kissed her.

"You still make me feel like a horny teenager," he whispered.

"You're not so bad yourself," she replied, trying to sound perky.

"I really love snuggling with you." He ran his hand along her thigh but stopped cold when she tensed, restrained his hand and pulled away. He slid back to his side and after a while slipped out of bed and tiptoed out.

Betty feigned sleep until she was sure he was gone. She pounded the pillow in frustration. Why doesn't he just leave me alone? But that's not what I want. Oh, I don't know what I want. And if I don't know, how can he? How can I get it through to him that all I want is a little tenderness, touching, snuggling and holding each other close? To him intimacy equals sex and nothing else. No, that's not fair. One of the things I love most about him is that he's crazy for my body, but he's always been considerate—never pressuring me to have sex—until now. That's silly. Once a month isn't pressuring. But my feelings are so different now than before. How can he understand if I can't?

This was only the fourth time they had tried to make love since Kelli's death. Every time, they both ended up with feelings of frustration, hurt, anger, selfishness, and guilt all jumbled together. They didn't talk about it for fear of hurting the other's feelings or of inflaming the situation. So the aggravation bubbled just below the surface, magnifying any other negative feelings each might have.

She lay in bed for almost an hour trying to make some sense of the contradictory feelings that whirled through her head. She yearned for how things used to be; how they had been once upon a time, long, long ago, in a life that she lived before. But once upon a time doesn't come twice, and everyone doesn't live happily ever after. Finally, with a huge sigh, she got up and wrapped her robe around her.

She found him sitting by the window staring up at the sky.

"Hi," she said.

"Hi."

"Okay if I come in?"

"Of course," he smiled and motioned to her.

She bent down and kissed him on the forehead, pulled the large ottoman over, and sat down leaning back against him. He folded his arms around her and kissed her on the side of the neck. He pointed to the glowing tapestry of glittering stars. "They say that they're not really stars but holes in the sky letting the love of our lost loved ones shine through. I like that."

"Me too."

He cleared his throat. "Honey, I'm sorry. Today was one of those rare, partly good days, and then I had to go and spoil it." He paused, thinking. "It's just that…that you were so full of life and looked so pretty. I don't know. I guess sometimes my overactive libido must muddy my brain."

"Hush," she said taking his hand and kissing the back of it. She pressed it to her cheek and went on, "I try so hard. I really do. It's not you; it's me. No matter how hard I try, I just don't feel anything. Used to be, you could simply touch me and I'd start to breathe hard. Now, nothing. Maybe it's because Kelli is a result of our love. Maybe I feel guilty enjoying something that brought her into being. Maybe I feel guilty about enjoying anything. I know this sounds crazy, but sometimes I feel as if she's watching us, and I just freeze up. It's not your fault."

"It's not our fault at all. It's Matt Williams' fault. He's like a leech that's latched onto our life and sucks any fun and joy that's left out of it. We're just the dried up husks of what we used to be." He got up and began to pace. "The frightening thing is that I don't think things will ever change. God, I hate him."

Chapter 4

Dave sat staring at the pictures of Kelli and Betty. Even though it was past eight, and he'd finished over an hour ago, he made no move to go home. What's happening to me? We have the first near normal evening since Kelli died, and I go into a deep funk for two weeks. I don't think it's entirely the sex thing. It just seems as if I've lost my wife as well as my daughter.

Chewing on a pencil, he reviewed his increasingly erratic behavior. He'd snapped at Millie, had two confrontations with patients—something he never did—and had even thrown a chart across the nurses' station at the hospital. More ominously, he had purposely distanced himself from Betty. It was frightening because he'd always felt anxious when he was not in control of any situation, personal or medical. Now he knew he was skidding out of control, and he didn't know how to stop it.

Finally he rose and went home.

Betty met him in the foyer. He gave her a perfunctory kiss and headed for the TV.

She wore a new slack suit, but he didn't notice.

"I fixed beef stroganoff," she said brightly. This was his favorite dish and one Betty always prepared for special occasions.

"That's nice." He clicked on the TV.

"Come on, let's eat before it gets cold."

"Okay." He left the TV on, came to the table and sat down, not bothering to help her serve.

"Here, light the candles."

He sighed and did as he was directed.

"Would you like some wine?"

"I guess."

When he made no move to get the wine, she served her plate and began to eat. She made several attempts at light conversation only to be answered by an absent-minded nod or grunt. By the time she served dessert, the only sound was the clink of the silverware on china.

When he finished his dessert, he went back to the TV and began to click from one channel to another, finally settling on a baseball game. Betty clenched her teeth and cleared the table.

He didn't notice when she left the room. It was almost midnight when the game ended. The bedroom door was shut. He started to open it, then hesitated, shrugged, turned and headed for the guestroom.

"Welcome home," he muttered beneath his breath.

Betty heard him early the next morning but made no move to get up until she was sure he was gone.

"Dr. DeMarco," Mary greeted Dave at the nurses' station. "You must be after the worm."

"Huh, what?"

"You know, early bird."

"Oh, yeah, sure."

Mary shrugged and returned to reviewing the previous night's reports.

"Davy, boy," Bob boomed and slapped Dave on the back. "Looking forward to seeing you guys Saturday night."

"Sounds like fun," Dave said without conviction.

Ignoring, or not sensing, Dave's mood, Bob blundered on. "I've got some good news and some bad news."

"All right, I'll play your silly game. What's the good news?"

"I saw Gino, the chef, in my office Tuesday. He says he'll hold the two thickest, juiciest steaks he has just for us."

"That's nice," Dave said, not looking up from his chart.

"Then there's the bad news."

"And that would be?"

"You've got fourteen delinquent charts in medical records that have to be completed by tomorrow, but," he looked at his watch, "that's probably why you came in early today."

Mary jumped as Dave slammed the chart shut.

"No, Bob, that's not why I came in early. I'll get to them when I'm good and ready."

"Dave, you know the hospital can't bill for the hospitalizations until they're complete."

"You're telling me the hospital is going bankrupt because of fourteen charts?" Dave said, his voice raising.

The nurses' station became silent. No one looked up from their work except to sneak a furtive glance at the two doctors.

"Hey, Dave, don't shoot the messenger. You're the one who assigned me to the records committee."

"How many times have I ever been late finishing my charts?"

"Well, this time for sure."

"Kiss my butt, Bob."

"Not until you finish your records," Bob said sweetly.

Dave stormed to the elevator and stuck in his arm to stop the closing doors. He winced as the doors squashed his arm then slid back open. He stomped on the elevator glowering as the doors closed, but not quickly enough to shut out the laughter that engulfed the nurses' station.

The following Saturday he finished breakfast early and changed into his work clothes.

Betty looked up from her newspaper. "It's awfully hot. Do you really think you should be working outside?"

"Yes."

"What are you going to do?"

"Split firewood."

"We have enough firewood to last into next year."

He shrugged, picked up his axe from the utility room and went out to the thick trunks of three dead oaks cut into two-foot cylinders scattered about the yard. Within minutes he was panting and sweating. I'm turning to flab. The wood was dry and the grain straight. Each slab split with one or two blows. One piece resembled a head.

Imagining it was Matt he split it with a single blow . He worked until well past noon, knowing Betty would have already eaten, then came in to eat lunch alone.

When he started back out, she called to him. "Dave, remember, we're having dinner with Bob and Sarah at seven."

Darn, I forgot. "Oh yeah, that's great," he said with false enthusiasm. "I'll be ready," he said and propped up another slab of wood.

"Dave, you'd better come in and get ready. It's six o'clock."

He split three more sticks then slammed the axe into a large piece and stomped in. He didn't deliberately dawdle, but it was almost seven when he finished dressing. Betty was standing in the living room with her sweater on. "I'm sorry. The time just got away from me." She glared at him but said nothing.

The Embers was brand-new, Hillsdale's only upscale restaurant; its valet parking assured an overpriced meal. A large waiting line filled the vestibule and spilled onto the sidewalk. Dave pushed through the crowd to the hostess' desk, but before he could give her his name, he saw Bob waving from a table toward the back. Taking Betty's hand he brushed past the hostess, followed by angry stares and a few snide remarks from the impatient, hungry crowd.

"Sorry, I lost track of time."

"No problem," Bob said, "It just gave Sarah more time to sort the family pictures."

Great. Sure am glad I rushed over Dave thought.

After placing their orders, Bob poured wine, and Sarah plopped a thick envelope of pictures onto the table by Betty, who seemed eager to share them. Alice was in medical school in Lexington. Robert, Jr. and the twins were in college. Jack and Julie were still in high school. "Doesn't Alice look professional with her white coat?" Dave grunted and took a large drink of wine. "Look how tall Bob's gotten."

"Yeah, he's really shot up." Dave did his best to feign some interest. Sarah glanced at him and tried to hurry through the rest of the stack, but Betty seemed to want to study each one. To his relief, their salads arrived and the pictures were put away.

"You seen any Lyme's disease?" Bob asked, trying to steer the conversation toward a safe topic.

"One, for sure, maybe another. Must be the increasing deer herd, or maybe it was always there and we just didn't recognize it."

"Well, vacation time seems to stress out everyone's heart. I did four caths and three angioplasties today. Good for tuition, but bad for the home life." Shop talk died a quick death. "The Wildcats have really recruited well. They may go all the way this year," Bob veered into another safe line of conversation. "If I can persuade Bob or the twins to give up their student tickets, we should all go to some games. On the other hand, they'll probably want to stick it to me. It might be cheaper to get them from the scalpers." Bob had season tickets and finagled two for Dave and Betty for most games.

Dave gave a weak smile and eyed his empty wineglass.

"That would be fun," Sarah said. "Do you remember when Kelli and the twins painted themselves blue, and Dave arranged for them to go to the bench and get Kyle Macy's autograph?"

Betty laughed. "I thought we'd never get their whiskers drawn to please them. I don't think any of them slept for three nights."

Dave said little all evening, for the most part sipping wine and listening to the others banter. After dessert, Bob looked at his watch.

"Nine-thirty. Time flies when you're having fun. We've got to go. I have an eight o'clock cath and need to get my beauty sleep."

Sarah kissed Dave on the cheek. "This was fun. Let's not wait so long to do it again."

"Yeah. Great."

Betty was quiet as they walked to the car. "I'd better drive."

"Why?"

"You had five glasses of wine."

"I didn't know you were counting." She didn't reply. "Whatever," he said and got in the passenger door. They didn't talk on the drive home.

Dave clicked on ESPN where someone was playing baseball, while Betty began tidying the room, slamming each item down after dusting under it. He tried not to make eye contact. "That was fun."

She stopped and glared at him. "It could have been if you hadn't sat there brooding all evening. Do you enjoy making people uncomfortable?"

Here we go. He stared at the TV and said nothing.

"I mean, they were just trying to be nice; they want so much to help."

"If they want to help, tell them to keep their pretty pictures at home. It doesn't help me to see other people's happy kids when ours is dead. It doesn't help talking about their future when we don't have one."

"What would you like for them to do?"

"I don't know. I really don't know. Why don't people just leave me alone?"

She started to leave but paused and turned to face him. "Look around, Dave. They already have."

Chapter 5

Dave was exhausted, but he couldn't sleep. His thoughts swirled and tangled as he tried to sort things out: Betty, Bob and Sarah, Matt, work, Kelli. It was still dark when he slipped out of bed and went to the sunroom where he pored through his Bible trying to get some insight or comfort. The familiar words sounded good but said nothing to him. Burying his face in his hands, he prayed as fervently as he ever had. "God, help me. I can't accept what's happened, so help me understand it. Why did you take Kelli? Give me one sign that anything I believed is true, and I think it will all hold together. Just one sign. God, I'm in the 'valley of the shadow of death' but you aren't with me. Where the hell are you?" He sat for a long time but heard no "still small voice," heard nothing at all, and, worse, he felt nothing.

At 5:22 Dave gave up on God. It wasn't a rancorous parting; he wasn't even that angry. It was more as if a trusted friend had turned his back on him when he needed him most. He picked up his Bible from the table, closed it and put it on the top shelf with the other books he was finished with, then went to the kitchen and put the coffee on.

Betty found him sipping coffee and reading the paper. She was dressed for church. She said nothing as she ate a piece of toast then put away her dishes and went into the sunroom. "Aren't you going to church?"

"No."

"Are you feeling bad?"

"No."

She started to say something but instead, put on her coat and left.

He was wearing his work clothes and watching another baseball game when she returned .

"What would you like for lunch?"

"I've already eaten a sandwich, thanks."

She changed clothes then ate alone.

Dave was standing by the window when she finished. "Those clouds are really dark, looks like rain." He rambled on about the weather but didn't mention last night or missing church. He seemed very calm, too calm. Betty went along with it for as long as she could.

"Dave, what's the matter?" He looked at her but said nothing . "You never miss church. You're acting strange."

He stared out the window and spoke in a monotone. "I saw a bumper sticker the other day. It said, 'Life's a bitch and then you die'. I think it was right."

"Dave."

"Look, Betty, you can't help, Bob and Sarah can't help, the church can't help, and God won't help. The only things in this rotten world that matter to me are you and my work, and I'm making a mess of those, but I'm going to try to do the best I can."

She grabbed his hand and pressed it against her cheek. "Oh, Dave."

He kissed her on the cheek. "The old Dave is dead. I don't know the new one very well, but I don't think I like him very much."

She watched as he went outside, yanked the axe free and began to split firewood.

℘

"Sarah, I don't know what to do," Betty said as they sat in Sarah's kitchen having lunch. "This last month has been terrible."

"What do you mean?"

"He barely speaks. He seems so calm, but I know he's about to explode. His fists are always clenched, even when he's reading the paper. If it's daylight, he keeps chopping wood until he almost drops. I don't know what he'll do when it's all split."

"Has he said what's bothering him? I mean other than Kelli's death?"

"No, he barely sleeps and he seems exhausted, but he still goes in early and works to all hours. When he gets home he eats, stares at the TV for a while, and then goes to bed in the guestroom. He's even stopped going to church."

"That is strange. Bob said he seldom missed, even in medical school." She toyed with the remnants of her quiche. "And how's this affecting you?"

"It's tearing me apart. When he's around, I feel as if I'm in a minefield, and the least misstep will set off an explosion. I need to talk about Kelli, but I'm afraid to even mention her because he can't stand to listen."

"I don't want to cause trouble, but I think you need to consider yourself first."

"What do you mean?"

"You can't fix Dave. It's not selfish to do whatever you need to help yourself."

"It's funny you should say that. I called Carolyn Sanders yesterday about the support group."

"That might be a start."

"But Dave seems so set against it."

"Screw him, Betty," Sarah slammed her hand down on the counter. "He doesn't have to go. It's about you, not him."

"You know, you're right."

The following Thursday he was eating breakfast when Betty came in.

"You're up awfully early," Dave said.

"I didn't sleep that well."

What was she so uptight about? What had he done now? He emptied his coffee, laid down the paper, and started to leave.

"Dave."

"Yes?"

"Do you have any plans for this evening?"

"I have a pretty busy schedule. Why?"

"Well…I'm going to the support group meeting in Lexington with Carolyn Sanders. I'll be gone before you get home. There's some fresh lasagna in the refrigerator. Just pop it into the microwave."

His hands clenched and unclenched. "Yeah, sure, I'll be okay." He slipped on his sport coat and left without kissing her good-by.

ꟷ

Betty looked out the window for the sixth time. Am I doing the right thing? What if it just makes matters worse? She said she'd be here at five. The clock read ten till. She rearranged a few magazines in the already immaculate living room and looked out the window as a white compact car rounded the last curve in the driveway.

Carolyn was slightly taller than Betty and much younger than she had expected, maybe early thirties. "Hi, I'm Betty, won't you come in? Have you eaten?"

"Thanks, I had a snack. We probably should get started. I'm a pokey driver."

They chatted as they left town. Carolyn had also grown up in Hillsdale. Betty recognized her family's name but had not known them.

"I was so sorry when I read about Kelli."

Just like that. She didn't seem uneasy mentioning her name. "Thank you."

"Tell me about her."

She really wants to know, Betty thought.

"The best way to describe Kelli is that she sparkled. She loved life, and she was my best friend." Betty was hesitant at first, but then the gates opened. She choked up from time to time but plunged on including all the details of the accident, the funeral and a sketchy description of the last four months. Finally she stopped. "I'm sorry, I've run on and on. It's just that I only have one friend who'll listen to me, and I don't want to be a burden to her."

"I had the same problem. I needed to talk about Billy, but there was no one."

"What happened?"

"I took him to the lake. While I was getting refreshments, he drowned."

"That's terrible."

"My husband never forgave me. For a long time I couldn't forgive myself, and I still feel guilty at times."

Betty nodded. "There are so many 'what ifs.' Do you have other children?"

"A daughter, Mary Lou. She's ten now."

"How did you and your husband work it out?" Betty asked. Carolyn grasped the steering wheel tightly and hesitated. "I'm sorry, I didn't mean to pry."

"No, that's okay. We didn't work it out. Fred could never accept Billy's death, and he blamed me. After about a year, he left, and we were divorced a year later."

Betty said nothing. "I'm so afraid. Dave and I don't talk. We seem to be drifting farther and farther apart, and I don't know how to stop it."

"I wish I could help, but I'm not the best role model. I've got my life back together, but I've resigned myself to being single. Hillsdale's not the social center of Kentucky. I dated a few times, but when things start moving toward intimacy, I freeze up. That was probably the final straw with Fred."

Betty bit her lip. "I know," she said softly.

They didn't talk for a while. "What's the meeting like?" Betty asked. "I've never been to a group before."

"It is a little scary at first, but I don't think I would have survived without it. You don't have to say anything. Just seeing other people in the same boat leading meaningful, productive lives seems to help."

"It's been a long time. Why do you still need to go?"

"Good question. Mainly, I think, it's to pay back the group for what they did for me. I probably don't need to go, but I still like to talk about Billy, and this is my only chance—or maybe I'm just addicted to hard chairs, bad coffee and dry cookies."

Their brief laughter seemed to break the tension. Betty was relaxed and talking easily when they arrived, but her relaxation was short lived.

The meeting room in the church basement was too large for the group. A table by the door was stacked high with hymnals, and a picture of an angel hovering over two children on a rickety bridge hung over the table. A circle of chairs filled one end of the room, and at the other about thirty people, mostly women with a smattering of men, milled about. Some who seemed to be regulars laughed and hugged, while others, like Betty, lingered on the periphery of the group, tense, saying nothing, just watching with a haunted look in their eyes. Several of the regulars spoke with Betty and asked about Kelli. After some refreshments—Carolyn had been right, the cookies were dry and the coffee weak—they all settled into the circle. The leader explained the rules and read a poem, then they began to introduce themselves.

"My name is Wilma Thomson. My son, Jake, was murdered two years ago. He was twenty…I'm Angela Martin, my son, Walter, died of cystic fibrosis three years ago. He was eighteen. …Jennie was killed by a drunk driver last May. She was fifteen…Donnie died of leukemia…My daughter, Emily, was stillborn."

Several struggled to say the painful words. Betty began to panic as the litany of horror slowly made its way around the circle, drawing ever closer to her. "My name is Carolyn Sanders. My son, Billy, drowned six years ago. He was seven years old."

Betty felt Carolyn grasp her hand. Her mouth was dry, and tears streamed down her cheeks. She tried to speak, but her throat was so tight she made only a strangled croak. She buried her face in her hands. Carolyn handed Betty a tissue and nodded to the next person.

"My name is Joan Billings. My daughter, Beth, was killed in an auto accident two years ago. She was twenty-five."

No one seemed bothered by her break down, and they moved on to the major topic for the meeting—how they were dealing with the beginning of school.

"Jennie just died three months ago. I have two other children. I'm afraid to let them ride the bus. They get angry because I'm so hovering and protective, but I just can't help it."

"Billy's been dead six years, but I still get depressed when school starts. I know it sounds crazy, but I drive two miles out of my way going to work to avoid passing his school."

"It took a long time, but I needed to be around kids his age. I volunteer as a reading aide."

After a while it became quiet. "Any other burning issues?" the leader asked. A short, slightly overweight lady cleared her throat. "Yes, Mary?"

"I know it sounds crazy, but sometimes at night I get so tense that I go out in the backyard and scream Jodie's name as loud as I can. I know it's weird, but somehow it seems to help. Have any of you ever heard of anyone doing that?"

"I do it in the car."

"I do it in my son's bedroom after my husband goes to work."

Betty spoke for the first time. "I've done that too, but I was afraid to mention it to anyone. I was sure I was losing my mind. It helps knowing that there are others as odd as me."

The meeting lasted about two hours, but Carolyn and Betty remained with several others, drinking coffee and talking for another half-hour.

"I don't think I've ever felt so emotionally spent," Betty said as they drove home.

"Don't be surprised if you're exhausted tomorrow. The meetings helped me cope, but I didn't realize what hard work coping was."

"I felt so foolish when I choked up and couldn't talk."

"I wouldn't let it bother me. It took me three meetings before I could say Billy was dead." She was quiet for a while. "I was crushed. At first the least little thing got the best of me: getting out of bed in the morning, fixing lunch, going to work. Later bigger hurdles: his birthday, the day he died, the first day of school, oh, and especially Christmas, but you get through it. You have no choice. You get up, you fix lunch, you go to work. A small victory, perhaps, but a victory nonetheless. You repeat this over and over, and you get through it. Life will never be the same, but you do learn to live again, one small victory at a time."

Dave was in the shower when Betty got home. She made a cup of tea and sat down to unwind.

" I'm glad you finally made it home," he said.

Ignoring his sarcasm, she asked, "Did you like the lasagna? It's a new recipe I got from Mary."

"I stopped at McDonald's."

"Oh." She sipped her tea. "The meeting was good. I think it will help."

"Yeah, fine." After an awkward pause he continued, "John Rankin called. He's coming over Saturday morning, probably to try to get me back in church. I told him not to waste his time, but he insisted. Why doesn't he mind his own business?"

"Dave. John has really stood by us since Kelli died. He's doing the best he can."

"A lot of help that's been."

"Please be nice."

"I'm always nice. I'm going to bed."

Dave was reading the paper when the doorbell rang. When he made no move to answer it, Betty glared at him and opened the door. "Hi, John. It's nice of you to come over. Dave's in the sunroom. Dave, John's here."

Dave laid the paper down as they entered but made no move to rise. "Have a seat, John." Betty shrugged, rolled her eyes and left.

John shifted in the large easy chair. "Dave, I've missed you at church."

"You might as well get used to it."

"What happened, Dave?"

"My daughter was killed. Don't you read the papers?"

John drew back. Better go easy. I've never seen him like this. "I can't imagine how you feel. Is there anything I can do?"

Dave clenched and unclenched his hands. "I don't want to fight with you, John. I've tried it your way all of my life and where did it get me? God killed my daughter and left me alone to fend for myself. No, there's nothing you can say or do that will help."

"God didn't kill Kelli."

"No, he let that worthless little drunk do it for him. Why didn't he let him die instead of Kelli? Someone told me that 'her time had just come.' What the hell does that mean? Did some arbitrary God just wake up last May and say, 'Oops, Kelli's time just ran out. I need to bump her off today?'"

"Dave, we've been given free will. Sometimes people abuse it, and others are hurt. You can't blame God for that. Think of all the good he does."

"Come off of it, John, you can't have it both ways. Something good happens, God caused it. Something bad happens, God couldn't stop it because of free will. A plane crashes and everyone from row 24 back survives. Praise God, he saved them, but he had nothing to do with what happened with those unfortunate souls in rows 1 through 23."

"I really don't know why Kelli died, but I'm convinced that God hurt along with you."

"Well, he's keeping it one deep, dark secret."

"What is it you want, Dave?" Dave gave him an incredulous look. "You know what I mean."

Dave pressed his knuckles into his temples. "At first I wanted to know why, but now I realize that, except at the most elementary level, I'll never know why or even if there is an answer to why. So I asked for some comfort, some sense that it wasn't all meaningless. Just a tiny bit of that 'peace that passes all understanding.'"

"We can't understand everything. That's where faith comes in."

"Faith. In what? I begged for just one little sign. Anything, just so I'd know that all I'd believed in wasn't a delusion. And what did I get? Nothing, just cold, dead silence."

"Then what do you believe?"

"I can't explain the universe without some Creator or First Cause or Prime Mover, whatever you want to call it. So I believe in a God. I just don't think He cares."

John sat in stunned silence. Dave stood up. "John, I appreciate what you're trying to do, but it doesn't help. Why don't you just go? I'll probably say things more hurtful than I already have, and I really don't want to."

"Okay, Dave, if that's what you want." Dave walked with him to the door. "I'll pray for you, Dave."

"Yeah, you do that." Dave started to close the door. "One more thing, John, and don't take this personally."

"Yes?"

"Please don't come back."

Dave leaned against the door and shut his eyes.

"Has John already left?" Betty asked.

"Yeah, he had to run." Catching her skeptical look, Dave added, "I was as nice as I could be."

"I see."

"No, you don't see."

She turned to leave.

"Betty."

"Yes?"

"If he calls back and you want to see him, fine; just have him come when I'm not here."

Chapter 6

"The group's really helped. It's hard to believe I've only been attending two months," Betty said. "I've really made a lot of progress. I still get blindsided by little things. Just the other day when I found a poem Kelli had written, and I went to pieces; but now I don't crash as hard, and it doesn't last nearly so long."

"That's the way it was with me," Carolyn said.

"Except for you and Sarah, the group is the only people I feel at ease with. There's no need to put on a smiley face or act chipper when I really feel rotten. When Dave was in Vietnam, he sent me tapes, and he was always talking about things back in the 'world' and how anxious he was to leave there and get back to the 'world.' I think I know why he said that. I feel as if I'm separated from everyone else by a big fence, and I'm living my life in this separate little world. They can't reach me, and I can't reach them. I blame them, but at times I wonder who built the fence, me or them, or was it a joint effort?"

Carolyn nodded in agreement. "You feel so isolated, so cut off. I get angry with them at times, but those who haven't lost a child can't understand no matter how hard they try. They don't know what to say, but, more than that, I think we frighten them, almost as if death were contagious, or maybe we just remind them that it could happen to their child, too."

"At least we have the group. Speaking about isolation, Dave has only Bob to talk to and, knowing Bob, I doubt if he can handle very much. I just wish I could help him, but it seems the better I feel, the worse he does, almost as if he resents my improving. The little time he's at home, he's surly and sarcastic, sometimes downright mean. He refers to the group as 'The Mutual Misery Society'."

Carolyn negotiated a hairpin curve. "What are you going to do?"

"With Dave staying away so much, I'm going stir crazy alone at home. I didn't realize how much Kelli and I did together. I've got to get out, so I've decided to go back into nursing."

"Have you mentioned this to Dave?"

"Not yet. I tried once but didn't. Now I have no choice; I have to tell him soon."

ജ

Dave tossed a chart onto the stack beside his desk and dialed the next number. He hated noontime callbacks, but it was better than putting them off until evening. He set the half-eaten apple on the remaining stack. Millie stuck her head in then started to back out, but he motioned for her to stay. "...yes, I'll call that in, Mrs. Watkins."

"I didn't mean to disturb you," Millie said.

"That's all right. It beats talking to more freeloaders too cheap to make an appointment. What is it?"

Millie fought the urge to question his uncharacteristic view of patients. "A lawyer called wanting to set up a meeting with you."

"What about? Who was it?"

"A Mr. Fourney, very evasive, said it was personal, not business. I tried to put him off, but he insisted that I check with you. I could clear some time for you tomorrow afternoon if you want."

"Just what I need, to finish out the week with a lawyer. Yeah, set him up, but tell him I only have thirty minutes and bill him the max."

"I'll be glad to." She eyed the apple and shook her head. "Is that all you're having for lunch?"

"I only have a few minutes."

"You'd better slow down; you're killing yourself. Why don't you take an afternoon off? You could use the break."

"Don't you start, too."

ꟿ

That night after dinner Betty brought him a cup of spiced tea.

"Hey, thanks." He took a careful sip. "Hmm, good."

"I want to talk to you about something."

"It's been a long day," Dave said.

"It's not about Kelli." He visibly relaxed, and she continued, "Remember last year when I said I might want to get back into nursing after Kelli graduated? Well, I think I'm ready. I'm going buggy rattling around in this empty house, and I need something worthwhile to do."

"I could talk to Mary Johnson in personnel and see what might be open."

"Thanks, but I want to do this myself. It's been over fifteen years since I did any patient care, and I need to get re-educated. There's an accelerated three-month nursing refresher course at the university in Lexington. They've accepted my application."

"When did you apply?"

"A couple of months ago."

"That's… good," he said. "Why didn't you mention it?"

"I tried to the night I wore my new suit and fixed the Beef Stroganoff. You weren't very friendly. You didn't want to talk," Betty said.

Dave winced. "I'm sorry. When do you start?"

"A week from Monday, October thirty-first. Since it's going to be ten to twelve hours a day, I've rented an apartment."

"You're going to live there?"

"It's too far to commute, but I'll come home on weekends. You're not home much during the week anyway."

He'd encouraged her when she'd first mentioned this. Ignoring the barb, he said, "Sounds good to me. Go for it."

She threw her arms around him. "Thanks, I'm so excited."

He pulled her to him and kissed her deeply. "I've heard nursing students can really be wild in bed."

"Oh, Dave, not tonight." He stiffened. "I'm sorry. I just can't."

His jaw clenched. "Yeah, sure. Can't, won't, couldn't care less, what difference does it make? You just go through the motions anyway. I know you're faking it."

"That's not fair."

"Life's not fair, Betty. Go on to Lexington. Hopefully, you won't be bothered by horny lechers like me there, and don't bother to come back on weekends; I'll get along fine. Think about it, you'll be closer to your precious group." Before she could reply he spun and stomped out.

He sat in the darkened sunroom after she went to bed, conflicting emotions ricocheting through his head: anger at her and himself, remorse for what he'd said, total frustration with their situation and with life in general, hopelessness about the future. More than anything else, at this moment he felt abandonment and an overwhelming sadness. Abandoned by Betty, and sadness as he watched his one small island of safety and intimacy slowly submerging.

He was pouring coffee the next morning when she came in. Her eyes were red and puffy.

"Dave, I…"

"I really don't have time to talk this morning."

She jerked out a chair, slammed it down and sat. She was trembling. Her lip curled up, almost in a sneer. "I don't want you to talk, I want you to listen. Just for once, I want you to listen."

It was as if she had slapped him. He sat and listened.

"You mope around here wrapped in your sorrow, and I have to tiptoe on eggshells to avoid upsetting you. You hide at work so you won't have to be with me, then expect it to be just like old times when you finally do come home."

"That's not fair."

"Life's not fair, remember, Dave? You dump on our friends, run them off and then wonder why you're so lonesome. I've had it up to here with you." She paused, breathing heavily.

"Maybe you should just stay in Lexington."

"You've got that right. You better just hope it's only for three months."

The chair crashed to the floor as she stood up, and she left without bothering to pick it up. He heard the bedroom door slam and sat in stunned silence. Finally he went and tapped on the bedroom door. She didn't answer.

That afternoon, Millie met him in the hallway as he exited the examining room. "The lawyer's here."

"I forgot. Any idea what it's about?" She shook her head. "I need a quick break. Just take him to my office. You'll probably have to clear a place for him to sit."

He was right. Millie lifted the pile of charts from the chair and set them on a box by the bookcase. She stepped into the waiting room where the lawyer was sitting very erect, briefcase on his lap. "Mr. Fourney?" He nodded. "I'm Millie Langston. Dr. DeMarco's almost finished. Why don't you come and wait in his office?"

"God, what a dump," he muttered under his breath, unfortunately, not quietly enough to escape Millie.

She was about to offer him some coffee, but she bristled and reconsidered. The edge to her voice was obvious. "Dr. DeMarco will be with you shortly." She left him standing there amid the clutter.

She found Dave in the break room sipping a Coke and finishing the cookies she'd brought that morning. "He's all yours."

Dave took a final swig and patted her on the shoulder. "Love at first sight?" She sniffed and went back to the business office. Fourney was studying the diplomas when Dave walked in. "Hello, I'm Dave DeMarco."

Fourney extended a limp hand. "Dr. DeMarco, good to meet you. Daniel Fourney representing Braxton, Braxton and Wallace." He turned to the plaques on the wall. "Eastern Kentucky boy, fine school." Dave said nothing. Fourney's voice softened, "Beautiful family," then became almost syrupy, "I'm so sorry about your darling daughter."

"Thanks." Dave tossed his white lab coat onto the pile of charts. He stepped over Fourney's briefcase and sat down behind his desk, and motioned to the now cleared side chair. "Have a seat. Who did you say you were with?"

Fourney seemed surprised. " Braxton, Braxton and Wallace. It's one of the largest firms in Lexington. J. Tyler Braxton, the senior partner, ran for governor several years ago. I'm surprised you haven't heard of them."

"Don't have time to keep up with lawyers," Dave said. He already didn't like him. Fourney was small, not more than five-six on tiptoe. He had a large nose and a receding chin, and moved with quick jerky motions reminding Dave of a ferret. His slicked-back hair accentuated his pointed features. Dave clenched his hands as Fourney chattered on, recounting the history and virtues of Braxton, Braxton and Wallace.

"Why are you here?" Dave cut him off.

Fourney almost stammered but regained his composure. "I was referred to you by some mutual acquaintances."

"What for? What mutual acquaintances?"

"I'm not at liberty to say, attorney-client privilege, you know, but they wanted to be sure you were aware of all of your legal recourses."

"Legal recourses?" Dave asked, a puzzled look on his face.

"Well," Fourney opened his briefcase, withdrew a sheaf of papers and laid them on the corner of the desk, "I have researched the matter of your precious daughter fully. You have a solid case for wrongful death. I think we could easily get three million, maybe more factoring in the loss of future earnings. It's almost November, and the statute of limitations is only one year, so we need to act expeditiously."

Dave frowned and rubbed his chin. "You want to make money off of Kelli's death?"

"No, no, I just want justice to be served. Besides we need to get these dangerous drunks off the road, make an example of them." He continued to rattle on.

Dave saw his lips moving and heard sounds, but he couldn't focus on what he was saying. As the familiar sick, hollow feeling in the pit of his stomach returned, he clenched his fists, fighting the urge to punch Fourney right then.

"Shut up!" Dave shouted. Fourney jerked back, then started to speak. "I said shut up!" Dave leaned forward, his eyes blazing. The lawyer shrank down in his chair making himself as small as possible, hands clasped in his lap, unmoving except for an occasional involuntary twitch. For months, Dave had been awash in a growing, unfocused rage, and now Daniel Fourney was in the crosshairs. "Mr. Fourney," his voice was flat and hard, "No personal acquaintance of mine sent you. They would've feared for your safety."

"What do you mean?" he stammered and licked his lips.

Dave rose and towered over him, "I mean that they'd be concerned that if you even mentioned something about Kelli, I would beat the stuffing out of you."

Fourney cringed down in the chair, making himself even smaller. "Don't you touch me. I'll sue."

"Wouldn't that look great for Braxton, Braxton and Wallace? Lawyer sues for getting butt kicked while unethically soliciting business from a bereaved parent." He leaned down, his face not two inches from Fourney's. "You ambulance chasing, blood sucking shyster. I'm going to haul you and Braxton, Braxton and Wallace before the ethics committee and nail your hide to the wall."

"You can't do that. I'm not a lawyer."

"What do you mean?"

"I'm just a representative of Braxton, Braxton and Wallace. I talk to potential clients for them to see if there's any interest."

"You bumbling blockhead. You're just a runner for them. If I complain, they merely claim they never knew you."

Fourney nodded, swabbing his wet forehead with his coat sleeve.

Dave grabbed him by his necktie and yanked him up on tiptoe. "If you have any desire to maintain your health, this is one doctor you'd better never see again." Fourney's eyes bulged as Dave half-dragged, half-carried him by his tie, stumbling on tiptoe down the hallway.

Millie dashed out when she heard the commotion, then backed into the waiting room, her eyes wide. Dave slowed as he passed her.

"Millie, don't you ever let this man or anyone else from Braxton, Braxton, and Wallace in here again. You hear?" Millie nodded and farcically ran to open the door. Dave hauled Fourney to the door then paused a moment. "If you ever mention my daughter again, I swear to God, I will pound you to a pulp," Dave snarled and shoved him out the door.

Fourney staggered but caught himself before he fell and scurried to the black Lincoln Towncar. "My briefcase," he wailed, turning back.

Dave sprinted back to his office, crammed the papers into the briefcase, ran back and hurled it out the door. It sailed upward in a slow arc then crashed in the vicinity of Fourney. Papers erupted all over the parking lot. The last thing Dave saw as he slammed the door was Daniel Fourney on his knees gathering the scattered sheets and stuffing them into his briefcase.

"Sonofabitch." Dave kicked the wastebasket across the waiting room.

"Dr. DeMarco, you've got to calm down." Millie was trembling. "What happened?"

Without answering he stomped back to his office, slammed the door and collapsed into his chair, heart racing, hands shaking. Sweat dripped from his forehead and chin, and his breath came in gasps. Forcing himself to take long, deep breaths, he gradually calmed, but his heart continued to pound, and he was left drenching wet with a queasy stomach.

After a while there was a soft knock on the door. "Come in, Millie." She stepped just across the threshold, alarmed by his gray pallor. "Are you all right?" Her voice quivered. "Is there anything I can do?"

"No, Millie, there's nothing you can do. There's nothing anyone can do."

"Oh, Dr. DeMarco."

He got up and put his arm around her shoulder. "Come on. You deserve an explanation, but first I need an antacid." They walked to the break room. He washed down three large tablets and sat down, motioning for her to sit. He gave her a brief recap.

"That's terrible." He nodded. "I hope you meant that about billing him the max."

"Doggone right I did."

"Good," she said without a quiver.

When he got home, Betty went to the foyer out of habit. Dave was pale, ashen, and he had a wild look in his eyes that she'd never seen. "What's the matter?"

"Don't ask." He brushed past her and went to his easy chair. He plopped a six-pack of beer on the coffee table and cracked one open. He sat in the dark, slowly drinking. He seldom drank at all and never more than two beers even on Super Bowl Sunday. He was on his fifth when she went to bed.

The next week seemed twelve days long. Betty packed, and, in what little spare time there was, tried to scan the textbooks she'd bought. Dave came home late, went straight to his chair and emptied the six-pack he brought home each evening. He picked at whatever she prepared, but seldom ate a full meal. He communicated in monosyllables and grunts.

On Sunday he helped her load her luggage into the car. After he slammed the trunk lid he stood uncertainly.

"Thank you," Betty said, "I've cooked up several things. They're in the fridge. Just heat them in the microwave."

"Thanks." He hugged her. "I'll call every night. "Betty, I..." He fumbled for words.

"I know. Good-bye, Dave." The door slammed and she drove off.

He didn't call every night—it was more like two or three times a week. He'd never been a good phone conversationalist, even when they were dating. When they did talk, she seemed more excited and enthusiastic than he could remember, telling him about each day's classes and asking for advice on difficult clinical questions. Answering her questions helped since it negated the need for small talk, but he felt a growing resentment at her obvious enthusiasm and sense of purpose . They were careful to avoid Kelli or anything personal. Maybe if they only had to talk superficially for fifteen minutes two or three times a week, they'd do all right.

Dave was in a downward spiral and didn't know what to do about it. After twelve to fourteen hours at work, he came home, sometimes called Betty, drank his beer and went to bed. He politely declined all invitations from Bob. Weekends were the worst, especially if he wasn't on call. All of the firewood was split and stacked, so there was little else to do except sleep late and watch TV. In desperation, he began cutting another large oak with an axe; the chainsaw didn't tire him enough. If he could keep himself exhausted, he stayed numb and didn't think. Even with all of this physical activity he felt decreasingly fit and found that it took less and less exertion to leave him breathless and exhausted.

He hated being in the empty house during the day. When he was too tired to work, he'd sit just beyond the salt lick on the edge of the hundred-foot precipice that Kelli had dubbed The Jump Off, stare at the ridges stretching off to the horizon, and wonder how anyone in the whole world could be happy. At times he wondered if it wouldn't be easier just to jump off.

ꟷ

"Crap!" Dave roared and slammed the refrigerator door. The spice rack wobbled for just a moment, then toppled from its place above the freezer compartment. He made a wild lunge but succeeded only in broadcasting jars and tins of pepper, cumin, cinnamon, and nutmeg all over the kitchen. A reddish cloud of paprika enveloped his foot when he kicked the can across the room.

The day had been a killer with no time for lunch and four walk-ins five minutes before the office closed. Betty's phone call hadn't helped. He'd feigned interest as she gushed about her studies and the wonderful evening that lay ahead with her instructor and the other four students: dinner at a posh restaurant and a concert afterwards. And now the final insult—no beer.

Sneezing all the while, he cleaned up the mess then slumped into his easy chair and stared out the window into the darkness, a perfect match for his mood. Unable to sit still, he began to pace.

"I need a beer," he said aloud and headed for the car.

Being alone had never bothered him before, but now it gnawed at him, making him more restless and edgy. "Oh, darn," he muttered as he zipped past the all night market four miles out the highway. Oh, well, a drive will help me unwind…maybe. He continued on for another ten or fifteen minutes until he reached a small collection of businesses—a service station, a seedy motel called the Dew Drop Inn, and a strip joint, The Play Pen. He pulled in at the strip joint to turn around. The lot was almost full of pickup trucks, motorcycles and vintage 70's autos with spoilers on their deck lids, a veritable redneck road rally.

Dave didn't turn around but sat for several minutes. Once after final exams, he, Bob and several other medical students had gone to a similar establishment for a wild night that he had never considered repeating...until now. Why should Betty have all the fun? He backed around and parked. What the heck, just a drink or two.

The Play Pen had no windows, just a single door in front. In the glow from the two mercury lights in the parking lot, the building's color was indeterminate but appeared to be some shade of pink, which harmonized nicely with the purple door.

"Hold it, buddy." A thick hand grabbed his arm. "There's a ten dollar cover charge." His head was shaved, and he stood a good three inches taller than Dave. Biceps the size of cantaloupes threatened to rip the arms of his T-shirt. He took the ten and noted Dave's full wallet. "I'm Hank. There's an empty table over there."

Dave picked his way through the crowded room to a small table by the wall and sat down. Loud, unfamiliar music pounded over the din of the crowd. Through a thick haze of smoke he saw a narrow, elevated stage jutting into the center of the room where two women wearing only thongs sinuously wove themselves around poles running from the stage to the ceiling. One had to be forty and reminded Dave of the old adage about horses who had been "rode hard and put up wet." An aura of boredom surrounded her as she mechanically went through the motions of her dance. The other one couldn't have been over seventeen but was enthusiastic about her work. Her enthusiasm was rewarded by loud hoots and cheers and bills tucked into her thong.

"Hi, honey, I'm Amber." The husky voice jerked Dave's attention from the floorshow. "Hank said you were alone. Like some company?" Smiling down at him was one of the most spectacular women he had ever seen. Her tawny hair was shoulder length. She wore something akin to a Dallas Cowboy cheerleader outfit—tight shorts emphasizing her tiny waist and long, well-proportioned legs and a snug halter tied in the front, barely covering the nipples of her full, firm breasts.

"Uh…I guess…sure," Dave stammered.

"I'll have to get us a drink to stay," she said almost apologetically. "What'll you have?"

"A beer will be fine."

"What is this?" he asked after sipping his drink.

"You looked like you needed a little pick-me-up so I added a splash of Jack Daniels."

"Pretty good." He drank in silence.

"You're not very talkative."

He threw down the last of his drink. "No, I guess not. You have another one of those?"

She gave him a radiant smile. "Coming right up."

Midway through his third drink he began to relax. Amber leaned forward and ran her fingers along the back of his hand.

"What's—"

"What's a nice guy like you doing in a joint like this?" she interrupted him.

Dave burst out laughing. "I guess I'm pretty easy to read."

She leaned forward giving him a full view of her breasts. "I see you're married," she said nodding to his wedding band.

"Sort of."

"What's that mean?"

He flicked the knot of her halter. "That doesn't look very sturdy," he said changing the subject.

She playfully slapped his hand. "You can look, but don't touch."

"That sounds familiar," he said, his voice becoming slightly slurred.

He had four more drinks, not noticing that she had drunk nothing after the first. On each trip back to the bar, she brought back two, simply giving him hers when he'd finished his.

"Oops." The last of his drink trickled across the table when he misjudged his grasp and knocked the glass over.

"That's okay, honey," Amber said. She grabbed a handful of napkins. "Here, let me help." She mopped up the drink, leaning across him, almost trapping his nose in her cleavage.

"Mmm. Nice." His voice was both slurred and muffled.

She pulled her chair next to his and slid her hand up his thigh.

"What's the matter? Don't I turn you on?"

"I guess I'm just not up to it," he giggled.

"How would you like to try somewhere private?" she whispered placing his hand on her thigh and nibbling his earlobe.

"And just where would that be?" he said very slowly and precisely, having difficulty coordinating his mouth, tongue and lips.

"I know the man at the motel across the road. Want to go for it?" she said slipping on a heavy coat.

"Sure, why not?" Dave's chair wobbled as he shoved back from the table . "Whoa!" He teetered when he tried to stand. Amber placed his arm around her neck, hoisted him to his feet, and guided him toward the door. The whole establishment seemed to rotate slowly, but he found that by hanging onto Amber and placing his feet wide apart he could remain almost upright. Hank smiled and opened the door for them.

"Hey, what're you doing?" Dave protested. He knew he was in a bed, but had no idea how he'd gotten there. Amber was pulling off his pants. "Cut it out. I can't do this. What would my wife say?"

With one final jerk, she yanked his pants off and began rifling his wallet.

"Seventy-two bucks? I froze my ass hauling you over here for seventy-two bucks?"

"Give me that," Dave said struggling to get up but succeeding only in sliding off the bed and landing with a thud.

Amber tucked his pants under her arm, threw the empty wallet at him and headed for the door. "You limp-dick loser. You better not come after me. Hank will squash you like a bug."

"My pants," he blubbered. "How will I get home?"

"Call your wife."

"You don't have any pants!" Bob almost dropped the phone laughing. "I'm sorry. I couldn't help it. It just tickled my funny-bone...Where are you?...The Dew Drop Inn." He tried but couldn't restrain another round of laughter. "Okay, just hang tight. I have one more case. I'll be there in an hour or so."

Dave's recollection of the preceding night was as fuzzy as the roof of his mouth. Bracing himself again the peeling desk he tried to dress. What's the use? Unable to knot his tie, Dave jerked it off and stuffed it into his coat pocket. He smiled ruefully at the red-eyed image in the dingy bureau mirror—dress shirt, sport coat, paisley boxer shorts, well-polished loafers, no pants—every inch the successful physician. Amber was right. He was a loser. Maybe the other was true, too. He sat on the edge of the bed and moved as little as possible to ease his throbbing head.

What in the world was I thinking? Betty's going to have a good time so I risk my reputation and marriage to get even. What if she finds out? Dave, you are stupid, stupid, stupid. He continued berating himself until he heard the gravel crunching outside. Seeing Bob's car, he dashed out unsteadily and flopped in.

Bob's face reddened and he gritted his teeth trying to suppress another gale of laughter. "Where to, sir, home first or straight to the office?"

Dave smiled. "Okay, wise guy, just take me home. I told Millie I had a bug."

"There's hot coffee," Bob nodded toward the cup holder. "You sounded like you could use some."

"Thanks, my head's about to explode."

Neither spoke on the short drive home. As Dave fished behind the mailbox for the key, Bob could resist no longer.

"When the lady of the house answers, tell her you're selling encyclopedias and intend to buy the rest of your suit with your next sale."

Despite himself, Dave joined Bob's hilarious laughter.

"Go take a shower. I'll make some more coffee," Bob said, then added as Dave headed toward the bedroom, "and for God's sake, put on some pants."

Bob was frying bacon and eggs when Dave returned.

"What'll it be?"

"Toast is all I think I can handle right now," Dave said.

Bob finished the last of his and Dave's brunch. "What happened?"

They sipped coffee as Dave gave him a brief sketch of his escapade.

"Did you…you know?"

"No, nothing like that, but the scary thing is that if I could've, I probably would've."

"You know that's crazy."

"Of course I know it's crazy. I just can't seem to avoid doing crazy things. Risking my marriage because I'm out of beer? That's not just crazy, that's absurd. I blamed it on Betty's being gone, but when she was here I did my best to avoid her, and when I couldn't, I picked fights with her. Why would she want to stick around?"

Bob said nothing.

"I'm coming unraveled, thinking crazy thoughts, and I don't know how to stop it. You know what I do when I can't sleep, which is most of the time?" Dave asked.

"What?"

"I lie in bed thinking about what I'd like to do to Matt. At first, I just wanted him in jail, but I'm a doctor. I can imagine better fates for that little twerp. I've finally settled on making him quadriplegic by severing his spinal cord at C-4, then destroying his vision and hearing with a laser. That way, he wouldn't die; he'd just lie there in the silent darkness unable to move …just like Kelli."

Bob stared at him wide-eyed.

"Didn't know your best friend was such a sicko, did you?"

"Is there anything I can do to help?"

"Yeah, don't tell Sarah about last night."

Frightened by his idiotic escapade, Dave struggled to regain some degree of control. The only time he felt reasonably normal was in the office where he was still tired, but at least his mind was occupied. Convinced he was becoming malnourished Millie started bringing some food almost every day. Today he was sitting in the break room wolfing down cold meatloaf.

"Don't you have anything to eat at home?"

"Lord, yes. Betty left enough food for an army. I just don't get around to fixing it very often."

"Dr. DeMarco, you've got to slow down. You look terrible."

"Well, thank you."

"I'm serious."

"Maybe after Betty gets back." If she comes back. She's flourishing and I'm going to hell, literally and figuratively. "What's the afternoon look like?"

"Not too bad. You have a new patient at four."

He finished lunch, brushed his teeth and slipped into his lab coat. "Back to the salt mines."

Dave scanned the new patient's chart outside the door. Walter Williams, age 49, security guard at International Chemicals. The rest of the chart was blank.

As he stepped into the room, Mr.Williams scrambled to his feet. "Mr. Williams, I'm Dr. Demarco. Sit down and make yourself comfortable."

Williams was a stocky, muscular man about five-eight, balding except for a fringe of gray-flecked hair. He fidgeted, his callused hands grasping the rolled up Co-op cap so tightly his knuckles turned white.

"What can I do for you?" Dave asked.

Williams' eyes darted around the room. The sweat beads on his bald pate glistened. Taking a deep breath, he looked at Dave. "I'm Matt's dad."

Dave did a double take, then sat down. "What do you want?" Dave asked, struggling to remain calm.

"I'm sorry to barge in on you like this. I wrote you a letter but you didn't answer."

No, I threw it in the trash, just like the one from Matt.

"Then the lawyer came and said you were going to sue me. Please, Dr. Demarco, I can't tell you how sorry I am for what Matt did. There's no excuse, but I have four children younger than him. We're barely making ends meet. Don't make them suffer for what Matt did."

"What are you talking about? What lawsuit?"

"The man from Lexington said you were going to sue me for three million dollars, and I needed an attorney to help me. I can't afford an attorney."

Dave stood up and began to pace. "Fourney. He's trying to play both sides of the fence." His face reddened, and his heart began to race.

Alarmed by Dave's appearance Mr. Williams could only stammer, "I...I'm sorry."

"Look. As much as I'd like to make Matt's life miserable, I'm not suing anyone."

Mr. Williams slumped back into his chair with a sigh of relief. Dave continued to pace around the tiny room, clammy with sweat. Finally, he sat back down. "I'm not going to sue you." Then out of habit he asked, "Is there anything else I can do for you?"

Tears welled in Mr. Williams' eyes. "I know it's too much to ask. I mentioned it to Mrs. DeMarco, and I wrote it better in the letter. Matt's a good boy. What he did was terrible, but he'd never drunk before. He's lost his scholarship and dropped out of college, he won't eat, and he's lost twenty-five pounds. He almost won't come out of his room. I'm afraid he ... might hurt himself. Could you please talk with him? He's so sorry. He just wants to tell you so."

Why is he doing this? His chest felt tight and his breathing was labored. Trying not to sound harsh, he said, "You're right, Mr. Williams, it's too much to ask. Matt made his bed, now he'll just have to lie in it." Without another word, he left the room. Karen, his nurse, stepped back as he stumbled toward his office.

"Millie, come quick, Dr. DeMarco looks terrible."

His face was flushed; his fist was clenched over the center of his chest. "Dr. DeMarco, what's the matter?"

He raised his twisted face. "Millie, I...I..." A heavy pressure in his chest choked off his breath and sweat dripped from his brow. The room began to do a slow swirl. "I think you should call 911," he gasped and fell to the floor.

Far away he could hear her shouting, her distorted voice sounded like a tape run at too slow a speed . "Hurry, please hurry, I think Dr. DeMarco's having a heart attack."

Chapter 7

He'd been in the cardiac care unit for about four hours. The pressure in his chest had subsided, and he listened through a mellow morphine haze as Bob spoke to him. "The TPA did its job. That clot's busted, and everything's settling down. The preliminary chemistries don't indicate any muscle damage. We'll plan on cathing you tomorrow if you remain stable. Any questions?" Dave smiled weakly and shook his head.

Bob patted him on the shoulder. " I'm really sorry," he said, choking up a bit. "After Kelli and all, it just doesn't seem fair." Embarrassed by this show of emotion, he avoided Dave's eyes and turned to leave.

"Thanks, Bob."

Dave watched as he walked to the nurses' station, slumped at the desk and began writing in the chart. From the unfamiliar perspective of a patient, the whole scene was out of kilter. The IV poles towered above him, and he had to strain to see what was in the plastic bags that fed the tubes running into his arm. The flimsy gown was bunched about his waist, and he kept getting tangled in the wires attached to his chest. A picture of a wooded stream spanned by a stone bridge hung on the wall directly before him. The EKG monitor was strategically placed out of sight above and behind the head of the bed. With some satisfaction he found that, by holding his head just so, he could see the rhythmic blips reflected in the glass of the picture.

Letting the morphine take over, he lay back, closed his eyes, and began to drift but was jerked back by a quivering in his chest. The alarm at the nursing station blared. The regular, sharp spikes reflected in the picture were now a chaotic, wavy line. "Oh, crap," he muttered.

"Code Blue ICU...Code Blue ICU," echoed in the distance.

His vision was blurring as Bob loomed over him, face contorted, clenched fist raised. As the fist slammed into his chest he faintly heard Bob screaming, "Damn it, Dave, don't you die! Don't you die!" Then everything went black.

ꟗ

Slowly the room came into focus. Dave had no sensation of floating, in fact, he felt nothing at all. He was just watching. From his vantage point somewhere above the foot of the bed, he surveyed the frantic activity below with calm detachment.

The scene was one of controlled pandemonium. His limp, naked body bounced as Jack Gibbons, the emergency room doctor, rhythmically compressed and released his chest. One nurse drew various solutions into syringes, injecting some into the IV tubing and setting others aside for future use. Another attached different monitors and took his blood pressure. After every fifth compression, the blue clad respiratory therapist squeezed a bag attached to the mask covering his mouth and nose forcing oxygen into his lungs.

Bob stood at the bedside giving brief, concise orders, his tension betrayed only by the strained urgency in his voice.

"Okay, Jack, give him five more, then let Ed intubate him."

Skillfully Ed slid the curved plastic tube down Dave's throat and into his trachea. The therapist attached the bag to the tube. The muscles of her forearms stood out as she squeezed and released, causing his chest to expand more fully than before.

Bob motioned to the nurse who stood beside a tall, red tool chest on wheels. She handed him the two paddles from the defibrillator atop the tool chest, then slapped moist conduction pads onto the front and the left side of Dave's chest.

"Give me 200," Bob said tautly, watching as the nurse turned the dial.

"Everybody back."

All activity ceased and everyone stood back, avoiding contact with Dave or the bed. Bob pressed the paddles onto the pads. Dave saw his body go rigid and bounce off the compression board as the jolt of electrical current coursed through his heart, but he felt nothing.

"Dammit, he's still fibrillating. One amp of epinephrine. Come on! Come on! Pump him, bag him, good, good. Okay, give me 300. Now, everybody back."

Distracted by a sensation of something behind him, Dave turned from the hectic activity. In place of the wall, a glowing tunnel of light stretched before him. The light was whiter and brighter than any other he'd ever seen, yet his eyes adjusted easily. The tunnel seemed endless. The only thing that surprised him was his lack of surprise. He felt no fear, no anxiety, just a vague sense of anticipation, of what he didn't know.

Within the tunnel he could see a separate concentration of light approaching him. It had no distinctive features, yet he recognized it as someone, or some thing, with personality.

"Who are you?" he blurted as the figure stopped before him. "Do I know you?"

"That's not important." Dave wasn't sure if he actually heard a voice, or merely perceived it in his mind. Whichever, it was clear and resonant.

Unable to comprehend what was happening, Dave asked hesitantly, "Are we in heaven?"

"No, you might think of this as a portal, a gate on the causeway to heaven."

Again Dave asked, " Am I going there?"

"Not now."

"Then why am I here?"

"You said you wouldn't believe without a sign. This is your sign, and for this, much will be required."

"I prayed, I begged, I pleaded, I tried so hard, but he wouldn't answer," Dave protested.

"Perhaps in your grief you cry out so loud you can't hear his voice. You call for his presence, when in truth he's always there."

"I don't understand."

"You're not asked to understand, but to believe. You can understand only a fraction of all that is, but be assured that all that is, has meaning."

"I just need to know why. If I can make sense of it, I can accept it. Why did God kill her? How can I trust a God who would kill my child?"

"God did not kill your child!" Dave threw up his hands at the force of the answer. Then in a more patient voice, "God wept with you when she died. She was his child before she was yours. She died because another child of his chose to do wrong."

"But she was so young."

"You have no concept of time and of age. Yesterday, tomorrow, today are the same. Everything exists in the eternal now. Time is not linear with God as with you. People live, and love, and sin, and their time moves on. God sees all as one and works backward into your time transforming evil into good."

"Why didn't he stop it?"

"It wasn't his will that she should die. However, when one chooses to do wrong, he seldom intervenes. If his children are not free to choose the wrong, neither are they free to choose the right, but he can absorb her death into his will and from it will come good. Of this you can rest assured."

Dave was silent, understanding no more than before, but in some odd way he seemed comforted. He stared intently along the incandescent tunnel. In the infinite distance he saw, or thought he saw, a myriad of similar glowing forms. "Is that heaven? What's it like?"

"With your earthly eyes and mind you cannot begin to comprehend. Consider the baby still in the womb. It feels, it tastes, it hears, it vaguely perceives something beyond itself – a bump, a noise, a startling jostle – just hints, hints to a mind incapable of imagining the world outside. So it is with you. Birth is the beginning of the pathway to death, and death is the birth to dimensions unknowable, except by hints. As life goes to term, by grace, you sometimes glimpse visions and vistas, and hear snatches of songs of unbearable beauty—just hints. Hints of a reality you can no more comprehend than that prenatal child could imagine others, and mothers, and moonbeams and stars."

Suddenly it hit him. "Is Kelli there?"

"Of course."

"Can I see her?"

"Not now."

"Why not? I'm so close."

"Now is not the time."

Oddly, this seemed reason enough.

They didn't speak for a while as they watched the frantic scene below.

"You must return soon," the entity said.

"Can't I go with you?"

"Not now. You're not ready, and God still has use for you here."

"Not ready?"

"Has it occurred to you that you may be here not so much to live as to learn? That his purpose for you is preparation, not gratification?"

"What does he want from me?" Dave asked.

"He wants *you*. Either God is of ultimate importance, the most important thing in your life, or he is nothing at all."

Dave jerked back as if he had been slapped. "My God."

"Indeed."

"What is it he wants of me?"

"By my visit, through no merit of your own, you have been given much more than most men get, your sign as it were. Far better are those who have had no sign and yet believe. As for you, the Father needs from you one great act that will benefit all mankind."

"How can I benefit all mankind in Hillsdale?"

"Everything you do has purpose. All of your acts, even the least, have meaning for good or ill that ripples outward through eternity. Matt's choice to get drunk at the prom was not a monumental choice, but the effects were catastrophic. Each of your choices, great or small, has eternal consequences, and one choice you will make, will affect all mankind for better or for worse."

"How will I know when that choice comes?"

"Listen to him."

"How will I know when he speaks?"

"He sent me to you, didn't he? Study his word and you will hear.

You hear him in the quietness of your heart; you hear him as you talk with him, if you choose to do so again." Dave winced as he said this. "Often you hear him through your fellow man. Many times you walk with angels unaware and hear the voice of God through your neighbor's lips. Listen with an attentive and a humble heart, and he will speak to you."

Slowly he began to glide away, and the tunnel began to dim.

"Wait. Wait."

"Peace be with you; you're not alone. Choose wisely," the voice echoed as the scene dissolved.

Dave felt himself fading also.

"All right!" Bob clapped his hands together. "We have a normal sinus rhythm. What's his blood pressure?"

"136 over 88."

"What's the time?"

"Nine-fifteen. Four and a half minutes."

"Come on, come on. Let's get him cleaned up. Judy, call the cath lab and tell them we have an emergency arteriogram and possible angioplasty. Call Dr. Spencer and tell him that we may need him for a by-pass."

The automatic doors on the emergency ambulance entrance swung open and Betty blasted through, ignoring the stares of the ER personnel as she dashed directly to the Coronary Care Unit. The charge nurse rose to meet her.

"Where is he? How is he?"

"He's okay. Dr. Maxwell has him in the cath lab right now."

Betty's fingers trembled as she fumbled with the buttons of her coat, unsure of what to say or do next.

The nurse grasped her arm. "Let me take you to the quiet room. Mrs. Maxwell's waiting for you there." She led her just outside the unit and opened the door with the stained glass panel.

Betty pulled back trembling uncontrollably, breathing in short, rapid pants.

"No, no, I can't go in there." Her voice became more high pitched. "That's where they told us Kelli was dead. I won't go in there."

Sarah hurried to the commotion, put her arms around Betty and began to stroke her hair. "I'm so sorry, Betty, I wasn't thinking."

"Should I get her a sedative?" the nurse asked.

Sarah shook her head. "She'll be fine. When Dr. Maxwell comes, tell him we're in the doctor's lounge."

Betty broke into hoarse sobs as Sarah led her down the hall and opened the door marked "Doctors Only." A large tin of stale holiday popcorn and two trays of partially eaten meals sat on the counter beside a coffeepot of thick, dark goo. Dirty scrubs and a potpourri of newspapers, medical journals, and hospital bulletins lay strewn about like debris from a hurricane, waiting to be removed by clean-up crews from housekeeping. Sarah guided Betty to the threadbare couch and removed a tattered Golf Digest and a TV remote gutted of its batteries. She and Betty sat in the small cleared area where she nestled Betty's head and let her cry herself out.

Finally, Betty sat up, pulled a ragged tissue from her pocket and blew her nose. "I'm all right. I'm just so tired and wound up—then that room." She didn't speak for several minutes. "What else can happen? It's just not fair." Sarah nodded but said nothing. "How is he? What can you tell me?"

"Well, he had chest pain at work and shortly after going into the unit, he fibrillated."

"Oh, God, no."

"Hold it; calm down. They got him back quickly. Bob said he thinks they dissolved the clot and has him in the cath lab right now to see if he needs a by-pass."

Betty leaned back and tried to relax. "I left as soon as Bob called. It was so frustrating. Pennington Gap was icy, and a truck had jackknifed. It took three hours to go twelve miles, and all that time I didn't know if Dave was dead or alive. I never should have gone to Lexington. He was so stressed out." Sarah let her ramble.

They both sprang to their feet as the door burst open, and Bob strode in. Betty grabbed his hand. "How is he?"

"Easy, easy," he said, prying her fingers loose and wiggling his fingers. "These magic fingers have to live to work another day."

"How is he?" she snapped, her voice rising.

"I'm sorry. It's been a little tense. He's fine." He led her back to the couch and plopped down beside her. "He's really lucky, as strange as that sounds. All of his arteries were wide open except one. He had a 95% blockage of the left coronary, the widow maker, but it was only a half-inch long and easy to get to. I dilated it almost back to normal. There appeared to be little or no damage from the earlier episode of pain, so he's actually better off now than yesterday. We just didn't know it then."

"Thank God. When can I see him?"

"How about right now? I had to give him some sedation for the procedure, so he's probably in La La Land."

She pulled him to her and kissed him on the cheek. "Thank you, Bob, thank you."

The nurse pointed to the open cubicle from which Dave's snores echoed through the unit. When Betty bent to kiss him, his eyes fluttered open. "Hi," he said and smiled. "You sure smell good. I love you."

She pressed his hand to her cheek. "I love you too, Dave. Oh, Dave, I'm so sorry." Still smiling, his snores resumed.

Bob had told the nurse that Betty could stay with Dave. Exhausted, she fell asleep holding his hand. Four hours later the rattle of trays woke her. It took a few moments to reorient herself, then she bolted upright and looked at Dave who was staring intently at her.

"How do you feel?" she asked.

"Much better now. I've been watching you sleep. You're so beautiful, and I love you so much."

She threw her arms around him. "Oh, Dave, I'm sorry. I never should've left."

He shushed her. "I'm okay. In fact, I think I'm better than I have been in some time."

She gave him a puzzled look. The nurse interrupted further conversation as she placed a tray on his serving table and brought another to Betty. He laughed, looking from his oatmeal, juice and skim milk to her bacon, eggs, coffee and grits.

"No mistaking who's the patient."

She smiled for the first time. "Well, we're not switching. I'm starved."

As she devoured her breakfast, he told her what he could remember, making her laugh with wry observations of how the world looked from the patient's viewpoint. He omitted Mr. Williams' visit and the weird occurrence during the resuscitation.

"Dave, I—"

He cut her off. "Before you say anything, I want to tell you something."

"Okay."

"I'm fine—and not just my heart. I'm not sure why, but I think I've turned a corner. I can't explain it yet, but somehow I'm certain we'll get through this."

What's he talking about? Betty couldn't quite follow his train of thought.

He seemed eager to talk. As he went on, she noticed that the tenseness around his eyes and mouth was gone, and he seemed more at ease and relaxed. His old easy smile was back. Maybe it was the sedative. If only it would continue after the medication wore off. At last he wound down, and for several minutes they sat, saying nothing.

"You look beat," he said. "I'm sure they'll move me to the floor in a little while. They need this bed for sick folks. Go home and get some rest, and we'll talk some more this afternoon."

Betty paced around in the house absent-mindedly clearing up Dave's clutter. What a mess. I'll bet he hasn't vacuumed since I left. She'd tried to sleep, but the night's events and thoughts of the future skittered about preventing any relaxation. Finally, she calmed enough to eat a carton of yogurt and soon began to wilt. She flopped onto the bed and crashed into a deep sleep. It was almost six when she woke.

Idly munching a sandwich, she sat in the fading light of the sunroom and mulled her options. There was no question she'd have to drop out of school and take care of Dave. Why can't someone take care of me for a change? What about my plans?

"Snap out of it, Betty," she said aloud. "Whining and self-pity don't become you." Maybe I can go back to school next fall. It's not as if people were lined up waiting for my services. Dave needs me now. Having an unresponsive ice-maiden for a wife didn't cause his heart attack, but it sure didn't help matters. I'm going to be a real wife to him. I'm just not sure how. Maybe we should get some marriage counseling. Maybe, Maybe, Maybe. Nothing's been stable since Kelli died. I wonder if it ever will. With a heavy sigh she slipped on her coat and headed back to the hospital.

"Hey, Betty," Bob's thundering voice startled her as she stepped off the elevator. He wore a fraying, dingy white lab coat over rumpled scrubs. "Boy, you sure look better."

"Thank you, I think, but you don't look so hot. You had any sleep?"

"I was just going, but I wanted to fill you in on Dave. Come in here." He led her into the nurses' lounge and poured two cups of coffee.

"Thank you for all you've done. How is he really?"

"He's fine. I wasn't just blowing smoke last night. I doubt his heart will bother him for many years, but just to be sure, I'm going to give him a mild stress test before he goes home to see how much, if any, damage he had."

"What will he be able to do?"

"Most anything, but I've told him to take a month off. He could go back to work next week, but don't tell him I said that. Physically he's in pretty good shape. I'm starting him in rehab next week just to impress him to be careful."

"I've decided to stay home with him."

"That's up to you. You've only got, what is it, six more weeks of school left? He can take care of himself for that long, and Sarah would love to baby sit him."

"I couldn't leave him alone again. The training will just have to wait." She stared at her coffee and hesitated. Finally she plunged on, blushing despite herself, "Bob, when will he able to… you know, make love?"

He burst out laughing. "Listen, little lady, there's nothing you could do that would hurt him. Why didn't I think of that? I'll just tell the rehab therapist to have him alternate sex and speed walking. Just don't get tangled up in the monitor wires."

"You would, you dirty old man." She said, punching him on the arm. "I'm sorry I asked."

He sat smiling, very pleased with himself. "Does he seem any different to you?"

"How do you mean?"

Bob chose his words. "He doesn't seem as wound up, or angry."

"I thought it was the sedation."

"He hasn't had any since the angioplasty."

"I hope he doesn't go back to like before."

He wrapped her in a clumsy bear hug. "Me too," he said and shuffled off without another word.

Betty tiptoed into Dave's room thinking he might be asleep, but found him standing by the window looking out at the business district. The hospital gown didn't reach his knees and gaped in back exposing his bare butt. She giggled. "I never have my camera when I need it." She gasped as he turned and crushed her against him, kissing her passionately. Surprised, she found herself responding.

"You certainly seem to be feeling better," she said.

"You do that for me."

Flustered, she retrieved the sack she had dropped. "I brought you some pajamas; you need them," she said giving his gown a tug. "Now, stop groping me and get back into bed before the nurse catches us and sends me home and you back to the intensive care." After he crawled in, she sat beside him and told of her plans to drop her classes to stay with him. He listened without interrupting. "I just feel so guilty," she concluded.

He took her hand. "The way I was acting, if you hadn't left, you'd probably have smothered me in my sleep." She started to protest. He held up his hand. "No, it's true. Now listen to me. I've been thinking about this all day. The blockage didn't start last month. It's been growing for years. If it hadn't happened now, it would have next week or the next, with or without all of our problems. You only have six weeks left, and there's a week break at Christmas. You've been so excited about getting back into nursing. It's important to you, but it's important to me, too. I want you to do it. Besides, I really need some time alone to sort things out and get my head screwed back on straight. When you finish, maybe we can take a little trip before I go back to work."

She considered for several minutes. "You'll be all right?"

"Bob gave me a twenty-year warranty. I'll call you every day. I promise."

"Let me think about it."

Chapter 8

Dave went home two days later. Even though the stress and blood tests had shown no trace of permanent heart damage, Betty was still uneasy, but she returned to Lexington.

A week ago he'd felt resentful and abandoned, hating to be alone, but now he welcomed her absence. In some inexplicable way, he was different. Since the strange event during CPR, the searing pain of grief had eased, replaced by a constant dull ache. The hollow feeling in the pit of his stomach had left, and the anger that bubbled just beneath the surface had subsided. He wondered what would happen when he went back to work.

At first he struggled to unravel the Event (that was the only way he could think of to refer to it) in the coronary care unit. He wondered if it had occurred at all. He remembered how he'd discounted the few patients who had related similar near death experiences to him as simple-minded and superstitious. It didn't make sense to him. Pop magazines, parapsychology, and New Age descriptions of psychic energy and auras, seemed just so much claptrap. Religious explanations based on carefully selected scriptures strung haphazardly together made no sense. Searching his journals and medical texts didn't help much either.

Other people consistently reported traveling through a dark tunnel and emerging into a brilliant light, yet in his experience all was light. Couldn't he even die right? Did that mean anything? What little there was in the literature speculated that chemical events in the brain, probably triggered by a lack of oxygen, were the cause.

That's got to be it; but if that's so, why do I feel so much more at peace? Maybe it's like electroshock therapy, but I have none of the memory loss that goes with that. Maybe I should just research Stephen King instead of the New England Journal. I could talk to Betty or Bob or John Rankin, but they'd probably patronize me and think I'd gone over the edge.

After two days of research, he reviewed the notes covering his desk. I had a very vivid dream, that's all there is to it. I'm glad I feel better, but if I'm ever going to get back to some semblance of normality, it's going to be through my own efforts. I'm not Abraham or Moses. God's not going to speak directly to me just to boost my spirits. Relieved that he had reached some conclusion, he cleared his notes from the table, put the books away and took a long shower. Before he turned back the covers, he knelt and prayed for the first time in months. It seemed different, almost as if someone were listening.

After breakfast the next morning, he wandered aimlessly around the house. From the bookshelf in the sunroom, he selected a book on coping with grief that Betty had gotten from her support group. He'd always retreated into reading when he was stressed, but he'd been unable to concentrate since Kelli died, and he'd refused to read anything from the group. Now, as he began to read, he found with relief that, in a typical masculine manner, he had reacted with frustration, anger and lashing out, and, to his surprise, most of what he read made sense. Much of it was what he had derided Betty for doing. Except for stopping to eat, he read steadily until bedtime. He highlighted one section: You can't go around it. You can't go under it. You can't go over it. You have got to go through it. You have to confront your grief head on.

With the methodical logic that often irritated Betty, he made a list of how he intended to confront his grief.

Go through the picture albums

Spend time in Kelli's room

Keep a journal

As he studied the list he came to a sudden realization.

"Dave, you jerk," he said aloud. These were the very things he had belittled Betty for doing. Not only was she having to cope with Kelli's death, but also with an out-of-control husband who was jealous that she seemed to be handling things better than he. He added two more things to his list:

Apologize to Betty

Try and talk about Kelli with Betty when she wants to, or at least listen

He spent the next few days poring over the picture albums, amazed at Betty's work. She'd spent hours in Kelli's room arranging pictures, report cards, newspaper clippings, poems and even Valentines, from her birth to her death. His throat tightened when he opened the first album and saw the black inkblot footprint and the birth announcement. He paged through from the first to the last, then started over, this time studying each picture in detail, trying to relive each moment. Usually he cried, but to his surprise, he felt better afterward. The last time he could recall crying before this was when he was eleven years old and his dog had died. Every few days a sense of tension or a vague anxiety built up, and he found that going through the albums or just remembering good times could trigger tears, and the pressure dissipated, as if tears were somehow therapeutic.

Keeping his promise, he called Betty every night. He sounded so much better that she finally felt reassured enough to stop grilling him about his health. He was very vague about his activities, saying only that he was doing a lot of thinking, but he was even able to convince her not to come home on weekends. "Your being tired and on the road would stress me out even more. Besides Christmas break is only two weeks away." Unspoken was the fact that he needed the time alone.

"You'll be all right?"

"I'll be fine." Two weeks to think and try to sort things out was just what he needed.

Three days after starting the albums, he decided to go into Kelli's room. Until now he'd entered it only far enough to shut the door. He and Betty had loud fights over this, and at his insistence, the door had finally remained shut. This morning he finished his coffee, read the paper and solved the crossword puzzle. You coward, quit stalling. Laying the paper aside, he walked to the closed door. His hand trembled, and he could feel his pulse to his fingertips as he grasped the knob. After taking a deep breath, he opened the door, stepped in, and sat on the edge of her bed until he calmed down.

As had happened so often in the last few days, the anticipation proved more stressful than the actual event. The frilly curtains, the rows of teddy bears, the trophies—nothing had been changed. Drifting around the room he picked up items at random and then replaced them . When he opened the closet, all of Kelli's clothes hung unmoved since May 16. On the shelf above the clothes rack lay a wool sweater that was his favorite. Easing himself onto the edge of her bed, he unfolded it across his lap and ran his fingers across the fabric as if some hidden message in Braille might be written there. When he had seen Betty smelling Kelli's clothes, he thought she was going crazy, but now he grasped the cloth in both hands and pressed it to his face, overwhelmed by his daughter's faint but unmistakable fragrance. Inhaling deeply, he drew as much of her as possible into himself, then as quickly as it had come, the pleasure gave way to hoarse sobs, which he didn't fight.

After he quieted, he refolded the sweater and resumed his exploration. The diary she had begun her sophomore year lay unlocked on her desk. "So much is happening, and it's happening so fast I don't want to forget," she'd told him. She had also told him that the diary was off limits. Fumbling, he opened it, hesitated a moment, then closed it with a snap and replaced it on the desk and continued to rummage for another hour. After one last, longing look at the diary, he turned and walked out leaving the door open.

Settling into a daily routine, he resumed trying to meditate and pray. Though he still had no mystical experiences, he now sensed that he wasn't alone, that someone heard and cared. When he prayed, he always ended with " Be with Betty, help me to make something meaningful come out of this, and please don't let Kelli be forgotten." He never mentioned the "one great act that would benefit all mankind." He couldn't forget he'd heard it, but what was he to do? Go looking for it? Let it find him? This always perplexed him, so he pushed it aside, feeling an uneasy, undirected sense of duty, but to what he didn't know. And he couldn't avoid the sense that all of his decisions, however small, were significant.

After his quiet time, he'd read for an hour or so and then drive to the hospital for his cardiac rehab. When he returned home, he had lunch then went to Kelli's room, the most satisfying thing of all. Ever since Betty had returned to Lexington, he'd tried to keep a journal, but he found that he had as much difficulty writing down his feelings as he had expressing them to others. This inability to record his feelings fed his greatest fear—that with time Kelli would fade, and he'd forget. So, just as Betty had done, he went through the picture albums over and over, memorizing every scene. Toward the end of the first week home an idea hit him. "Yes," he pumped his fist and began jerking open the drawers to her desk until he found a thick stack of notebook paper. Opening the first album, he began to write down whatever the pictures brought to mind. As he wrote her story, he found his feelings naturally flowed out, and with each page he wrote, a tiny bit of the pain seemed to ebb away.

The next Sunday he went to church. Without making a conscious decision, he slipped back into the ingrained Sunday routine of years—eat breakfast, read the paper, shower, get dressed. Not until he opened the front door did it occur to him that he hadn't been to church for almost four months. As inconspicuously as possible, he drove around until the services had begun then slid unnoticed into a back pew. The familiar liturgy and hymns were comfortable, but in some way different. No longer just an observer, he was a part of something beyond himself. As he hurried out on the heels of the benediction, another small load lifted.

Tuesday morning John Rankin called. "Dave, John Rankin. I saw you at church Sunday."

"Yes?"

"Well… uh… I was really glad. I've missed you."

"I wasn't feeling very motivated."

"No, I didn't mean it that way." John hesitated. "Would it be all right with you if I dropped over? I could bring sandwiches from the deli."

Dave bit his lip remembering his nasty behavior the last time John had come. "Yeah, John, that'd be nice."

"I don't mean to intrude. I mean, it's okay with you?"

"It's okay."

"You sure?"

"I'm sure."

"All right then, see you at noon. Bye."

Dave leaned back, hands clasped behind his head, gazing at the ceiling. Okay, Buddy, now what are you going to do? Had it been four months? Since he couldn't get at God, he'd been deliberately cruel, verbally beating his surrogate to a pulp and heaving the remains out the door. Betty didn't talk to him for days afterward. A time or two he'd been tempted to call John himself, but he'd been uncertain if he wanted forgiveness, guidance or just the chance to go another round or two. He busied himself straightening the house and brewing another pot of coffee. The doorbell rang. "Hi, John, come on in," he said leading him to the sunroom.

"I brought chicken salad. Hope Bob won't object."

"That's fine. I've fixed some coffee and have some low-fat cookies that Sarah brought."

They chatted about safe topics as they ate—the weather, Kentucky's basketball team. John sat on the edge of his seat, very straight, tense, as if ready to run if pounced upon. They finished the cookies in an uneasy silence.

"John..."

John jerked, sloshing coffee on the floor. "I'm sorry," he blurted, fumbling with his napkin to blot it up.

"John, relax." Dave said, "I'm not going to attack you. Actually, I want to apologize. I'm really sorry for the way I treated you the last time you were here. You meant well."

"Oh, that's all right."

"No, it's not all right. I was frustrated and angry—at Matt, at God, at Betty, at everyone, even Kelli. You were just an unfortunate, but convenient, target. I had no right to treat you as I did."

"I can't imagine the pain you were in. Your daughter—"

"Kelli, her name is Kelli. I wish you'd say it."

"It's hard to know what to say. Kelli was so special, and you two were so close. I still can't think of anything to say that might help except that I'm so sorry."

"That's good enough."

"It's been so frustrating because I've wanted to help but couldn't. I've wrestled with what you said, and I still have no answers."

Dave stared into his coffee cup. "I remember you saying that if we had all the answers there'd be no need for faith. I'd been asking Why? I thought if I could just understand why, then I could make some sense of it, but I know now that I'll never know why, and it will never make any sense. Even if I did understand why, I'm not sure it would help. If the hand of God wrote a concise explanation on that wall, Kelli would be just as dead, her chair at the table would be just as empty, and Betty and I would be just as alone."

John nodded but said nothing.

"I decided that instead of asking 'Why?' the proper question might be 'What now?' How do I bring some meaning to this? How can I bring something good from Kelli's life rather than create chaos because of her death?"

John leaned forward, no longer on guard. "I've never heard it said quite that way, but it makes sense." He stroked his chin. "So what now?"

Dave laughed. "I wish I knew."

"You seem different, Dave. Was it the heart attack?"

Unwilling to mention the Event, he said, "Sort of, it's hard to explain, and I don't fully understand. I'm still working on it."

Treading softly, but determined, John asked, "Is there anything I can do to help?"

"I'm not sure. Maybe just listen and let me bounce ideas off you. Right now, God and I are working out a rapprochement, but there are a couple of things I might want to talk about with you later. I'll give you a call."

"I'd like that." John stood to leave but hesitated. Having come this far he continued, "Dave, if I learned anything from our previous conversation, or confrontation, it's that platitudes don't help." He reached into his jacket pocket and drew out a folded sheet of paper and handed it to Dave. "I don't know why, but right after we talked on the phone I jotted this down. I'm not trying to dump religion on you, but this once helped me during a tough time I was going through."

Dave took the paper and shook John's hand. "Thanks." He shut the door and returned to the sunroom. Outside, the birds were swarming around the feeder. He poured another cup of coffee, sat down and unfolded the note. Jeremiah 29:11. To his surprise he was curious rather than angry. After all, religion was John's life and the Bible his tool. If all you have is a hammer, then everything looks like a nail. Dave picked up his Bible from the coffee table, quickly found the reference, and read it several times. *For I know the plans I have for you, declares the Lord, plans to prosper you and not to harm you, plans to give you hope and a future*. It was like a small flicker of light on a very dark night. I wonder how I missed that before.

After pouring the last of the coffee, he returned to the window. The single cardinal, who seemed to be a constant diner, fixed Dave with a steady gaze. Dave raised his cup and nodded, "You're my favorite too."

For the most part Dave and Betty's nightly conversations were upbeat and positive. Finally, unable to avoid it any longer Dave asked, "What will we do for Christmas?" There was a long pause.

"I avoid thinking about it as much as possible. I don't even go to the stores or listen to the radio. Carols just wipe me out."

"Yeah, I know, I felt like the Grinch when I told Millie that an office party was just too much for me this year. Do you want me to come to Lexington?"

"No, I want us to be in our home. It'll hurt, but to stay away would seem like abandoning Kelli." Betty hesitated for a moment. "I want to give gifts, but let's keep it simple, and let's not have a tree this year. I just couldn't bear hanging all her ornaments." They were silent for a while and then she continued. "I got an idea at the support group last week that I'd like to do if it's okay with you."

"Anything you want is fine."

Betty arrived home two days later. A growing sense of sadness pervaded the house, but there was none of the former tension and anger, just an overwhelming emptiness. They avoided town and friends, choosing instead to talk, leaf through the picture albums together, and relive happier times.

Christmas Eve was bitter cold. The sun had set when they arrived at the cemetery, and stars were just beginning to ignite in the indigo sky. The growing darkness added an extra bite to the wind whipping up the hill. Frozen grass crunched beneath their feet as they walked up the familiar path to the granite marker.

Neither spoke as they knelt by the grave. Betty laid a large holly wreath before the headstone. From a bag she took out a small storm lantern, shielded it with her hands as Dave lit the candle, and placed it in the center of the wreath. They didn't move for a long while. Then Betty reached into the bag and withdrew a Winnie the Pooh clad in a parka and earmuffs and propped it against the wreath.

"Merry Christmas, my darling."

They rose and walked to the bench and watched the flickering candle through tear-filled eyes. Huddled against the cutting wind, they felt like two trivial transients, abandoned by the fates in a vast, frozen wasteland surrounded by death.

When Betty began to shiver, he asked, "Are you ready to go?"

She nodded.

Holding hands, they walked back down to the car where they paused for a moment and turned for one last look at the glowing candle.

"Kelli, we love you." Dave's whisper was swept down the valley by the wind.

They drove without talking, each lost in their private memories of Christmases past and sorrow for what might have been. They arrived home exhausted, but in some odd way uplifted by the experience. Later, they snuggled on the couch before the fireplace and talked quietly until almost midnight.

In bed he slid over, wrapped her in his arms, and felt her stiffen.

He nuzzled her and kissed the nape of her neck. "Not that," he said softly. "I've just been so lonely; I need to hold you close to me. You're the best thing that ever happened to me, and I've been so afraid I was going to lose you."

She turned and nestled in his arms. "Oh, Dave, I love you so much."

They were still entwined when they woke the next morning.

After breakfast they read the Christmas cards they'd been saving.

"I've sat around feeling sorry for myself, and I forgot how much people care for us," he said. "I resent their ignoring us, yet they want to help and just don't know how. Maybe I need to reach out to them instead of waiting for them to come to me. John mentioned something about me talking to the church some evening. I may just do that."

They re-read the cards with anecdotes about Kelli or ones with especially touching messages and set them aside for future readings. When they finished, Betty went to the kitchen and returned with a flat, rectangular gift with bright red wrapping and a large green bow. He removed the wrapping, as usual taking care not to tear the paper.

"This is beautiful," he said, setting the "glamour picture" of her in her new nurse's uniform on the coffee table before him. "This is the same girl that thunderstruck me when I was an intern. Thank you, thank you, thank you." He retrieved a gift for her from the chair at the end of the table. "This is for you."

Her eyes danced as she ripped the paper from a package that resembled a large jewelry box. "Oh, Dave, thank you," she said lifting a gleaming stethoscope engraved with flowing script: To my favorite nurse with love, Dave.

"I figured the best nurse in the class needed the best quality instruments."

"Thank you, Dave. Thank you for everything."

Betty returned to school the following Sunday. They talked nightly and the three weeks slid by almost unnoticed. On the Monday night of the last week of her school Betty called after dinner.

"Hey, it was my night to call," he said.

"Oh, I know, but I just couldn't wait."

"Wait for what?"

"I have the greatest surprise for you, so don't make any plans for the week after finals."

"Why?"

"Well, if I told you now it wouldn't be a surprise." Dave smiled at her logic. "Besides, I want to tell you face to face."

"All right, when do you tell me face to face?"

She was talking so fast he could hardly keep up. It had been a long time since he had heard this much enthusiasm in her voice.

"I have finals tomorrow and Thursday—I really think I'm going to ace them—then we have exit interviews Friday morning. I should be home mid-afternoon." She rattled on, slowed, and was quiet.

"Betty, I've missed you so. I didn't realize how much I needed you. We have so much to talk about. I love you."

There was a catch in her voice. "Thanks, I needed that." A pause. "I've got to go before I get all blubbery. I love you too."

Dave spent most of the next day at Kelli's desk with the picture albums, working on his journal. He was barely into the third album and had already written fifty pages, no editing or rewriting, he just wrote. Perhaps sometime in the future he'd organize it and type it up, but for now it was simply therapy. Betty knew nothing about it, but he realized that he'd have to confide in her if he continued to write after she returned. He had no intention of telling her, or anyone else for that matter, about the Event. If they didn't think he was crazy, they'd at least be watching to see if he could pull off one great act.

Dave had picked up the diary from time to time, but he always fought off the urge to read it.

Betty was excited but obviously tired when he called. "I'm sure I did really well on the Anatomy, Physiology and Chemistry exams today. The notes you sent were really helpful. Thanks."

"My contribution to a budding career."

"I think I'm ready for Pharmacology and the practical, but they're the ones that bother me most because there's so much new equipment and so many new medicines to know."

"You'll do fine. Those were always your strong points," Dave said.

"But that was a long time ago. I'm going to go over my notes one more time."

"You know as much now as you're going to know. Take a Benadryl and get a good night's sleep, doctor's orders."

"Yes, doctor."

"Great. They're teaching you civility and respect, too." I don't know if I ought to say anything. She's on edge now, but I really need to know. "Betty."

"Yes."

"I don't want to upset you, but I have to ask you something."

"Ask what?" She sounded anxious.

He took a deep breath. "You know the diary on Kelli's desk?"

"Yes."

"Do you…do you think it'd be okay if I glanced through it?" A long pause. Oh, God, what have I done.

"Of course. I read it several months ago, and it really helped. I just didn't know how to talk to you about it." She sounded almost relieved.

"Thank you, darling." They were silent. "I was serious about getting a good night's rest."

"I will, I promise."

"I can't wait until Friday. I love you. Goodnight."

Dave woke early. He skipped meditation, finished his rehab exercises and went straight to Kelli's room, taking the coffeepot with him. At her desk, he ran his fingers over the diary's cover. His hands shook slightly as he undid the gold latch, opened it and began to read.

He wasn't sure exactly what he'd expected. Most of the entries were about simple everyday events and common teenage worries but ordinary though they were, they touched him. Some were more personal, things you can tell your dad at thirty but can't at eighteen. At times it seemed almost as if she were talking to him.

Matt bailed me out in geometry. I never would have passed without him. He's so nice. He never hits on me. He's just a wonderful friend.

He read it several times in disbelief. There were several other references to Matt. I didn't even know they were acquaintances. What a crazy, upside down world .

If I could have had a brother, I'd want him to be just like Matt.

When she was young she'd ask for a baby brother for her birthday or Christmas. She'd quit as she got older, and Betty explained that there probably wouldn't be any brothers or sisters.

Mom said Daddy saved a baby's life today. He didn't mention it. I hope I can be like him.

Tamika cried when I gave her my blue sweater today. She had admired it at school. She's so sweet. And so talented. I'll bet she makes All-State next year. Coach asked me to help her with her dribbling and passing. That might be fun. She probably can't go to college if she doesn't get a basketball scholarship.

I am so glad coach let Mollie be our statistician. I really had to bug him, but he finally agreed. She's so shy and sensitive about her weight. Maybe this will help her get some confidence.

How many other kids did she help? She'd never mentioned any of these to me.

I know daddy wants me to be a doctor, but that's not for me. Mom says a good nurse can help people in ways a doctor never can. Besides, I want to have five children. Mom and daddy love kids so much. They'll be great grandparents.

There were many entries about her and Betty's conversations, which helped him to understand why they were so close.

I got Mom to give me a note to Dr. Bailey saying it was O.K. to go on birth control pills. I probably won't need them, but I'd hate to make a dumb mistake. I was afraid to ask Daddy; he'd have a cow.

I wonder if she ever needed them. In a way, I hope she did. If she did, who was it? God, I hope it wasn't Matt.

Although it was obvious she admired him, entries about him were less personal.

I hope I meet someone like Daddy someday. I just hope he doesn't work so hard.

Some were not so admiring.

Daddy missed the big game with Danville. I don't think I've ever played better. 26 points and he missed it. I know he had an emergency, but he's always having emergencies. I just wish I was as important to him as his work.

His throat tightened as he re-read this entry several times, growing more irritated, but at the same time more guilty, each time he read it. He tried to read on but was unable to get beyond the damning entry. Finally, he closed the diary, put on his jacket and hiking boots and went outside. About halfway down the quarter mile driveway a trail veered off into a small hollow that sloped down around the ridge toward the river and a large flat area along the bank of the river. Jeb Hawkins, short for J.E.B. Stuart Hawkins, a descendant of one of the original settlers had owned it and lived there in a small, one hundred fifty year old log cabin. His name left little doubt where their sympathies had lain during the Civil War. About five years after he and Betty had moved to Hillsdale, the old man had paid them a visit.

"I have two hundred acres of prime bottom land and no family," he'd said. "I'm eighty years old and can't earn a living farming anymore. I'll sell it to you for five hundred an acre, if you'll let me stay here until I die. I don't know how soon that'll be, but probably not too long from now."

At that time, the price was a little more than the going rate, but they loved the land and didn't want it developed so they immediately borrowed enough to purchase it. Uncle Jeb, as Kelli came to call him, lived for fifteen more years, due in large part to the medical ministrations of Dave and Betty. Vastly improved nutrition provided by frequent meals shared at their home or casseroles taken to his cabin, first by Betty, but later by Kelli, who loved visiting his log "playhouse" helped also . They shared many picnics on the riverbank in front. When he died, they buried him in the small family plot above his cabin.

Dave hadn't been on the "back forty" since Kelli died, and now as he walked down the weedy path, his mind a muddled medley of emotions, recollections of past trips here with Betty and Kelli spilled over him. In the spring the area was a riot of wildflowers: yellow and red trillium, deep blue bird's-foot violets, pink and yellow lady slippers and jack-in-the-pulpits that grew knee high. If you sat very quietly, deer, raccoons, and wild turkey would often wander by. Happy memories seemed to seep out at every bend in the trail: the pool in the bend of the Beaver river where he'd taught Kelli to fish, the rope swing for cannon-balling into the river in the heat of July and August, and the muscadine vines which produced a hail storm of purple fruit when jerked in September.

The cabin sat at the far end of the flat stretch, just beyond a huge barn Jeb had built in the late sixties. By the time Dave reached it, his irritation at Kelli for not understanding the conflicting obligations that constantly pulled at him had given way to the realization that she was right—that being a doctor provided him with a ready excuse for neglecting his family. Who could argue with his being dedicated to suffering humanity, even if that dedication often was nothing more than maintaining an image and a desire to be liked? Besides, he'd thought he could always make it up to Betty and Kelli later.

He sat in the porch swing of the cabin and gazed out at the river, almost overcome with regret and remorse. A month ago this would have triggered an outburst of anger or irrational behavior lasting days, but now he sorted through his emotions. I can't undo the past. What was it I said to John? "The proper question is 'what now?' How do I bring meaning from this?"

He sat for over an hour then slowly made his way past the Hawkins burial plot and up the steep return trail that emerged in the yard near the salt lick and the Jump Off.

He fixed a cup of spiced tea, returned to her room and opened his journal. I will never again put my family second he wrote, then closed the journal, opened the diary and began with the next entry.

He choked up at times and laughed at many of her observations. He'd forgotten how funny she was. Betty had called her the "Funmaker" with good reason.

When he flipped to the next page, his hands began to tremble. The right-hand page was blank. The left was dated May 15.

Daddy's going to help Mom chaperone the prom. I'm so glad. I'm going to dance with him and make all of the other girls jealous.

The page became blurry. He yanked out his handkerchief, wiped his eyes, blew his nose, then snatched a piece of paper and began to write.

Dear Kelli,

I am so sorry.

He stared at the paper for several minutes, then put it in the back of his journal promising himself he'd finish later, but just having written those six words made him feel better.

Chapter 9

"Okay, Okay," Dave shut off the vacuum and ran to the dryer whose buzzer brayed from the laundry room. I should've had Mrs. Thomas come over and help. I'll never get everything cleaned up before Betty gets home. He set a vase of flowers on the coffee table and another in the dining room. Friday's paper lay unread on the couch. That'll have to do; I've got to shower.

The grandfather clock was chiming 12:45 when he heard Betty honking the horn all the way up the driveway.

"Oh," she squealed as he crushed her in a hug and then kissed her.

"I'm so glad you're back. I missed you."

She caught her breath. "I can see that." Arm-in-arm they went in. "The house looks so nice, and the flowers are beautiful."

"Have you eaten?"

"Just a pop-tart at six."

"Like a late breakfast? Bacon, eggs and pancakes. I'm cooking."

"Who could turn down an offer like that? I'm glad I didn't stop."

"Actually, you know that's all I know how to cook."

He watched as she went through two stacks of pancakes.

She pushed her plate back. "You'll be pleased to know you've just fed the top student in my class."

"Pleased? I'm overwhelmed, but I'm not surprised. I'm so proud of you. To accomplish that while dealing with Kelli and then with me, you deserve it."

They talked for over two hours before Betty jumped up from the table. "Oh my gosh, look at the time. I've got to run into town."

"What for? I'll go with you."

"No, there's something I have to do. Be back in an hour."

Millie met Betty at Dave's office door.

"I've got it all set up. Dr. White and Dr. Hawkins are happy to keep covering for him until next Monday. They've really wanted to do something special but didn't know how until now, so they're glad you asked . And..." dramatically she held up an envelope, "I hold in my hand, two first class tickets and reservations for the balmy Caribbean. No sleet, no cold, no wind-chill factor for five glorious days."

"You're amazing. No one could book this on a week's notice during the peak season."

"They could if a certain travel agent was desperate for an insurance physical before next Wednesday."

"You didn't."

"I did. Like I told Dr. De Marco, good Christmas bonuses pay off in the long, or in this case the short, run."

She hugged her. "Thank you, Millie, you don't know how much I appreciate this."

"You both need to get away. A change of scenery might help."

"I hope so."

"I'll see you when you get back. Give Dr. DeMarco my love, and as for you, I can always find work for a well-trained nurse."

He met her at the door, the foyer routine in reverse. "Does this have something to do with that big surprise you were talking about?" he asked.

"What surprise?"

"Don't jerk me around."

"Well, I may have done something really crazy." She led him to the sunroom and sat down. "Remember how you said we could take a vacation before you went back to work?"

He nodded. "I think a break would be nice, but where'd we go? I'm not ready to go back to the mountains yet. What did you have in mind? Louisville? Atlanta?"

Her eyes sparkled as she smiled and held up a thick envelope. "No, not Louisville, not Atlanta, nowhere that's cloudy or cold, nowhere we've ever been, nowhere with reminders."

"Then where?" he asked.

"Aruba!"

"Aruba? What's an Aruba? Where's an Aruba?"

Laughing, she threw her arms around him. "An island in the Caribbean with lots of sun, miles of beach, and, where we're staying, not many people."

"How did you pull that off?"

"Millie did it. You ought to give her a raise; the lady's a genius."

"She is at that." Dave walked to the window and looked out at the low, gray clouds. "When do we leave?"

"Tomorrow morning at eleven."

"Tomorrow?"

"Tomorrow."

"Then we'd better get packing. We'll have to leave by six to make our flight."

"No frocks, no coats, no ties," she ordered, tossing their luggage on the bed.

This was like old times. Often, before Kelli was born, when things had gotten too stressful in his residency or the early years of his practice, they'd pitch the bare necessities into their old VW Beetle and take off, usually without the slightest idea of where they were going. They were convinced that Kelli had been conceived in a tent in the Smoky Mountains on just such a trip.

It was almost midnight when they placed their bags by the door and prepared for bed. He hugged her. "You're one remarkable woman."

☙

Heat, reflected from the Tarmac, engulfed them as they clamored down the steps from the plane. In less than an hour they were zipping along the coast road in a rattling baby blue 1967 Chevrolet cab covered with bright floral designs. To the seaward side, blue water, low-cresting waves, and a ribbon of white sand stretched as far as they could see. Two miles past the last resort hotel the cabby stopped at a cove with five cabins, painted bright pastel colors—blue, yellow, peach, a pale green and a near mauve—nestled in the palms. Each had storm shutters and a covered porch with a table and four chairs. Cactuses sprawled about the yards, and strange, sideways bending trees, their foliage streaming out like a woman's hair, partially shaded each cabin.

The proprietor, dressed in shorts, a flowery, loose shirt, and a broad brimmed hat, stepped from the nearest house and strode briskly to them. His trim gray-flecked moustache contrasted with his deep tan. Smiling broadly, he removed his hat revealing thick hair that matched his moustache. "Dr. and Mrs. DeMarco, I presume. I am Juan Estaban." His speech was formal and had a Spanish lilt to it, but at the same time there was a Germanic hint, perhaps picked up from the Dutch on Aruba. "Miss Millie said you'd like some privacy so I gave you the last cottage." He picked up their luggage and led them to the farthest cabin, which was painted a cheery yellow. One of the strange, tilted trees stood by the porch. "Ah," he said when he saw Dave studying it, "you've found the divi-divi tree. Visitors call it the 'one way tree'. The wind here always comes from the northeast, so the branches grow down-wind." He took the bags inside. "There's water and food in the cooler. I brought you several bottles of sun block, and there's an umbrella for the beach. I'd suggest that you make full use of both. You northerners tend to burn quickly in the winter. There's excellent snorkeling in the cove. I can get you the equipment if you would like. Breakfast is at eight and dinner at seven each day in the cabana on the beach if you care to join us. If I can be of any assistance, please call on me." He gallantly kissed Betty's hand and left.

They unpacked and slipped into shorts, a welcome change from the overstuffed clothes they had crammed into the closet as they left.

"I'm not hungry," Betty said.

"Me neither, let's go for a walk."

Juan waved at them from the cabana where the other guests were gathering for dinner. Hand-in-hand they walked down the beach to the point at the end of the cove. The sun hung suspended just above the horizon casting a golden glow on several resort hotels far down the beach toward the airport. In the distance wind-surfers skittered across the waves toward the hotels. They lounged in the sand and watched the sun sink into the ocean. Neither had said anything since leaving the cottage.

"It's beautiful," Dave said softly, "so quiet, so peaceful."

"So comfy," she said as Dave poured warm sand over her feet.

They sat, seldom speaking for over an hour. Dave yawned, and very shortly Betty followed suit. After the third repetition of this sequence, she laughed. "We'd better go back and get some sleep, or we'll flake out on the beach and be washed out by the tide."

Thin strains of music and laughter drifted from the cabana across the cove as they walked back. The moon was just starting to push up out of the sea when they fell into bed and, for the first time in months, slept all night without taking a pill.

The sun was already bright and warm when a chattering bird in the divi-divi tree woke them.

"I wish we had some corn flakes," Betty said as they dressed.

"Juan could probably get some."

"No, it's not the corn flakes. I just don't want to meet a lot of strangers. As soon as you're introduced, the first thing they ask is what do you do, and the second is how many children do you have. I'm still so uncomfortable with that."

"Yeah, me too."

"I mean, I just can't bring myself to say none, but I don't want to explain either." She took a deep breath. "I'm starved; let's do it."

They stepped out onto the shaded porch.

"Look," Betty squealed and clapped her hands. On the table sat a large bowl of chilled fruit: pineapple, strawberries and bananas and to the side was a covered bowl of muffins, a thermos of coffee, a bottle of water and a pitcher of orange juice. They gave a simultaneous sigh of relief.

"Juan is a saint," Dave said as he hurried back in for some dishes and utensils. They hadn't eaten since the flight the previous afternoon and dug in greedily. He laughed at the pineapple juice dribbling down Betty's chin. In a few minutes, their dishes were clean save for scattered muffin crumbs. Bright blue and green birds fluttered around the yard, and small lizards darted across the sand. They leaned back in the growing warmth, sipping coffee and watching sail boats and wind-surfers fan out from the distant resort.

"It's so nice not to have anything to do. Several months here and I'd probably go stir crazy, but for the next few days it's just what I, the doctor, ordered. My bones are just beginning to thaw from the Kentucky chill. I feel naked without a parka, cap and goose bumps."

"No obligations, no schedules, no reminders to jump out and slap you down. I can use some of that, too," Betty added.

They sat watching the waves and chatting.

Juan rounded the corner of the house. "I see you're awake."

"Oh, Juan, thank you for the breakfast," Betty said.

"Just put it on our bill," Dave added.

"No, no, it is part of the service, just like these bag lunches." He set two brown paper bags on the table. "There's no lunch service at the cabana, so this is provided. I suggest you put them in the cooler until you are ready to eat."

"Thank you so much," Betty said, giving him a radiant smile.

"Part of the service," he repeated. "The other guests are going into town to shop or to the resort for windsurfing. There's plenty of room if you would like to join them."

"No," Dave said slowly, "we're just going to lounge around and maybe explore down the beach a ways today."

"That's fine." Juan gestured toward the beach. "About a mile beyond the point, the beach ends in a small mangrove thicket. I wouldn't go into it, but many different birds and sea creatures live in and around it. If you'd like to go snorkeling, the cove here is one of the best spots on the island. I can bring you some equipment if you like. It's—"

Betty laughed, cutting him off in mid-sentence. "I know, it's part of the service."

"We'll try that tomorrow. Okay with you?" Dave asked looking at Betty.

"Fine, sounds like fun."

"Good, just relax and soak up the heat," Juan said. "I saw on the weather channel that it's snowing in Kentucky." He pronounced it

Caintookey.

After he left, Dave burst out laughing. "I'm glad we're not in Caintookey."

"You're a fine one to talk. You didn't even know what an Aruba was."

While Dave unfolded two beach chairs, Betty retrieved an old hardback copy of Wuthering Heights from the cottage. "Getting a little high-brow aren't you?" Dave held up the latest Tom Clancy novel.

"I read it years ago and just loved it. I wanted to see if the magic was still there."

They read quietly for a couple of hours. "How'd you like to go on a picnic?" Dave asked, closing his book.

"Sounds good to me," Betty agreed, more than ready to leave the damp moors of her novel. She loaded the lunches, two bottles of water and some sunscreen into her large straw tote basket. "Let's go."

They ambled along the beach in the firm sand where the tide washed farthest up onto the shore. Every seventh or eighth wave broke higher than the others and lapped around their ankles, tugging at their feet. Small crabs washed up by the waves scuttled franticly to bury themselves in the sand. From time to time they found an odd shaped or particularly pretty shell and tossed it into the basket. This stretch of beach was devoid of tourists and undeveloped except for an occasional private dwelling set back behind the low dunes. Around a bend far down the beach the first patch of concentrated greenery they'd seen hove into view. Upon drawing nearer, they could see that it stood twelve to fifteen feet high. The mangrove trees crept out into the water on matted stilts of roots. They walked up to the edge, but the thicket was so dense they could see only a few yards into it. Birds flitted in and out of the thicket; brilliant patches of green, yellow and blue that disappeared before the eye could focus on them.

Betty shuddered "They're pretty, but I'll bet it's full of poisonous snakes."

They climbed a small adjacent dune and spread their beach towels. Their lunches were basic, but filling: ham and cheese sandwiches, pickles, chips, an apple and oatmeal cookies. As they ate, a curious iguana crept from the mangroves and slowly sidled toward them. Betty stood up and threw her apple core at it.

"Shoo! Scat! Get out of here! I told you there were poisonous snakes in there."

"That's not a snake; it's a lizard, and it's not poisonous."

"Not much difference," she said, edging further away. "Get rid of it."

Laughing, he chased it back into the thicket. Betty kept a sharp lookout for several minutes, but, once reassured that it was gone, she sat back down on the beach towel, being careful to keep Dave between her and the mangroves. They lolled in the sun and gazed up at the sky.

"Look," Betty pointed to a large cloud, "Richard Nixon."

Dave laughed as he recognized the ski-jump nose. "Charlie Brown," he said outlining a particularly rounded one.

"Mickey Mouse."

"Dolly Parton."

Betty rolled over and smiled down at him. "Only you could find Dolly in a cloud." She leaned down and kissed him fully on the lips. Surprised for a moment, Dave took her in his arms and kissed her back. For the last six months, there had been no spontaneity to their love life, actually, no love life. Their kisses had been formal or indifferent, wary, lest they lead to intimacy, which to Dave's continued disappointment, Betty still seemed to find distasteful. Their sex life had always been a wonderful blend of passion and lighthearted fun, but now they seemed to tiptoe around the whole subject, or they didn't talk about it at all for fear of hurting the other's feelings or of making matters worse.

"That was nice," Dave murmured.

"Yes, it was." She stood, ending any further activity, and began cleaning up the lunch debris.

The sun was setting as they walked back up the cove. Juan was just leaving their porch as they neared the cottage; he waved but continued toward the cabana. On their table sat two covered pans and a bottle of Cuban rum.

"He must have been watching for us," Dave said

Betty removed the lids. "This smells wonderful."

They ate slowly, savoring the spiced pork and a tangy black bean, rice and herb dish, all washed down with rum.

Dave inspected the empty pans. "Either Juan knows exactly how much we eat, or we'll just wolf down however much he brings us." They sat listening to the waves and sipping rum until the bottle was empty.

"Whoa." Betty swayed precariously as she stood up. They very seldom drank, and when they did, it was usually one glass of wine at dinner.

"I'm a little lightheaded myself," Dave said, purposely slurring his speech. "I think we should sit the hack, or is it hit the sack?"

Betty laughed and put her arm around his waist. "Why don't we just go to sleep?" she said

The sun was well up when again the birds in the tree woke them. Dave had put the clock in the dresser drawer when they arrived, so they had no idea what time it was.

Dave rolled over and kissed her. "My head feels like a balloon." She groaned in agreement, watching as he got up, splashed cold water in his face, and slipped on a polo shirt and shorts. "I could sure use some coffee."

Betty walked carefully to the door, testing her sea legs. "Dave, he did it again," she exclaimed, spying the spread on the porch table. "Get some dishes while I slip into something."

"Just part of the service," he laughed, carrying the tray of dishes and silver to the porch.

"Eating, reading and loafing, I could get used to this," Betty said, pouring their coffee. They ate more leisurely today as the coffee and food eased the throbbing in their heads.

"It looks like Juan has our day planned for us," Dave said, pointing to the snorkels and fins on the step.

"I'm not sure I can swim well enough to use those," Betty said.

"He probably doesn't think so either." He held up the boogie boards. "These will brand us as mid-western tourists, but at least we won't drown. It's still a little chilly for swimming," he said retrieving his Clancy tome. "Until it warms up, I'm going to see if Jack Ryan can save the free world."

"I could use a couple of hours to get completely over the wobblies, and I'm still trying to see how you compare with Heathcliff. So far it's about a dead heat; today may be the tie-breaker."

They read for almost three hours, stopping every now and then to chat or to point out a new, exotic reptilian creature or a ruby-throated hummingbird buzzing around them. It wasn't so much the books that gratified them, as just the sense of freedom, of being able to do nothing productive. Their Calvinist backgrounds were so deeply ingrained that any idleness was equated with sloth and required a generous serving of guilt whenever they indulged in it.

"More service on the way," Betty said as she saw Juan coming toward them. He was smiling and holding up the brown sacks.

"Corned beef today," he said proudly.

"Sounds good. Thanks for the gear, we're going out in a few minutes."

"The best place is midway between the points at the mouth of the cove. One visitor said he counted one hundred and twenty-two kinds of fish there. I won't swear as to his accuracy, but there are a lot of different ones out there."

"Are there any sharks?" Betty asked.

"A few small reef sharks, but no one has ever been hurt here."

"Good."

"Enjoy yourselves," he said turning toward his cottage.

They ate the bananas from the lunches and put the rest in the cooler, then changed into their swimsuits. Catching Betty topless, Dave gave an appreciative whistle.

"You're just a Peeping Tom," she laughed as she whirled away from him.

She squeezed a glob of sunscreen into her hand and tossed the bottle to him. "Help me with my back," she said spreading the oily goo over her arms and legs. He greased her back, letting his hand slip inside her panties.

"Just the exposed parts, please," she said with a playful smile.

"Just trying to protect your fish belly white buns."

As she laved sunscreen over his legs, she noticed the growing bulge in the front of his trunks.

"You're impossible," she said slapping the container into his hand and scampering to the porch. "Grease yourself, and let's go while you're still presentable."

They picked up their gear and trudged toward the cove. Near the water's edge they stopped to don their flippers and masks. Laughing at each other's awkward, high-stepping gait they splashed into the water and lay forward on their boogie boards, quickly becoming accustomed to the equipment, and soon paddled with confidence. Fish darted below in water that must have been twenty feet deep, though it seemed they could reach the bottom with their outstretched hands.

"Look, Dave," Betty raised her head and pointed below to a school of angelfish swimming by. She swam in circles, excitedly pointing to each new species she saw. Happiness welled up in him watching her smile and point in wonder like an uninhibited little child. The sun was well past its zenith when they made their way back to the shore.

"Wasn't that fantastic?" Betty gushed, her eyes dancing with pleasure. "I've never seen anything quite like it except on TV."

"It was really nice. We'll have to do this again tomorrow."

Betty remained animated all the way back to the cottage. They laid their snorkeling equipment in the shade on the porch and washed the sand from their feet at the spigot by the steps. She sat drying in the sun while Dave retrieved the remainder of their lunch and soft drinks from the cooler. As they ate, Betty continued to replay all the different fish they had seen. Seeing her so lively almost made things seem like they had been before. They lolled in the sun for a while, but finally Dave rose, gathered up the dishes, took them inside and began to wash them. Betty took a cloth and dried. When they finished, Dave picked up his book and started out to the porch.

"Dave."

He turned. She took the book from his hands and laid it aside. Standing on tiptoe she put her arms around his neck, pressed against him, kissed him deeply, then released him and stepped back. He said nothing, unsure of what he should do next. Smiling slightly, she loosed the tie on her bra and let it drop, then without pausing she stepped out of the panties.

His voice was thick. "God, you're beautiful."

She took his hand, led him to the bedroom and undressed him. They kissed softly, hesitantly as if this were the first time they had made love. Then she drew him to the bed and snuggled against him. He slid his hand across her hips but drew back when he felt her tense, then she softened and pulled him closer. "Don't stop. I really want to, I just need some help."

He began to slowly kiss and caress her. Gradually she relaxed, and her breathing began to quicken as suppressed sensations started to return, gently at first, like a soft shower of rain, then harder and more insistent, finally pounding down with the intensity of a storm. "Yes… yes… now, oh, now." She pulled him tightly against her, swept away in a thunderous, quivering release.

Later she lay against him, her head nestled in the crook of his arm. "I had forgotten how good you make me feel. I was afraid that might be gone forever."

"It's much nicer when I feel like we're making love together rather than you're just letting me have sex."

"I didn't mean for it to seem that way. I just couldn't do any different." She nuzzled his neck. "I'm glad I'm finally over that hump."

He burst out laughing. "I'm sorry, I can't help it. 'Over that hump'."

"You." She began laughing and pounding him on the chest with her fists. "You know what I meant." She threw back the sheet, crawled on top of him and kissed him long and deep. "All right, Mr. Smarty," she smiled down at him. "You asked for it. I'm going to see if Bob was right about how strong your heart is."

They barely ventured out of the cabin the rest of that day or the next.

After the usual breakfast the following morning, they lingered over their coffee. Dave felt more relaxed than he could remember, muscles loose, lacking the tenseness he hadn't even realized was present until it was gone. The lines around Betty's eyes and jaw had softened. They made no sound as separately each savored this sense of well being that they both feared would be fleeting, especially when they returned to the real world.

"It's hard to believe we've been here four days," Dave said.

"That means that we have to go back home tomorrow. Do we have to?" Betty whined, trying to put on a pouty-face. "Can't we stay for another week or two?"

He laughed. "I wish." He looked up and saw Juan coming up the walk with the familiar brown bags. "Right on time."

"Good morning, Miss Betty and Doctor Dave," he said doffing his hat. He set the bags on the table. "What will you be doing today?"

"We enjoyed snorkeling so much we're going to do it again," Dave answered.

"I know of a special place where very few people go. I can give you directions if you like, it isn't far."

"Sounds good. Where is it?"

"You remember the mangrove thicket?" Dave nodded. "There's a path just behind the dune that leads around the mangroves to a cove. It's very deep so take your float boards. There are more kinds of fish and sea creatures there than anywhere else on the island." He smiled at Betty, "But no sharks."

"What do you say?" Dave looked at Betty.

"Let's do it."

"Good." Juan hesitated, then spoke as if uncertain that he might be violating protocol. With great formality he continued, "Doctor Dave, Miss Betty, I would consider it a great honor if you would have dinner with me tonight . The other guests are all going into town to the casino."

Betty touched him on the arm. "Juan, we'd love to."

He broke into a broad smile. "Would seven be OK? I know you must leave early in the morning."

"Seven would be fine."

Without another word he sauntered off toward the cabana whistling a lively Latin tune.

They stuffed the tote basket with snorkeling equipment, swimsuits, bottles of water and the lunches. Dave tied the boogie boards together then eyed the almost-round basket and the boards dubiously.

"I hope we can make it with all this stuff."

"Dave, you wimp, come on, I'll carry it all," Betty jeered at him. She grabbed the basket in one hand and the boards in the other and staggered off down the path. Laughing, he took the basket.

"Give that to me before you dislocate your hip."

They reached the mangroves in thirty minutes. The path was just as Juan had described. Multi-colored birds flitted before them as they circled the thicket. After about ten minutes they stepped into a large clearing, bordered from the mangroves to the beach by tall palms. In the center of the clearing was a small stone chapel and to one side, a cemetery enclosed by a low wrought-iron fence. Beyond the church, the cove's deep blue water glimmered. The chattering of hundreds of birds filled the air.

"It's beautiful," Betty whispered, not wanting to break the spell.

The cornerstone by the chapel door was inscribed "1872." The chapel didn't appear to have been used in years. A thick layer of dust covered the pews and pulpit.

"Are you ready to swim?" Dave asked, opening the basket, and tossing her swimsuit to her. "Go ahead and change, I'll just watch."

"You dirty old man," she snickered. She grabbed up the swimsuit and ran to the confessional, jumped in and closed the door. "Eat your heart out," she called from the tiny room. When she came out, he had changed as well and stood smiling at her.

They slowly swam into the cove where thousands of fish, ranging in size from tiny ones to up to four feet in length darted and cruised below them. From time to time a slow moving sea turtle drifted by. Great piles of coral almost reached the surface at the mouth of the cove. In three hours they'd barely had time to scan the entire cove.

"I have never seen a National Geographic show that beautiful," Betty said.

After changing back into their shorts and tees, they spread their lunch in the shade of a large palm tree. Anticipating that they might be hungry, Juan had made them both two sandwiches. When he'd finished his lunch, Dave lay back in the shade and dozed off, waking in about twenty minutes. Betty wasn't there. He found her in the cemetery where most of the tombstones had Dutch names and were dated in the early 1900's. Here and there were a few Spanish names, two that appeared to be German, and one that was English.

"Dave, come here," Betty called from the far end near the back gate. She gently traced the inscription with her fingers.

TEOFILO ESTABAN GONZALEZ
September 19, 1954 December 14, 1976
'El placer que el dio nunca morira'

"He was so young, not much older than Kelli," Betty said, mentioning her name for the first time since they got there.

Although a bit more somber than before, they continued to explore.

"I really hate to leave," Betty said as they loaded up their gear and headed back for the cottage. "It's been so quiet and peaceful, and so beautiful."

Since they were leaving early, they packed their luggage before dinner. They'd brought no dressy clothes at all, but Betty found a fresh flowery sundress, and Dave put on his last clean pair of shorts and a bright paisley shirt.

Juan's cottage was larger than the other four, the porch lit by a single yellow light. He rushed to greet them before they could knock at his door.

"I am so glad you agreed to have dinner with me," he beamed ushering them inside where a medley of spicy aromas swept over them. "Please, sit down, it's almost ready."

The living room opened directly into a large kitchen equipped with an oversized stove where several pots were steaming. In a small alcove to one side was a candlelit table with three place settings. Betty walked into the kitchen and stood to one side watching as he coordinated all of the steaming dishes.

"You do that so easily," she said.

"I've had a lot of practice," he smiled. "This is where I prepare most of the food that I serve at the cabana."

"Or the food that's just part of the service?" she teased.

He smiled, not looking up from his preparations.

ꟹ

Dave wandered around the living room. Bookcases filled with neatly arranged books covered one entire wall. Most were in

Spanish, but he recognized Hemingway, Steinbeck, and T.S. Eliot and also Marx and Mao Tse Tung. On the opposite wall two large pictures hung in the center of a grouping of smaller ones. One was a beautiful dark-haired woman in her twenties, tall and slender with a regal bearing. A tall rather muscular young man dressed in combat fatigues who also appeared to be about twenty smiled from the other. Smaller photos of both at younger ages surrounded these and to the side was a blurred black and white photograph of a group of twenty or thirty young men dressed in combat fatigues standing against a jungle backdrop, cockily brandishing their weapons and smiling for the camera. Dave could swear that the two in the center were Fidel Castro and Che Gueverra.

"Dinner is served," Juan announced with a formal bow, taking Betty's arm and leading her to the table. After they were all seated, he took their hands and, bowing his head, said a simple grace. "Amen," they echoed after him when he had finished. He first served their plates and then his.

The spicy pork and chicken dish was savory and moist, but not the least bit greasy. The side dish of black beans, rice and small bits of shrimp was seasoned just enough to taste, but not enough to readily identify the ingredients, all of which were accented by a mellow Portugese rosé. As they ate, Juan gave a brief, but thorough history of Aruba.

"Were you born here?" Betty asked.

"No, I came here from Cuba about ten years ago. I would imagine that Aruba is somewhat different from Caintookey," he said, diverting the conversation to them. "Miss Millie told me that you were a doctor," he said to Dave and listened with obvious interest as Dave described his practice. "And you, Miss Betty, are you employed outside the home?"

"I'm a nurse," she answered, "but I had retired some time ago." She tensed awaiting the inevitable next question.

"Perhaps you will go back to nursing sometime?"

"Yes, I've just finished a refresher course," said Betty, relaxing somewhat.

"Ah," he nodded to Dave, "but what better a teacher?"

They talked easily as they sipped coffee and ate a spongy textured cake with a sweet, but tangy, fruit compote. It seemed odd to Betty that he always steered the conversation to them, seldom revealing anything about himself, and he never asked about children. After dessert they went into the living room where Juan served them small glasses of rum.

"What did you do in Cuba?" Betty asked. "Were you born there?"

Juan hesitated, sipping his rum, almost as if he were debating with himself whether or not he should lower his defenses. Sensing that they could be trusted, he replied, "Yes, I was born in Havana. Before the revolution I was a college student and a cook in the Hilton hotel there. About ten years ago, I moved here, before the tourist boom. This area around the cove was miles from anywhere, and I got it for a very good price. I built the cottages and have been here every since."

"The woman in the picture," Dave pointed to the grouping, "is she your wife?"

Juan stood up and walked to the pictures. His voice tightened. "Yes, she was my wife."

"I'm sorry," Dave said, "I didn't mean to pry."

"No, that's all right," Juan said. He almost seemed relieved that he'd asked. "I moved here to be able to control my contact with people. When I came, I had a real need to limit my contact with others. You know what I mean."

"You know," Betty said softly.

"Yes. Miss Millie told me. I'm so sorry for your loss. I'm sure the holidays were particularly hard." He turned back to the picture. "We met at the university." He smiled wistfully at Dave. "I didn't set out to be a chef. I was a pre-medical student when Maria and I married. She quit school and worked full time so I could continue my studies. Then came the Revolution."

Dave walked to the pictures. "Are you in this picture?" He pointed to the soldiers.

"Yes, here." He pointed to a slender young man in the rear holding an AK-47."

"You were in some pretty heady company."

Juan laughed. "I was in middle level management. The highest rank I attained was lieutenant." He paused. "When the Batistas discovered that I was involved in the opposition, they took her away. I never saw her again." His tone invited no pity.

Betty flinched. "That's horrible."

They sat sipping their rum. Dave studied his drink, debating whether or not to ask the obvious. The silence stretched on.

"Who's the young man?" he finally asked.

Juan looked at the picture, but his gaze was fixed somewhere far away. "That is our son, Teofilo. He was three years old when Maria was taken away. After the Revolution, my mother lived with me and cared for him. By then, medical school was impossible. Times were hard. There were no jobs due to the embargo, so I got my old job as a cook in the Hilton." He smiled. "The Russians didn't know I was a terrible cook. I guess even my cooking was better than what they were used to. My mother taught me the basics, and I studied cooking as diligently as you did medicine. In time, I became the head chef, not as good as chief of orthopedics, but not bad considering the circumstances." He paused, a faint smile playing on his face.

"Teo was special, even as a child. He had his mother's looks but, where she was reserved, he was outgoing. He never met a stranger, especially of the opposite sex. When he became a teenager, the girls swarmed around him like bees around the sugar mill—young girls, older girls, some grown women. I never had such a problem. He was a pitcher on the provincial championship baseball team, and, oh, how he could use his hands!"

He walked to the bookshelves and picked up an exquisitely carved Madonna and handed it to Dave. "He carved this when he was eleven. I just put the twenty figure creche he carved back into storage."

"This is remarkable," Dave observed running his fingers over the smooth flowing curves, then handed it to Betty.

"Yes, it is." Juan's voice cracked a bit as he said, almost to himself, "He would have been an excellent surgeon." He dabbed his eyes with his handkerchief and was silent.

"Oh, my God," Betty gasped. "The chapel, the cemetery, that was his marker wasn't it?"

Juan nodded.

"What happened?"

"After the revolution, Castro made poor choices. He distrusted

America for its support of the Batistas, so he embraced the communists. He saw this as the only way to realize the fruits of the Revolution for the Cuban people. Initially, I supported him in this, but as time went on, he began to drift from the goals we had when we were fighting in the hills of Oriente. We wanted only the freedom of our people. Whether he actually was dedicated to expansionist Marxist ideology or just needed to ingratiate himself to those providing us with aid, I don't know. Regardless, this led to the sending of a Cuban brigade to Angola. That picture was taken just before Teo shipped out aboard a Russian ship. He was killed two months later in the jungle of a country I had never heard of, for a cause neither of us believed in."

Juan continued, unable to stop. "I was so filled with rage. He had wanted to do nothing but play baseball and go to medical school. He didn't care about politics. I was so helpless, but what could I do? Kill Castro?" He emptied his glass and refilled it with rum. "I don't remember much about the months after they brought him home. I must have been pretty crazy because later when I became more rational, it was obvious that I had said too many of the wrong things and had to leave Cuba. Perhaps because of my service in the Revolution, I was allowed to leave, provided I did not go to the United States. After I had settled in Aruba, some of my friends smuggled Teo's body out of Cuba, and I buried him here. I couldn't allow him to rest among those who were responsible for his death, and," he said almost as an afterthought, "I needed him nearby."

"I'm so sorry." Betty's eyes were moist. "The cove with the chapel is so quiet and peaceful. Do you go there often?"

"Not as often as at first. Early on, I went daily, and it hurt so much. Now I go on anniversaries and holidays, times when he should not be alone, and there are times when memories arise, or when I should not be alone, and I go and visit. In some odd way it comforts me, and now I feel a warmth and closeness where I once felt only pain. I still miss him. I wonder what he would have accomplished if he had been given the chance, but I'm better for having had him, if only for a short while." He smiled. "Do you know what has helped me the most?" They shook their heads. "Although sometimes I cannot do it, I try to do some good deed every day in his memory. I have this sense that he is watching me, and I want him to be proud. If I had remained as I was, I would have shamed his memory. In this way I can bring some meaning to his life."

"That's beautiful," Betty said. "There have been others who have received kindness that were 'just part of the service' haven't there?"

He blushed through his tan. "You are the only ones I have ever told about this."

"The inscription on his marker, the part in Spanish. What does it say?" Dave asked.

He seemed a bit embarrassed. "My one attempt to be poetic. In English it says roughly, 'The happiness he brought will never die'."

For a moment they both looked stunned. "Unbelievable," Dave whispered, "That's what's on Kelli's marker."

Juan hesitated, and then asked, "Would you tell me about your Kelli?"

Betty began talking about her, and, to Dave's surprise he joined in. They talked, laughed, shared, and sometimes cried, until well after midnight.

The sun was just rising when they left the next morning. Except for Juan indicating a few last points of interest, they spoke little on the drive to the airport. He helped them with their luggage.

"I have enjoyed meeting you. It helped so much talking with someone who understands. I hope someday you will visit me under happier circumstances."

"We will, I promise," Dave said firmly shaking his hand.

He kissed Betty's hand. "I will pray for you, Miss Betty."

She held both of his hands in hers and kissed him on the cheek. "Thank you so much."

After they boarded the plane, he remained beside his battered car and waved until they were out of sight.

Betty gazed at the blue-green sea below. A white rimmed cay with a coral reef slid into view. As it passed behind the plane, she closed her eyes and was again back in the cove floating, weightless, fixated by the flashing fish beneath her, all alone, cradled by the water, just her, the sea, and the flickering forms beneath.

"Could I get you something to drink?" The flight attendant's voice reeled her back into the present.

"I don't think so," Dave was saying.

"Wait, yes, two glasses of white wine," Betty spoke up.

She sipped her drink and nestled her head on his shoulder. "Ummm, just what the doctor didn't order."

"He didn't order the trip either, but it's been unbelievable in so many ways. I really feel like we've moved forward."

"Me too."

Neither spoke for a while.

"You know," she said, "I haven't had time to process all of this, but it's just too much for coincidence. In the peak of the tourist season Millie picks a place out of the yellow pages that just happens to be quiet and private and run by a kind, generous person who's lost a child. And what about the inscription on the marker? It's as if God were trying to tell us that he hasn't forgotten us and that there is hope."

To her surprise Dave agreed. "Something like that occurred to me too."

"It's been so nice to be able to talk and share," Betty said. "Let's try and keep it up when we get home."

Dave nodded. "Okay, but if I tell you that I can't right then, give me a little space."

She squeezed his arm. "Agreed, and the same here."

For the next hour they were like two kids returning from camp, replaying all the fun things they'd done: snorkeling, Juan's food, the dinner.

When they reached the mainland, thickening clouds smothered the sparkling sun, the brilliant blue sky, and their conversation. The airline magazine lay open on Dave's lap. He stared at it but had not turned a page for half an hour.

"What are you thinking?"

He took her hand. "Remember when I was in Vietnam and met you in Hawaii for R and R?"

"Do I? Yes."

"On the way to Aruba, I was afraid that when we returned, I'd feel just like I did on the flight back to Danang."

"How was that?"

"For four glorious days I was able to forget the hell I'd left. But on the way back, I knew that nothing would have changed—the rain, the filth, the shattered kids, the body bags." A long silence. "With this trip, I was afraid that we'd have a much needed break, but when we got back to the real world, nothing would be any different. People would be just as ignorant. The reminders would still be there, and Kelli would still be gone."

"Didn't the R and R help?"

"Oh, yes, I would've had a hard time lasting without it. But I knew if I could just survive five more months it would over. I've wondered if this will ever be over."

"I don't know." Betty felt her spirits plunging.

He saw her expression. "That's just it. I know nothing out there has changed, but we have. We're not the same two people who left Hillsdale last week." He took both of her hands in his. "We'll never be the same as we were before Kelli died, but look at Juan. We're going to be different, but, by God, we're going to know happiness again We're going to be normal—maybe a different kind of happiness and a new type of normal, but it's going to happen.

There were ten inches of snow on the ground and the temperature was eighteen when they landed in Lexington. They struggled to the car with their luggage. "No snorkeling tomorrow," Dave said as he unlocked the door.

Chapter 10

"This is wonderful. We've been home two weeks, and you're still home by six," Betty said. "With this new work schedule, I may get to keep you around longer."

"The folks at the office are happier too."

"Has Millie made any progress finding the new nurse?"

He winced. "I forgot to tell you. She starts next week."

"Well that makes two of us."

"What do you mean?"

She was beaming. "Bill Talbot called today. They have an opening on pediatrics Monday, Wednesday, Friday, and every other weekend. I'll still be able to go to my meetings on Thursdays. What do you think?"

"That's great. With two incomes we might make Caribbean vacations a routine."

"That, too."

හ

The world hadn't changed in their absence, but Dave was right—they had. Betty always met him in the foyer and dinner was again the high point of each day. They said grace. Once again they lingered, discussing the day or reminiscing about Kelli, who still hovered, but didn't dominate every waking moment. That Dave was no longer a lit fuse waiting to explode dissipated the tension at the office, at the hospital and at home.

"Dave, what's happened?" Betty asked him. "You're so different, calmer, even quieter than before Kelli." Without thinking, they had fallen into referencing events to Before Kelli and After Kelli.

"I don't know, but I can see it, too. Maybe almost dying just helps you get your priorities straight," he said, elaborating no further.

He continued to journal his way through the albums, and even allowed Betty to read what he had written, unedited as it was.

"That's beautiful, Dave," Betty said. She'd never seen this side of him and hadn't realized how, and how much, he loved Kelli.

Rereading Kelli's diary became his favorite pastime, almost like visiting her. Usually it comforted him, but parts of it still made him uneasy—so uneasy that at last he decided to act.

The Saturdays that Betty worked were Dave's day to sleep late, but this one he had wakened early.

"What are you going to do today?" she asked.

"I don't know, maybe split firewood." He laughed as her head jerked up. "Just kidding, I have some things to do in town."

After she left, he read his Bible and stalled, irritated by his indecision. I don't see any way around it. I have to do it, but even knowing it's what Kelli would want doesn't make it any easier.

He double-checked the address, 228 Washington, and recognized it was just down the street from old Mrs. Perkins where he made frequent house calls.

Even though it was still February, there were hints of spring everywhere—the wind had lost its bite. Crocuses shouldered their way through oak leaves along the walk giving splashes of purple, white and yellow against a backdrop of brown, winter drabness. Daffodil buds swelled, but were holding out for two more weeks of warm weather before bursting open.

The houses on Washington Street were for the most part neat, well-kept five room post-war bungalows, but now most had been expanded. Some almost covered the small lot they sat on. Definitely blue-collar. The roof on 228 had been raised in back to incorporate the attic into the house; the side porch had been enclosed and extended to the rear—neat, utilitarian, but not designed by an architect.

After sitting at the curb for several minutes, Dave got out of his car, walked up the uneven sidewalk and knocked on the door.

Mr. Williams opened the door and his eyes widened. "Dr. DeMarco." His gaze dropped. "I heard you had a heart attack. I'm sorry. It seems that everything my family does hurts yours. Are you all right now?"

"I'm fine. May I come in?"

"Excuse me," he said stepping back, "It's just…you surprised me. Please, come in."

The living room was cramped, but clean. A sagging couch and two threadbare easy chairs faced a small TV with rabbit ears.

"I started to call, but I didn't know quite what to say."

"That's all right. What can I do for you?"

"Is Matt home?" Dave asked.

Williams bit his lip. "Yes, he doesn't go out much."

"Is he awake?"

"I'm sure he is. He doesn't sleep much either."

"Could I talk with him?" This was like pulling teeth.

"Dr. DeMarco, he's barely hanging on. Please, don't do anything to hurt him." He hesitated, ambivalent about what he should do. "Wait here," he said and disappeared down a narrow, dimly lit hallway from which Dave could hear muffled voices. Williams returned and motioned for Dave to follow him to a tiny bedroom. "Matt, this is Dr. DeMarco. He wants to talk with you." He stepped back to let Dave enter. "I'll just leave you two here. Holler if you need anything," he said to either, or both, of them, then shut the door and left.

The room barely accommodated a bed, a clothes chest, a small desk and chair. Dave pulled out the desk chair and eased down almost knee-to-knee with Matt, who sat hunched forward on the edge of the bed staring in the direction of his bare feet. He wore a rumpled T-shirt and jeans. His unkempt hair, unshaved, hollowed cheeks, and sunken, blood-shot eyes gave him a wild, wraith-like appearance . Now Dave remembered having seen him several times in the past, but then he had been robust and muscular as opposed to his present near skeletal appearance. Dave shifted uncomfortably wondering what to say. Matt solved the problem by burying his face in his hands and bursting into tears.

"Dr. DeMarco, I'm so sorry," he blubbered. "I wouldn't have hurt Kelli for the world. She was my best friend. Oh, God, why didn't I die instead of her? I wish I was dead." He paused and tried to compose himself. "I'm not that kind of person. I'd only drunk one or two beers ever before prom night. I don't know why I did what I did. Why? Why?" He pounded his leg with his fist.

"Matt, I know you didn't mean to hurt her. That doesn't excuse what you did, but I know you meant no harm."

Matt dried his eyes and blew his nose on his sheet. "Then why are you here?" His voice was hoarse, small and miserable.

"To tell you that, as best I can, I forgive you. Hating you is destroying me, it's destroying you, and it won't bring Kelli back." He laid his hand on Matt's arm. "Kelli thought very highly of you. In her diary she said you were one of her best friends. In fact, she said you were like the brother she never had."

"She said that?" For the first time there was a glimmer of life in the sunken eyes.

"Yes."

"What can I do to make it up to you?"

"I have to be honest. There's nothing you can do to make it up to us." Tears began to stream down Matt's face again. "A better question might be, 'Given the situation that we're now in, what would Kelli want us to do with our lives?' If her life is to have any meaning at all, we're the ones who'll have to give it meaning—by the way we live. If we continue to tear ourselves and each other apart, then her life will have had no meaning at all."

"What should I do? What can I do?"

"What do you want to do with your life? What would make it meaningful?"

Matt ran his hand through his hair. "I know this may sound silly, but the only thing I ever wanted to be was a doctor. I had a pre-med scholarship to UK but I lost it after…you know, Kelli."

"Then I think that you should become a doctor, a superb doctor, or a teacher, or a truck driver. I don't care what you do, just do it in a manner that would make Kelli proud. Do it for Kelli. Do it for me if you like, but, most important of all, do it for yourself."

After a prolonged, awkward silence, Dave rose to leave. Matt grabbed his hand in both of his. "Thank you, Dr. DeMarco, thank you. I won't let you or Kelli down, I promise."

"Or yourself, that's all I ask."

ꟗ

"Hey, buddy, good to see you back at work. Ooh, some tan. Does it go all over?"

"No, Bob, we had to wear bathing suits," Dave said.

"Too bad. I was thinking about taking Sarah there. Now I'll have to do some more research."

"Yeah, I can see the tabloids. Nanuck the Naked Frightens Small Children on Nude Beach."

Mary Bolton laughed. "Dr. DeMarco's been back for almost two weeks. If you'd crawl out of that hole in the basement, you might know what was going on."

"Just saving lives. The captain of the cath lab, which, in case you didn't know it, is the money pump that keeps this hospital afloat."

Dave rolled his eyes and picked up the next chart. "Eliza Jane Thompson. I can't remember. Am I supposed to say 'Hey' when I see her?"

Mary stifled a giggle. "No, silly, you're supposed to say 'Ho'."

"What in the hell are you two talking about?" Bob said.

Dave gave Mary a high five and began to sing, "Hey, little Liza, little Liza Jane."

Mary followed with, "Ho, little Liza, little Liza Jane." The song ended as they dissolved into laughter.

"Damn," Bob muttered, "I'd hoped I'd blasted your silly jokes out of you with the defibrillator."

Dave grabbed Mary's arm. "Hey, let's go see Liza."

"Ho-kay."

Bob smiled, shook his head and ambled down the hall.

"Mike's home tonight, and I've fixed spaghetti," Mary said when they returned to the nurses' station . Why don't you and Betty come over."

"Sounds good," Dave said, picking up the phone. Mary's spaghetti was legendary. She'd learned to make it from her Italian grandmother. "She's all for it, says she'll bring a low-fat dessert that Mike and I will love. I'm going to bribe Bob to tell her to get off my dietary back. What time?"

"Seven?"

"Fine. See you then."

"I'd forgotten what good spaghetti tastes like," Dave said. This was the first time they had gotten together since Kelli died.

"More wine?" Mike reached the bottle to Dave.

"No, thanks. I have a two glass limit."

Mary and Betty were engrossed in Betty's refresher course and imminent return to work.

"So how's crime, Mike?" Dave asked. "Hillsdale always seems so quiet."

"It used to be, but now there's a lot of drugs coming in from Louisville and Lexington. Crime's going rural—lower overhead for the bad guys and less manpower for the cops. The scary part is that it's starting to spill over to our kids. A couple of months ago, we busted a group out of Cincinnati cooking up crack cocaine and LSD. Few people realize it, but marijuana is the largest cash crop here and in the surrounding four counties."

"I guess I'm really sheltered from the shadier aspects of Appalachian life."

"Just watch out for the chronic pain guys. Doctors are such an easy touch. Narcotics are a lot cheaper by prescription than on the street. Ten hydrocodones at the pharmacy costs about eight dollars, but can go for fifty to seventy-five on the street; good way to support a bigger habit."

"You're probably right. We just naturally trust people and assume they tell the truth."

"They don't. That's a fact I learned in my line of work."

"How's the girls basketball team?" Dave asked.

"They're pretty good," Mike said, sensing the topic was safe now. "They're not as good as when Kelli was there. Before the season started, I thought they had an outside chance to get back to the state tournament, but the Peterson girl got sick. Too bad, she was heading toward being All-State."

Mary interrupted them. "We have some dessert if someone will clear the table."

"I think that's our cue," Mike said.

"Decaf and Betty's special skinny cheesecake, totally organic and no fat, just the thing for you tubbies," Mary said.

"Great," Dave said, "counterfeit coffee and fake fat."

"He's not accustomed to being healthy," Betty said. "You might as well get used to it because I have a vested interest in keeping you around, or…" Betty pulled his serving away, "I could just give it all to Mike."

"No, no, I have to humor you. I'll eat it."

"Don't put yourself out."

He took a large bite. "That's good," he said, acting surprised.

"Naturally, no pun intended," Betty said with a snicker.

"That was nice," Betty said on the way home. "Mary's going to be my mentor for two weeks when I go back to work."

"That'll help. She's good, very smart with a large load of common sense thrown in. They're nice folks. You know, I actually enjoyed myself. It was nice that Mike would talk about Kelli, and it was nice that I could listen."

80

"Good sermon, John, you kept me awake almost the whole time," Dave said, wincing as Betty poked him in his ribs.

John Rankin shook Dave's hand. "That's all right, Betty. Next week I'll show that Jesus was a socialist and favored government control of medicine. I'll bet that keeps him awake."

They walked hand-in-hand to the car. "Let's just grab a quick snack at the deli," Dave said. "Tom and Dan were glad to cover for me while I was off, but they're even more glad to give my call schedule back to me."

"That's fine. Anyway, I need to get ready for tomorrow. Two weeks orientation seems intimidating, even with Mary."

"You'll do fine."

After lunch he dropped Betty at home and returned to the hospital. On the long straightaway just past the cemetery, he braked hard and pulled onto the shoulder of the road. He dragged a large limb that had fallen across the sign into the ditch.

Hillsdale pop. 34,146
Home of the 1987 Girl's State Basketball Championship
A Good Place to Live.

He straightened the sign, brushing the dead bark from it. Yes, it is, and Kelli, you made it better.

He had barely started on rounds when his pager and the intercom sounded simultaneously .

"Dr. DeMarco, emergency room stat. Dr. DeMarco, emergency room stat."

He took the stairs. "What've you got?"

The nurse pointed. "Seizure. Room 5."

A slender African-American girl lay on the stretcher and gave several spasmodic jerks before lying still, her breath coming in hoarse gasps. "I've given her IV Valium and started an IV," Jack Gibbons, the emergency room doctor said.

"Thanks. Any history?"

"Not yet."

Dave began a methodical, step-by-step examination of the unconscious girl. She was tall and slender, sixteen or seventeen years old, and had a scaly rash on her trunk and arms. Somehow, she seemed familiar. He motioned to the nurse. "Is there any family?"

"Her mother's in the waiting room. She's pretty upset."

"Could you get her, please?" he said and resumed his examination.

"My baby, my baby, is she going to be all right?"

Dave turned. Oh, no. "Mrs. Peterson."

"I told you she was sick. I told you, but you wouldn't listen."

God, I knew it, I just didn't care. "I know. Why didn't you bring her back?"

"I tried to, but you was sick."

"I'm sorry. She's stable for now. We've stopped the seizures, but I need to talk with you. Let's go to the consultation room where it's quieter." Mrs. Peterson followed him. They sat down. "Could I get you some coffee or a coke?" She shook her head. "I need to know what happened today."

"She done a little better after she was in the hospital last summer. She started trying to practice basketball, and she went straight downhill. She's been getting worser and worser, won't eat, hands been trembling." She dabbed her eyes. "She ain't been to school for two weeks. She's just too weak." Mrs. Peterson paused. "Then last night she started talking out of her head. We called the emergency room, but they said to bring her in today if she wasn't any better." Mrs. Peterson began to shake. "Then this morning, all of a sudden her eyes roll back and she commenced to jerking and twitching and foaming at the mouth. I thought she was going to die." She burst into tears. "Is Tamika going to be all right, Dr. DeMarco?"

"I'm sure she is," he lied. He stayed with her until all of the lab work and X-rays were done. The girl was resting but mumbling incoherently when he left.

He slammed the neurology book shut. "Somebody ought to kick me right in the butt. She told me she was sick, and I knew she was sick, but I didn't do anything."

"Dave, you did the best you could," Betty said.

"No, I didn't. I just blew them off."

"You were under a lot of stress."

"Then I should've had someone else see her." He rubbed his temples. "The scary part is that I haven't the foggiest idea what's wrong with her. She's delirious, having seizures, and covered with some weird rash. Except for being anemic her work-up is normal. The spinal tap and CT scan are cold normal. No one else has any ideas either. I'd send her to the University except the family can't get back and forth and can't afford to stay in Lexington. I may send her anyway, or take her myself if I have to."

"Don't be too hard on yourself."

"It's hard not to be. She was Kelli's friend. Kelli mentions her several times in her diary. It's almost as if I'm letting Kelli down."

"Would it help if you called someone from the University?"

"That's a good idea. I'll do it first thing in the morning."

The next morning he made sure to see Tamika first and found Mrs. Peterson was waiting at the door to her room.

"I think she's a little better, Dr. DeMarco. She seemed to recognize me this morning and there ain't been no more seizures."

"Good, let's take a look." She was a little more alert. "How do you feel, Tamika?"

Tamika looked puzzled, struggling to process his question through her memory banks.

"All right."

"Do you hurt anywhere?"

Again a long pause. "My tongue's sore."

He shined his penlight into her mouth. The edges of her tongue were blue from where she had chewed it during the seizure. She still had a noticeable tremor of her hands, and the rash was unchanged.

"She does look a little better," Dave said. "She was pretty dehydrated yesterday, and the IVs have perked her up."

Mrs. Peterson nodded. "What do you think is wrong with her, Doctor?"

"I have to be honest. I'm not really sure." Mrs. Peterson bit her lip. "Try not to worry. At least she's not worse. I'm going to call the head neurologist at the University medical school to see if he has any suggestions. I'll let you know as soon as I find anything out. I promise. Have you had any sleep?" She shook her head. "Look, she's going to be here for several days. You must get some sleep if you're going to be able to help Tamika. The nurses will take good care of her, and I'll call you if there are any changes. Now go home and get some rest."

"I will. Thank you, Doctor."

༄

"Can I be of any assistance, Doctor?" a husky voice asked from behind him.

"Huh? No, thank you." He turned. Betty and Mary were smiling at him. "I was a thousand miles away. Betty, you look great, just like old times." They chatted for a few minutes. "I've got to finish rounds and get to the office. Keep a close eye on Tamika for me."

"We will," Betty said. "We might just diagnose her while you're gone."

"You have my permission. Go to it. Someone needs to, and fast."

It was 11:45 when Millie paged him. "Dr. Wistrom is on line two."

He rushed to his office. "Dr. Wistrom, Dave DeMarco from Hillsdale." He gave him a thorough summary of Tamika's case.

"Is she on drugs?"

"I don't think so. The family says not and I believe them. I did a complete drug screen anyway, and it was totally negative."

"What medicine is she on?"

"Nothing except some vitamins and iron pills."

They continued for over half an hour. Finally Wistrom concluded, "Dr. DeMarco, this sounds metabolic or toxic. It could be an unusual form of multiple sclerosis except the rash doesn't fit that. I'd do a complete metabolic survey and a screen for toxins and heavy metals. Would you like to transfer her here?"

"I sure would, but for now the family won't hear of it."

"Well, good luck. This is a tough one. Call back if we can help and give me a follow-up when you find out what's wrong."

"Sure, thank you for your time and help." If I find out what's wrong.

He was encouraged when Tamika seemed a little more alert that afternoon.

He helped Betty with dinner, and afterward they sipped coffee and talked.

"Well, how was your first day back?" he asked.

"Better than I'd anticipated. The refresher course really helped, and Mary's marvelous. It's starting to come back."

"Did you see Tamika?"

"Yes, I recognize her now. Kelli brought her home several times. She was a very good basketball player, but she's lost so much weight. Was the fellow from the medical school any help?"

"He just reinforced what I'd already read, but it helps knowing I was thinking in the right areas. Now there're two of us in the dark, which beats being alone and without a clue."

He scoured several journals he'd gotten from the hospital library. "I'm going to run back to the hospital for a quick visit."

"Remember, you have other patients."

"I know, but I won't sleep without a quick check."

She kissed him. "All right, go, but drive carefully."

"Yes, ma'am."

A feeble night light by the door glowed in Tamika's darkened room. Dave stepped in but then retreated when he saw the figure kneeling beside her bed. He walked to the nurse's station and waited until he saw some movement in the room. A tall man standing at least six feet-four, his bald, ebony scalp ringed by a fringe of gray, rose and stepped out to meet him. He appeared to be about seventy years old.

"She's sleeping," he said.

Dave reached out his hand. "I'm Dr. DeMarco."

"Sorry to make you wait, but I was talking to the Lord. I'm glad to meet you. I'm William Peterson, Tamika's father." His voice was deep and resonant and he bore himself with a quiet dignity. His huge hand swallowed Dave's.

"I just dropped back by to be sure she's okay."

"Thank you, Doctor, I do appreciate it."

Dave led him to the small visitor's lounge. "Would you like some coffee?"

"Yes sir, that would be real nice. Black's fine."

As they sipped their coffee, Dave had him go through Tamika's history, hoping to get another clue, but he told Dave nothing that Mrs. Peterson had not. He had eight other children, still worked as a janitor at the chemical plant and was the lay minister of the church in Boogertown.

"Tamika's my youngest, the smartest, too. She was going to be the first to go to college, but that probably won't happen since she can't play basketball." He sat silent for a few moments. "She sure loved your Kelli."

"You knew Kelli?"

"Oh, yes sir, Kelli ate with us lots of times when she came over to help Tamika with her basketball. Tamika really liked your wife, too. I think the two of them are who got Tamika interested in being a nurse. Going to college and being a nurse was that child's dream."

"I talked with a doctor from the medical school and we have some ideas about what might be wrong with Tamika."

"Is she going to die, doctor?"

Dave groped for the right words. "I hope not."

"I appreciate what you are doing, Dr. DeMarco, but in the end she's in God's hands. Lord, it would hurt to lose her, but you know all about that. You know better than me, but, doctor, I've been thinking. Tamika was a gift from God to an old man who never dreamed he'd have another child, and she's been everything I could want a child to be, but I don't own her. She's a gift." He rubbed his huge hand over his bald pate. "Lord knows I want her to live years longer than me, I told Him so. But I'll tell you this, if I had to choose whether to have her for seventeen years and then let her go or to never have her at all," he snapped his fingers, "I'd take her for seventeen years just like that. Yes sir, I would."

Dave didn't speak for several minutes. "Thank you, Mr. Peterson. I'd never thought of it like that, but you are absolutely right." He stood and took Mr. Peterson's hand. "You keep on praying, and I will, too, but I'm going to do my best to see to it that you don't have to make that choice."

As he drove home he couldn't get the tall, black man out of his mind. Just as he turned up his drive it hit him. "…and hear the voice of God through your neighbor's lips." He stopped for a moment. "Thank you," he whispered and drove on up to the house.

Chapter 11

"Don't they know this girl is seriously ill?" Dave snapped.

"I'm really sorry," Bill Blakely, the pathologist said. "I've called the lab and asked them to put a priority on them, but, at the best, the metabolic screens will take three or four days and the heavy metal screens will take at least ten days to two weeks."

"Okay, Bill, thanks for trying. Do you think they might could do it faster at the medical school?"

"Yeah, if you're a professor and have a research grant."

Although her rash was no better and her tremor hadn't changed, Tamika was more alert and she seemed to feel better. Two days later Betty and Mary went into Tamika's room with Dave. Her eyes brightened and she smiled. "Mrs. DeMarco."

"She never greets me like that," Dave said, feigning hurt feelings.

"I'm sorry. Hi, Dr. DeMarco."

"That'll do, I guess. How are you this morning?"

"I'm better. I ate my oatmeal and drank my milk."

"That's great. Anything else bothering you?"

She looked down avoiding eye contact. "I look terrible. My hair's like a rat's nest and my nails are all chipped."

"I can help that," Betty said. "Remember three years ago when I helped you and Kelli learn to use make-up?" Tamika's eyes brightened. "I'll come here after work and give you a once over. Would you like that?"

"You don't have to do that, Mrs DeMarco," but her obvious anticipation overrode her protest.

"I really want to."

"Oh, thank you, Mrs. DeMarco. I'd love it."

Dave laid down his journal. "That was a nice thing to do. I'll bet Tamika was thrilled. Did you know you were sort of her hero?"

"Yeah, I learned. She's such a sweet girl, and she really wants to be a nurse. Evidently she and Kelli had talked a lot about it." Her throat tightened. "Kelli loved people so much. She would've been a great nurse herself."

"Or doctor."

"No, we talked about that. She wanted to have a family, and she saw how much time you put into your work. She thought nursing would give her the best of both worlds." They were quiet. "Be sure to compliment Tamika in the morning. We got her hair done and put some make-up on her. She's very pretty. I even painted her nails; they really needed attention and they looked so strange."

"Strange?"

"Every one of her fingernails had this white line about a quarter inch wide that went all the way across it."

"What did you say?" Dave asked.

"There was this funny white line across each nail. Why?"

He began rummaging through the stack of books on the coffee table. "That's it, by golly, that's got to be it."

"What's it?"

"Look at this picture. Did they look anything like this?"

Betty studied the colored illustration in the book. "Yes, exactly like that."

"They're called Mees lines. I have no idea how she got it, but I'll bet everything I own that Tamika has arsenic poisoning. The seizure, the rash, the delirium, the tremors, the anemia, it all fits."

"Arsenic? Where would she get arsenic?"

"I don't know, and it's too late to do anything tonight. I hate to have you do it, but take off that fingernail polish tomorrow so I can see her nails. You can put it back later."

He called Dr. Wistrom with his findings and opinion the first thing after seeing Tamika. "That's got to be it."

"It sure sounds like it," Wistrom said, " although I've never actually seen a case."

"Is there any way you could facilitate the arsenic tests?"

"I'm sure I can. This patient sounds pretty sick, and if she does have arsenic poisoning, we need to get some BAL started as soon as possible. It probably won't reverse all the symptoms, but it should keep them from getting worse and might help make them better. Would it be all right with you if I brought a couple of residents down to examine her? We could bring the urine specimens back with us and save a day or two."

"That would be fantastic. I had them start the collection last night, anyway."

"Good. We'll see you this afternoon."

"I think you're right," Dr. Wistrom concluded after his own examination. "I can let you know the day after tomorrow, but where could she have gotten it?"

"I've been working on that since we talked," Dave said. "There's been no spraying, so I doubt she inhaled it. She lives near the chemical plant, but if she drank it, why aren't others sick? She hasn't eaten much, but what she has eaten is the same diet as her family. It's a real mystery."

"I could see if the environmental science and maybe the public health people from the graduate school might like to tackle this."

"That would be great," Dave said, "I'm going to look over things with her father tomorrow, but I'm not sure I know what I'm looking for. I'd appreciate any help you could give me."

"Tamika and her family are thrilled that we know what's wrong. They think you're a genius," Betty said.

"I'd have been a genius if I'd diagnosed it six months ago. We won't be sure until tomorrow." Just then the phone rang.

"I'll get it," Betty said. "I sure hope it's not the emergency room." She picked up the phone. "It's Dr. Wistrom."

"Fred, what's up?"

"One of the residents is in tight with a girl in the lab, and he got her to run the sample this morning. The arsenic in Miss Peterson's urine was so far off the scale that she ran the test three times just to be sure. I'd start her on some BAL in the morning. Here's the dosage. I had to look it up."

"Fred, I don't know how to thank you."

"You made the diagnosis. Thank you for letting me horn in. By the way, a graduate student from environmental science and one from public health are champing at the bit to come down. They have visions of grants, publicity, and Ph.D. theses dancing in their heads. Would Saturday be okay?"

"That's fine. I'd like to see how they go about it."

He hung up and told Betty what Wistrom had said.

"What's BAL?" she asked. "I don't remember it from my pharmacology class."

"It's British antilewisite, an old chemical developed in World War I as an antidote for arsenical war gas. It combines with arsenic and removes it from the body. The only problem is that it may take several weeks to do it, and it may not reverse all of the effects of arsenic on the body."

"Dave, I know you're excited, but pace yourself. You cut back after your heart attack, and you told me it was permanent. Having you around more has been nice, so please don't go back like you were."

"I've thought about that. I'll get the grad students to do most of the work. I'm a doctor, not an investigator, but it's nice to have something positive to focus on. Helping Tamika and her family is almost like helping Kelli, and I think Kelli would like that."

Betty hugged him. "I do, too."

ᘓ

"That was delicious," Will Martin said, cleaning the last crumb of the cherry pie from his plate. "Letting us stay with you tonight will sure make it easier to get everything done tomorrow." The graduate student was short and solidly built with neatly trimmed reddish hair.

"Yes, thank you so much," said Sue Wilson as she rose to help clear the table. She was at least five-eight, had short cropped hair and moved with the fluid grace of an athlete.

"Why don't you get the material we need for tomorrow while Betty and I clear the table so we can have some work space," said Dave.

"They're not what I expected," Dave said when they had left.

"What do you mean?" Betty asked.

"I expected a couple of hippy tree huggers. You know, pony tails, wire rimmed glasses and granny dresses. Instead we get two clean scrubbed Mormon missionaries."

"You old fogy."

Will had a large contour map spread on the table. "Here's Boogertown." He paused. "How did it get a name like Boogertown?"

Dave smiled. "Where're you from?"

"Upstate New York."

"There are about fifty or sixty African-Americans who live there. Kentucky's not the deep South, but we're still below the Mason-Dixon line and old habits die hard."

"Oh." Will re-oriented himself. "I did a little research. One of the major products International Chemicals makes here is insecticides, so no doubt they use a lot of arsenicals. There's also something about chemical warfare work for the government, but that's very hush-hush. You said that all of the residents get their water from wells." Dave nodded. "It's unlikely she inhaled the arsenic. Boogertown is here between the road on the east and Hickory Ridge on the west, about a half-mile below the settling ponds. Groundwater can do funny things, but usually it follows the contour of the terrain. I'll bet the ponds are seeping into the wells."

"That's the only thing I could think of," Dave said.

Sue spoke up. "What we thought we'd do tomorrow is take water samples from all of the wells and check it for arsenic. The only thing that puzzles me is why only this one girl got sick."

"That doesn't make sense to me either," said Dave.

"First things first. We should make certain the water is safe, and if it is, try to figure where else she could have gotten it."

Saturday and Sunday passed in a blur of nonstop activity. They had walked the entire perimeter of Boogertown. Thanks to Mr. Peterson, the residents had been organized and cooperative in helping gather water and soil samples.

Sunday afternoon they helped Will and Sue pack their van with boxes of soil and jugs of water, each tagged and identified as to where it had been collected.

"It's going to take a while to process all of this," Will said. "We'll call you as soon as we have any results."

"Thank you so much," Dave said. "Let me know if there is anything else you need."

"I'm beat, and they don't even seem winded," Dave said as they drove off. "Oh, to be young again."

☙

Dave didn't come to the cemetery often, but today he needed to be alone and think. He leaned back on the curved concrete bench and inhaled deeply. The warm breeze was laced with a mixture of lilac and honeysuckle. Bees flitted from one bird's foot violet to another, their weight bending the delicate blue blossoms almost to the ground as they siphoned the nourishing nectar. The cemetery rules forbade flowers except in the designated vase because they interfered with mowing. Kelli had liked this particular variety of violet so much she had transplanted some from Uncle Jeb's place around the base of the bird feeder where they flourished in soil made rich by bird droppings. It had been a simple thing to collect some, slip them in a few at a time and plant them close against the base of her marker . Evidently they didn't qualify as flowers since the caretaker had left them alone.

Spring was different this year. This beautiful time of renewal and new life grated against the life that was gone and wouldn't return. Who cared if the violets bloomed, if Kelli wasn't there to enjoy them?

In the two weeks since the graduate students had left, a cloud of malaise had settled on the DeMarco house. The flurry of activity with Tamika's illness had distracted them, but like the optimistic enthusiasm after their trip to Aruba, it dissipated. The searing pain of those early months was gone, replaced by a continuous emptiness. Gone were the bitterness and sniping of last winter. If anything, he and Betty were closer and talked more now than they ever had. Gone were his erratic behavior and the need to stay busy, although he welcomed the demands of his practice which at least kept him focused. Their lives had taken on a semblance of normality, but still ground along day-to-day, sometimes hour-to-hour, with the cloud of Kelli's absence always hovering nearby. What future they could imagine stretched before them as a lonely path of near meaninglessness.

"Come on, Dave, snap out of it," he said aloud, and began reviewing what he should do next. It strained credulity to think that someone had arsenic poisoning less than a mile from a company that used vast quantities of arsenic and the two were somehow unrelated. Still, most of his patients worked for the plant and were covered by their insurance. His relationship with their employer had always been good, and he had never had a hint of a disagreement with them. Should he rock the boat? This was a tough decision, but had he not been telling himself that all of his decisions were important? He ran as many scenarios as he could imagine through his mind and finally decided.

Heaving himself up from the bench, he poured water from a small bottle into the vase of fresh cut flowers which Betty replaced weekly, brushed some grass clippings from around the marker, and headed for the car.

Betty met him in the foyer and hugged him, holding him against her longer than usual.

"Were you at the cemetery?"

"Yeah. The flowers are really nice. I just feel so helpless."

"I know."

After a quiet dinner they sat on the patio.

"I saw Tamika today," Dave said.

"How's she doing?"

"Actually, very well. She's much more alert. The rash is completely cleared, and her tremor's almost gone, but she still has some nerve damage to her legs."

"Does that mean she won't be able to play basketball?"

"Most likely. From all I can read, there's usually some permanent damage."

Betty bit her lip. "That's a shame. She was so good, and it was her ticket to college." She hesitated, thinking how to broach the subject. "Do you suppose …No, forget about it."

"What?"

"Just a wild thought about Tamika and college."

Before he could pursue the matter, the phone rang. It was Sue from the university.

"Dr. DeMarco, this is getting stranger all the time."

"What do you mean?"

"All of the wells have arsenic levels that are slightly above normal, but not dangerously so. Odd thing though, the soil and water samples were significantly higher toward the ridge, not toward the plant."

"It still had to come from the plant," Dave said.

"I don't see any other explanation. As Will said, groundwater can do funny things. We'd like to come back next week. Will thought it would be helpful to see if any other residents have elevated arsenic levels. We should get urine samples from as many residents as possible."

"Tamika's father is the community leader, and I'm sure he can arrange it. Just say when. One more thing, I'm going to talk with International's CEO; I'm sure he'll want to help."

"I wouldn't count on it. Most industries want to keep a low profile, especially if they're doing sensitive government work, and they particularly don't like people raising environmental concerns."

"But surely they wouldn't want to harm the community," Dave said.

"No, but they wouldn't want to spend a lot of money on clean up either."

"I'm still going to talk with them."

"Do what you think is best." She sounded dubious. "We'll see you next week."

He told Betty what Sue had said.

"Do you really think you should talk with them?" Betty asked.

"I don't like to make waves, but they should know that there may be a problem."

"I guess so. It's just that we have enough to deal with without adding more."

Chapter 12

The road over Indian Gap in the spring was one of Dave's favorite drives. The lush new foliage on the hills would dull and darken with the heat of summer, but for this brief time they glimmered with new life. Red buds and dogwoods dappled the green palette with shimmering splotches of pink and white, and the warm April air wafted new aromas around each bend in the curvy road. Briefly the impending date in May receded, replaced by the beauty of the moment. The highway that led to International Chemicals arrived too soon, interrupting his reverie. After Dave explained the nature of his visit, the guard at the gate called somewhere then gave him directions and waved him through.

The receptionist ushered him into a spacious office, richly paneled with what appeared to be solid cherry. Three men rose as he entered and were introduced in an unspoken pecking order. A stocky, broad shouldered, squared jawed man behind the desk rose and extended his hand. He looked like a bulldog.

"Dr. DeMarco, Josh Albritton, CEO."

The man to his right stepped forward. As tall as Dave, he had a patrician bearing and manner accentuated by his expensive tailored suit and gleaming silver hair.

"J. Tyler Braxton of Braxton, Braxton and Wallace."

"I've had dealings with one of your associates," Dave said shaking his hand.

"Really, who?"

"A Mr. Fourney."

"You must be mistaken," he said, his voice cold. "We have no one by that name in our firm."

Dave let it pass.

Sensing some tension, Albritton hurried on. "And this is Jim Wheeler, our director of environmental affairs. Let's all have a seat." Without giving him a chance to shake Wheeler's hand, he indicated a chair set before his huge desk. "Would you like some coffee or something stronger?"

"No, thank you," Dave replied and sat in the straight back chair feeling like the subject of an interrogation.

Albritton leaned forward. "On the phone you made some very serious charges."

"No charges. I said I have a patient who lives just down from the plant who had near fatal arsenic toxicity, and that the most likely source was your plant. I felt like you'd want to know."

"We appreciate your concern, and we, too, are concerned—so much so that we had Jim review all of our testing for the last three years. Jim, show him what you have."

The engineer spread a large map on Albritton's desk and motioned for Dave to join him. "Here are the settling ponds," he indicated, his finger sweeping over the large blue areas on the map. "They're constructed on compacted clay covered with six inches of concrete and a composite liner, the latest technology and practically leak proof."

Dave was impressed.

"And here below the ponds are three concentric rows of bore holes, each three hundred feet deep, extending from the base of the ridge on the east to the base on the west between the plant and any residences. We wanted to cover the entire area because groundwater can do funny things," he said, echoing Will Martin's words. "We test these wells monthly and as of last Thursday, the levels of heavy metals, specifically arsenic, and other toxins have never even approached the levels the EPA considers high."

Dave studied the map. "Then how could they have gotten arsenic? And why would their wells and soil show elevated levels of arsenic?"

"How do you know they were elevated?" Albritton asked.

Dave told him about Will and Sue.

Albritton wrote something on a note pad. "I'm not sure how much credence I'd put in the work of two college students." Dave said nothing. Albritton looked at Wheeler.

"Oh, yes," the engineer stammered, "even assuming their values are valid, and I'm not ready to concede that they are, the whole area you indicated is built on a landfill used by the railroads from around 1900 to 1947. God knows what they may have dumped there."

Dave studied the map for a few minutes longer and then sat down.

"Your patient may have gotten into some arsenic, but it wasn't ours. For all we know it may have been contaminated drugs. You know how those people are." Dave was silent. "Have we answered your questions?"

"I'm not sure," Dave said and rose to leave.

Albritton cleared his throat. "Dr. DeMarco, we appreciate your concern and admire your dedication to your patients, but you must realize that a company's image, just like a doctor's, is a precious commodity." Dave nodded, wondering where this was heading. "We can't have our corporate image damaged by unfounded rumors and innuendo. It would be wise if you dropped this matter altogether. We wouldn't want to have to take legal action against you."

Dave was stunned. He chose his words carefully. "I've spread no rumors. I brought my concerns directly to you."

"How about contacting the university?" Albritton snapped.

"Aside from doing what was necessary to treat my patient, I have discussed this with no one except you, nor do I intend to."

Braxton started to speak, but Albritton cut him off. "We're not trying to intimidate you, Dr. DeMarco."

The heck you aren't.

"But," Albritton continued, "we work hard to be a responsible corporate citizen and are very jealous of our reputation. I'm sure you understand." He came around the desk and shook Dave's hand. "If we can be of any assistance, please feel free to call us."

Dave returned his handshake. "Thank you very much."

As soon as the door shut, Albritton slammed his fist on the desk so hard that the phone receiver bounced onto the floor.

"Can I help you, Mr. Albritton?" the receptionist's voice called from the dangling handset.

"No!" Albritton roared and jabbed off the intercom button with his stubby finger. Red faced, he leaned on the desk. "Jim," his voice was strained, "get Slade over here. Now."

"They seem to have checked things out fairly thoroughly," Dave said, not mentioning the thinly veiled threat from Braxton. " I still can't think of anywhere else Tamika could have gotten the arsenic from." He paused because Betty was staring out the window. Her mind seemed far away. The lack of sound snapped her back.

"I'm sorry, I just can't seem to concentrate," she said.

"I know. This commotion with the poisoning serves as a good distraction, but when things get quiet, it all comes flooding back. It's hard to believe it's been almost a year."

"For a little while, after our vacation and starting back to work, I thought I was out of the woods, but now I think I'm worse than ever. I expect her to come bounding through the door any day."

"Yeah, I know," Dave said. "I try to think about the future, but it seems so hopeless; there's nothing to look forward to."

Too restless to sit in silence, Betty began to pace around the room. When she finally sat down beside him she asked hesitantly, "Have you thought about what we could do on...that day?" There, she'd said it.

He took her hand. "I've been stewing over it for a month. I just didn't know how to bring it up."

"I know what I don't want to do. I don't want to be with other people. I don't think I can stand another memorial service, and I certainly can't go to work, but I don't think I can just sit at home and feel sad. I try not to make such a big deal out of it, but it just sits there and grows."

"You're reading my mind," he replied. "I did have one idea, but it seemed sort of far-fetched."

"What's that?"

"Something Kelli wrote in her diary. She said that I was always making big plans to do something, but then would get busy at work and never do them." His voice tightened, "Like the prom."

"So what's your idea?"

"Remember when we went camping in the Smokies? We always said we wanted to climb Mt. Leconte, but I never had time."

"Yes."

"I thought we might do that on the sixteenth. If we get tired enough, we might not be as sad, sort of grief therapy by fatigue. I think Kelli might like that."

Betty said nothing for several minutes; then very softly she said, "I think she would."

Three days later Sue called. "All of the residents have minute traces of arsenic in their urine, but not dangerously so, except for two boys. Their levels are extremely high. I'm surprised they haven't gotten ill."

"Who are they?"

"Eric Porter and Michael Peete, both teen-agers. Will and I can come down Saturday if that's all right with you."

Mr. Peterson met them when they drove up, and Dave told him what they'd found.

"We'd like to talk with these two boys and Tamika. Since they're the only ones with high levels, maybe we can find something in common among them."

Mr. Peterson nodded. "They're all up at the basketball barn."

"The basketball barn? Where's that?" Dave asked.

"I guess I forgot about it when you were here before. It's just beyond that little knoll. We used to raise some cows. When we quit, we made it into a basketball court and a place for the children to play in the winter."

"Dr. DeMarco," Tamika shouted and ran to them breathing heavily, her dark skin glistening with perspiration. She nodded in understanding as he told her the purpose of their visit.

"Hey, Eric, Michael, come over here." She introduced them to Dave and the students. "Let us wash our hands and get a drink of water, then we'll be able to talk better." When they returned they sat on a wooden bench like attentive students.

"This is where Kelli practiced with me when we couldn't get into the gym," she said, then remembering why they were there, she asked, "What is it you want to know?"

After an hour of close questioning, Dave was becoming frustrated. Playing basketball was the only thing the three had in common. Sue asked about any drug use in the community, which they all denied.

"Wait a minute," Dave blurted.

"What?" Will asked.

"Tamika, do you have a cooler up here?"

Tamika shook her head. "No sir."

"Where did you get the water to wash your hands and drink?"

"At the well out back"

"What well? Show me," his voice rose.

They followed her to a shallow, hand-dug well behind the barn.

"That's got to be it, it's got to be." Dave almost danced with excitement. "Does anyone else use this well except those of you who play basketball up here?"

Tamika shook her head.

"I'll bet you're right," Will said. "I'll get some samples of the water."

"You'd better get some soil samples from here and over there." Sue had walked to a dry wash running down the side of the ridge just beyond the well. It had a brownish-yellow tint with only a few scraggly weeds growing in it.

"Sue, let's walk up this a way while Will gets his samples," Dave said.

They followed the path of the wash through a small stand of pine trees beyond which it continued up the rocky slope. A hundred yards beyond the trees a barbed wire fence blocked their way. Every few yards plastic No Trespassing signs hung from the wire. They crawled through the wire and were half way up the ridge when the crack of a rifle brought them to a halt.

"Get the hell out of here! Can't you read?"

They could make out the shape of a man on the crest of the ridge, a very large man, so large he blocked the sun behind him, which obscured his features but not the rifle he held in his right hand.

Dave shielded his eyes with his hand. "We were just—"

"I don't care what you thought you were just doing," the huge figure shouted, "What you are doing is trespassing." He moved the rifle the slightest bit. "Now get your asses out of here and don't come back."

Giving Sue a light shove back down the hill, Dave called out, "Calm down, we're leaving."

Rocks broke loose and rolled down the wash as they scrambled back. After reaching the cover of the trees, Dave paused to look back. The man was still there, the rifle still held ready.

ꟷ

Will called two weeks later.

"Dr. DeMarco, I have some good news and bad news."

"Give it to me."

"On the positive side, you were right. The arsenic in the well water was off the scale. More than that though, it was a witch's brew of chemicals including high levels of PCBs and cadmium among other things. The soil samples were extremely high around the well and up the wash. I'll bet it's leeching out from above."

"Where someone doesn't want us to look," Dave said. "What's the bad news?"

"I feel like a jerk, but I can't work with you any more."

"Why's that?"

"Thank goodness we'd already measured the samples because the head of the department called me in yesterday and told me in no uncertain terms to drop it. Otherwise, my fellowship would be in jeopardy. I'm almost ready to start my dissertation, and I just can't risk it. I told him that I had already called you with the results last week. He didn't like it, but what he doesn't know can't hurt him. Cover for me if you're asked."

"I understand and I appreciate all you've done. Someone really wants this to disappear. How about Sue?"

"She said she'd been warned too."

"I didn't intend to cause you any trouble, I'm sorry."

"That's OK. I just wish we could finish it."

He was mulling over calling Sue when the phone rang.

"Dr. DeMarco, it's Sue. Do you know what's happened?"

"Will just told me."

"Well, they're not going to intimidate me. They can't tell me what to do."

"Who do you mean?" Dave asked.

"International Chemical. I dragged it out of my faculty advisor. They give big bucks to the university and think they can run the place."

"Evidently they can."

"Well, I'm not going to drop it. I may just make an anonymous call to the newspaper."

"I don't want you to do that," Dave said firmly. "You and Will have both been invaluable, but we know what we need to know. I don't want you risking your future. Do you understand? Not another word to anyone, please."

She said nothing.

"Sue?"

"All right," she said, "on two conditions. You keep me updated, and you promise to call me if you need any further help."

"Agreed. And Sue?"

"Yes?"

"Do continue to drop in from time to time. Betty was saying the other day how nice it was to have a young woman around again."

"Thank you, Dr. DeMarco, I'd enjoy that."

He warned Mr. Peterson to cap the well so no one else could use it and began treatment on the other two children. With the well off limits no one else could be hurt, but what about the soil where the children played? What if more of the poisons washed down and contaminated the other wells? No, they were too deep. Or were they? At the moment he didn't have the motivation to take on any other problems. He tried not to dwell on Kelli, but May 16 loomed and cast a pall over everything, so he buried himself in his work and tried to forget poisonings, chemicals, and death dates.

A few days later, Millie caught him between patients.

"Dr. Maxwell called and said to meet him at Charlie's for lunch. He didn't leave a number. He just said to be there at one."

Dave smiled. Bob always got his way. Just leave orders for everyone and disappear.

Bob motioned from a rear table when Dave walked in.

"Good to see you, buddy. I hear you've been busy dazzling the staff with your diagnostic acumen. I'm even a little impressed myself." Dave started to speak, but Bob rattled on. "As a reward, just this once, I've ordered you one of Charlie's deluxe double cheeseburgers, but tomorrow, its back to rabbit food for your flimsy heart."

"Thanks," Dave said. "It's good to see you, too. I've caught glimpses of you disappearing around corners, but I guess we've both been busy."

Charlie brought their burgers and they ate in silence.

"How are you guys doing?" Bob asked. "It's hard to believe it's been a year."

"Next Monday just hangs there, but we're doing okay. They say the anticipation is worse than the actual day. I sure hope so."

"Want to get together?"

"Thanks, maybe afterward. I think we need to get away, just the two of us."

"Where're you going?"

"It may sound weird, but we're going to climb a mountain. A new theory of mine, distraction by exhaustion," Dave said. "We've rented a cabin for the fifteenth and will try to climb Mt. Leconte that Monday. It'll give me a chance to see how well your angioplasty works."

Bob took a long swig of Coke. "It's different, but whatever works."

"Since you're being so generous, I think we should split a piece of coconut cream pie."

"Just this once," Bob laughed, "My work can stand up to a little dietary abuse. Just don't make a habit of it."

"Yes, doctor."

After finishing the pie, they sat sipping coffee.

Bob cleared his throat. "I wanted to talk to you about one other thing."

Dave said nothing and waited.

"I've been hearing rumors about some bad blood between you and the plant."

"What did you hear?"

Bob shrugged. "Nothing specific, something here, something there. Anything to it?"

"I met with them once to tell them about the arsenic. Nothing since then."

"I wouldn't push it. They employ the bulk of our paying practice. Don't want to make Big Daddy mad."

Dave told him about the two students, the soil and well contamination and the man on the hill. "What's his connection to International Chemicals? The plant property doesn't come anywhere near there."

"It sounds to me like you've warned the people sufficiently. Why don't you just back off? You have enough on your plate already."

"You're probably right." Dave grabbed the check before Bob could get it. "This is thanks for your good deed of the day, particularly the burger. You can get the tip."

That evening Dave drove home by way of Boogertown to talk with Mr. Peterson. The children were still allowed to play basketball, but now they got their water from the large cooler Dave had donated earlier. When he entered the barn, Tamika was intent on her practice and didn't notice him. She swished shot after shot from both long and short range, but she still couldn't fully coordinate her feet and hands when she dribbled.

"You're looking good," Dave called.

She ran to him and threw her arms around his neck. "I can shoot as good as ever, but I just can't handle the ball like I used to."

"Just stick with it," Dave said and turned to leave.

"Can't you stay and play a game of horse?"

Dave laughed. "No way. I remember how you clobbered me last time. I'm just going to walk a ways up the hill." She started to follow. "No, you stay here and practice. I'll just be a few minutes."

The large man hidden in the trees saw him coming and retrieved a camera with a long telephoto lens from the bag next to the rifle. Dave reached the fence and stood looking up the hill. Using a low branch to steady the camera, the man snapped three pictures, set the camera down, picked up the rifle, and stepped out of the trees in full view. Dave saw him and turned back.

Dave put two small bags and their backpacks into the trunk of the car and slammed the cover. Betty carried a fresh arrangement of irises and lilacs to the car. Neither spoke as they drove to the cemetery. When they reached the grave, Betty moved a small bouquet of daffodils lying beneath the headstone to one side and placed the irises in the center. Silently they stood holding hands. The savage onslaught of grief that had pounded them for months had given way to a deep, dead yearning for the presence that was gone and the future that would never be. They retreated to the bench and sat together as the sun set, each immersed in private memories.

"It can't have been a year." Betty shuddered. "It seems like yesterday."

"I know." Dave said nothing for a while. "I wonder who brought the daffodils?"

Betty debated with herself. "I'm sure it was Matt." She braced for his outburst.

"That was nice. How do you know?"

"I saw him here one evening several months ago. He ran off when I got out of the car. His mother said he has a small garden where he grows whatever is in season to bring here."

Dave said nothing, remembering the numerous little bunches of flowers he'd seen but had taken little note of.

It was dark when he spoke again. "We'd better get going if we're going to reach the cabin by ten."

She nodded and hand-in-hand they walked back to the car.

"Hey, slow down," Betty called out from several yards behind him. "I thought you were the one who had the heart attack."

Dave waited as she clambered up the steep rocky trail. "I guess Bob was right about all of that rehab. I feel good—tired, but good. It's only about another quarter mile to the top."

The nip in the wind on the crest was made worse by their being soaked with perspiration. After slipping on light jackets and catching their breaths, they walked out on an isolated point to see the view, but also to avoid having to talk with other hikers.

"You can almost see forever," Betty said, gazing out at the endless rolling ridges below them. "I think you were right. I'm sure Kelli's giving us a thumbs up."

They spread their lunch from their backpacks and ate ravenously.

"I didn't realize how hungry I was," Dave said lying back and staring up at the clouds. He was about to doze off when Betty spoke.

"Dave, there's something I've been wanting to talk to you about but never could seem to find the right time."

He propped himself on his elbow and looked at her. "What's that?"

"Remember I said I wanted something good to come out of all of this?"

"Yes."

"I've been thinking. You know, we have the college fund we put aside for Kelli."

"Yes."

"Well," she rushed on not wanting to give him a chance to object, "Tamika's not going to get a basketball scholarship. What do you think about our setting up a scholarship for her? She wants so much to be a nurse." She waited as Dave pondered the idea.

"I think that's a wonderful idea, but it would have to be anonymous because Mr. Peterson is too proud to accept what he'd view as charity, even for her."

She hugged him tightly. "Thank you. You remind me of the man I married."

The trip down passed quickly, and they reached the bottom exhausted but uplifted.

Dave settled into his old routine but finished work early to get home at a decent dinner hour. Surprisingly, he found that at times he could even look to the future, but he couldn't rid himself of nagging questions about the arsenic. What if someone else was injured? He'd talked to Bob who continued to advise him to let well enough alone. He had prayed earnestly for guidance, which made him uncomfortable, because he always came away with the sense that he already knew that he should do something.

Chapter 13

Sarah and Betty sat on the patio drinking lemonade.

"It seems as if you turn a corner and all that's there is another long desolate road. It was such a relief to get past that day," Betty said. "How do you say it? Death date? Remembrance date? The day she died? In my head I knew nothing would be changed, but I thought somehow having gone through the cycle of every reminder—birthday, Thanksgiving, Christmas, graduation, school starting, death date—that somehow it would be better."

"It may not be any better, but you are," Sarah said.

"You're right. I'm not as overwhelmed, and, when some reminder blindsides me, it doesn't cut as deep or last as long as it once did. I guess I just want things to go back like they used to be, even though I know that's never going to happen." She sipped on her lemonade. "I really appreciate your being willing to listen. If it hadn't been for you and Carolyn, I don't think I would have made it."

"You would have. I'm just glad I could help. How's Dave doing?"

"In some ways he's accepted the loss better than I have. I can't say it to him, but I think the reason it takes longer for women to adjust than men is that, to men, children are something they love deeply but are more like some cherished possession. With women it's different. There's something about carrying them around in your belly for nine months that produces a totally different, more intimate bond. It's not as if I've just lost something I cherish deeply; I've lost an integral part of myself, and I don't think I'll ever feel whole again."

"That makes sense, but I think you're right to keep it to yourself. I doubt that Dave would see it the same way." She paused for a moment. "You've been doing some heavy thinking."

"The group has really helped, but back to Dave. He's different, more at ease. He hasn't mentioned Matt since his heart attack. He's still wrestling with what to do about the plant and that arsenic thing. I just wish he'd let it go, but he seems to be on some sort of mission or something that I don't understand."

"You know, it's almost five. Bob and Dave have staff meeting tonight. Why don't we go to that new little bistro by the river for an early dinner? I've really wanted to try it out, but Bob never has the time."

"Sounds fine to me. We can leave a message with the hospital operator."

"Managed care will be the death of all of us," Bob griped as they left the meeting. "Do more work, get paid less. Just do what some pencil pushing bean-counter tells you and to hell with the patient."

"Ease up, Bob," Dave laughed, "I can't do an angioplasty on you if you have a coronary here in the parking lot."

Bob snorted. "I've got to check one more person in the ICU. See you later." He lumbered toward the hospital.

Dave always parked at the far end of the lot to insure he got some exercise each day. He fumbled with his key trying to find the door lock in the dimness of the one light at this end of the lot.

"What the…?" His breath whooshed out as he was thrown face forward into the side of the car. He struggled but was held immobile by each arm. "Ohhh," he moaned as a fist slammed into his kidney.

"Just hold still, doc, and I might not hurt you too bad. Hold him tight, boys." The voice had a nasal twang and reeked of alcohol.

Dave jerked back trying to see his captors, then went rigid as he was punched again.

"I said be still."

"What do you want?" he gasped. "My wallet's in my left hip pocket."

"I don't want your money. You just shut up and listen." Dave stopped struggling. "If you know what's good for you, you'll stop snooping around above Boogertown."

"I don't know what you're talking about."

The man grunted as he hit Dave again. "You're a damn liar. I got your picture." He paused a moment. "Too bad about your daughter, but you wouldn't want anything to happen to that pretty little nurse wife of yours, now would you?"

"You leave her alone."

"Then you don't go poking your nose where it doesn't belong. You hear?"

Dave nodded. "Yeah." He cried out as they hit him one more time, then dropped him to the pavement. He heard them running as he pulled himself up. Before the red pickup cleared the parking lot, he made out ADE on the door and a Kentucky license plate with the last four numbers-3941.

Gasping for breath, he pawed in the dark until he found the keys, then jabbed at the lock three times before he could insert the key. He flopped into the car and locked the door. Any motion sent spasms of pain up his back. He jotted the license number and description of the truck on a prescription pad before he forgot. Finally, he started the car and drove slowly home. Betty met him in the foyer .

"Dave, what's the matter?" He clung to the doorframe until she helped him into the living room and eased him onto the couch. "What happened?"

He lied with a forced smile. "I'm not as agile as I used to be. I missed a step on the stairs in the doctor's parking lot. Nothing seemed broken, so I just dragged myself home."

"Shouldn't you go to the emergency room?"

"All they'd do is take a lot of x-rays and tell me to go home and lie on the couch. I'm way ahead of them."

"What do you want me to do?"

"I could use some aspirin and an ice pack, and could you call Millie at home and tell her I won't be in until Monday?"

She let him lie there until ten and then half-carried him to bed.

He could scarcely move for the next three days and was careful that Betty didn't see the ugly bruises over his kidneys.

"Do you think you should go to work?" Betty asked Monday morning.

He forced a reassuring smile. "I'll be fine as long as I don't bend, stoop, move or try to breathe."

On the drive to the hospital he studied each red truck he saw, but none had the license or lettering he'd written down. All day he reviewed his options, knowing it was only a matter of time before someone else would be harmed if the mess in Boogertown wasn't cleaned up. But International Chemical had shown they were willing to play very rough, and he couldn't put Betty at risk. After he had finished the day's business, he called Mike Bolton.

"Mike, I need to talk with you."

"Sure, what's up? I get off in another hour. I could stop by your house. Maybe Betty has another of those healthy cakes."

"No, don't come to the house."

"All right," Mike sounded puzzled. "Where you want to meet?"

"Could you just stop by the office? And Mike, come in your car rather than the squad car."

"No problem. Is something the matter?"

"I'll tell you when you get here."

"Why didn't you call the police?" Mike asked after Dave described the attack.

"For one thing, I could barely move, and I didn't want to frighten Betty. She's been through enough without this."

"But this is really serious. You should let us handle it."

"Maybe so, but I think the best thing is just to drop the matter."

"I don't think that's very smart, but it's your decision. So why am I here?"

Dave hesitated. "Do you think you could find out who it was from the description of the truck and the license number? I'd at least like to know who to watch out for."

Two days later Mike called.

"Dave, you're fooling around with a really nasty crowd. Before I go any further, I want to tell you again to let us handle it."

"I just want it to go away," Dave said. "If you start putting the heat on them, they might hurt Betty."

"I knew you'd say that, so I'll tell you if you'll promise me one thing."

"What's that?"

"You are not to do anything on your own. This is out of your bailiwick. Don't go playing cowboy on me."

"I swear. So who is it?"

"A fellow named Frank Slade. He runs a small strip mine, but I think that's just a cover. You remember I told you about how the drug dealers were moving into rural areas? Well, Slade's the number one dealer in this area. He's a very dangerous person. He's been implicated in several drug-related murders, but we haven't been able to pin anything on him yet."

"Why is he concerned with me?"

"I don't know. I can't feature him being in cahoots with the plant. Maybe he has something up on that hill. You just stay away and stick to doctoring. You understand?"

"Absolutely. Thanks, Mike, I'll keep my nose clean and my eyes peeled." He started to hang up. " Mike, don't breathe a word of this to Betty."

ꟹ

"Dave, are you feeling well?"

Dave closed his journal quickly and looked up at Betty. "I'm fine, why?"

"You've just been so quiet and distant since you fell. I know I've been sort of down since the sixteenth, but you had really been upbeat. Is there something you're not telling me?"

He pulled her into his lap and hugged her. "No, my little worry wart," he lied, "I guess I still have ups and downs too."

"Want to talk about it?"

"Not right now."

She stood up and yawned. "I'm beat. Are you coming to bed?"

"I'm really not sleepy. I'll just read for a while."

She kissed him and left.

Dave left the journal closed on the table and stared out the window into the darkness feeling some heightened sense of duty or obligation as bits and pieces of the Event kept running through his mind.

I know I'm doing the right thing. One act that will benefit all mankind. Well, all of mankind won't benefit from doing something in Boogertown. I can't put my family at risk for a delusion. All our choices, great or small, have eternal consequences. What is it you want from me? Isn't it enough that I believe? Can't I just be a good doctor, husband and person? Either God is the most important thing in your life, or he is nothing at all. Please, help me know what to do.

ꕥ

Three days later Dave was writing a prescription when Karen, his nurse, cracked the door to the examining room.

"Dr. DeMarco."

Dave finished writing the prescription. "Yes?"

"It's Dr. Gibbons from the hospital on line three. He says it's an emergency."

Dave excused himself and picked up the phone in his office. "What you got, Jack?" He frowned and bit his lip. "I'll be right over."

"A two year old, Nicole Hodges. She came in vomiting and seizing. I was worried about meningitis so I did a spinal tap, but before we could do much else, she went into shock and died."

"The grandmother's my patient," Dave said. " I think the mother is only seventeen or eighteen. Is she here?"

"Yeah, they're down in the quiet room. I haven't told them yet."

"I'll do it." He started out the door.

"Hold on, Dave. She didn't have meningitis. The spinal tap was normal."

Dave didn't move. "No, it couldn't be."

"Probably not, but with that thing earlier with the arsenic, I thought you might want to check it out."

The hallway outside the quiet room was full of African-Americans. Mr. Peterson was leading a small group in prayer. When Dave's eyes adjusted to the dim lighting he saw a slender girl on the couch between her mother and Tamika. She clenched a handkerchief, trying to control her trembling.

"How's my baby?"

Dave knelt before her and took her hands in his. "I'm sorry, there was nothing we could do for her. She's gone."

The girl went rigid and began screaming hysterically, her keening echoed by the group in the hall. When several women came in to tend to her, Dave motioned to Tamika and Mr. Peterson to follow him into a consultation room.

"The family's too upset to talk. Can either of you give me some idea of what happened?"

Tamika dabbed her eyes and snuffled. "She's been sick for several days, colicky-like. She didn't have any fever."

"Had she drunk any water from the well?"

"I'm sure she hasn't," Mr. Peterson spoke up. "That well is locked tight."

"Has she been around the well?"

"Mary, that's her mother, brought her to the barn a lot when the other children were playing, but she just played around in the yard."

Dave thought for a moment. "Did the little girl do anything funny, like, did she ever eat dirt?"

"Lord, Dr. DeMarco," Tamika blurted, "Her face was muddy all the time. You couldn't keep her from eating it."

Dave's heart sank. Even our smallest choices have eternal consequences, and I chose wrong.

"Dave, you've got to calm down. It's not your fault," Betty was almost pleading.

"Then whose is it? I knew that soil was full of arsenic, and I didn't do anything about it." He rose from the chair and resumed his pacing.

"You don't even know if it was arsenic or not."

"What else could it be? An infant is much more sensitive to toxins than an older child or adult. I knew how some small children eat dirt, pica they call it. I could have done something about it, but I didn't want to make waves at the plant. Now a little girl is dead."

"I just think you should wait until you're sure."

"Well, the autopsy didn't show anything grossly, but Sue should be calling today or tomorrow with the test results. Then we'll know."

She called later that night. He was right.

When Betty got up the next morning Dave was still in the sunroom where she had left him.

"Have you slept at all?"

"No. I've been thinking." He didn't raise his voice. He had the same eerie calm that he showed just before he started unraveling months ago.

"Dave, please don't go back like you were. We've made so much progress."

"I won't, but I know what I have to do. I'm going to get that place cleaned up, even if it means taking on the plant."

"I'm not sure, but if you think you should…" Betty was uncertain what to say, but she wanted to keep him talking. "I guess so."

"It's more complicated than that, and I can't leave you in the dark any longer."

"What do you mean?"

He sighed. "I guess I have to go back to the first. You remember how I had such a dramatic turn around after my heart attack?" She nodded. He went on to tell her about the Event. "I know it sounds strange, and I tried to ignore it, but I couldn't. I can't explain it, but something real and important happened and somehow all of this with Tamika and the plant is tied in with it. It's something I have to do."

Betty chose her words carefully. "I'm not sure I understand, or believe, what may or may not have happened. I don't think God speaks directly to us. He certainly doesn't to me. I think he wants me to help, and be helped by, other people like us—not all of mankind, just a few hurting parents. It may have been lack of oxygen as you said or something else even, but it obviously had a powerful effect on you. Why don't you talk to John about it?"

"I started to once but backed off. Talking with him might be a good idea, but I don't think it will change anything." He paused, debating whether to go on. "There's more." He told her about the man on the hill and about Slade and the beating.

"Why didn't you tell me then?"

"I should have, but you've had so much to deal with, and I thought if I just let it lay, it would just go away. Well, I let it lay, and now someone else has a dead daughter."

"What are you going to do?"

"I'm going to try to reason with the plant but if they won't act, Will and Sue say the only thing left is to go to the EPA."

"What about Slade?"

Dave tried to keep his voice steady. "I'll talk to Mike. I'm sure Slade's all bluff," he said without conviction.

Betty took his hand. "Dave, it's terrible about that little girl, but that's over. Mr. Peterson can just fence off the whole area. Please, don't get involved any further."

"Betty, I don't have any choice. I have to do it."

"You have no right to do this. You do have a choice, and just like always, your family comes last." Her face reddened and tears of frustration brimmed in her eyes. "You're going to risk our futures, and maybe even our lives, because you think that while you were unconscious, God told you to save the world? I've had about all that I can take. Why don't you do one great act that will benefit us?"

I know she's right. She doesn't deserve this. "I'm just going to talk to them."

She started to reply, then gave him one last baleful look and stalked from the room.

༄

"Dr. DeMarco, I thought you'd dropped this unwarranted vendetta you have against our company."

Dave was surprised at how calm he felt. "I don't have a vendetta against you. I appreciate what your company does for Hillsdale; however, there's a little girl dead and another with permanent neurological damage. Both lived in close proximity to your plant, and both were caused by one of the major chemicals which you use."

Albritton's voice became hard and flat. "We've redoubled our surveillance of the test wells, but there's still no evidence of elevated arsenic levels. I'll show you the data if you want, but I doubt it would convince you."

"I believe you," Dave said. "It must be getting out some other way."

"There is no other way," Albritton said through gritted teeth.

"Maybe you should have the EPA check it out."

"Dammit," Albritton roared, "they have checked it out. We called them in ourselves." He motioned to Wheeler who scuttled to Dave and handed him a folder of papers. "These are their findings, and they exactly match ours. You can't take that report with you, but take as long as you like to read it." He leaned forward on his desk. "I want to warn you—"

Braxton cleared his throat and started to speak.

"Can it, Braxton. I'm tired of legal pussy-footing." Turning back to Dave, he said, "I want to warn you. I've had it up to here with your interference. One more thing from you, just one more, and you'll regret it. You understand?"

"Fully," Dave said.

"My secretary will show you out when you're done." With that, they all three rose and left.

After poring over the report for more than an hour, Dave jotted down the name of the EPA investigator, Michael Underwood, and left. As soon as he got home, he called Underwood who informed him the report was accurate.

Betty and Carolyn had just left for the support group when John Rankin rang the doorbell.

"Hi, John, come on in."

Dave gave him a brief explanation of his meeting at the plant, and a very detailed description of the Event. John said nothing until he had finished.

"Have you ever heard anything like that?"

"Yes, but not nearly so detailed. Most of the time the person experiences a brilliant light and just feels comforted and at ease."

"What do you think it means? I have a hard time accepting that God just waltzes in and talks with us, even through glowing emissaries," Dave said.

"I honestly don't either."

"But why do I feel so compelled to be guided by what I think I heard?"

John rubbed his chin and appeared lost in thought. "I think we can know some of God's will through what we've studied, but more through what we've experienced and found to be true. Then, there are things we act upon which we accept by faith, even though we have no concrete evidence."

Dave nodded. "Go on."

John continued, "I know you, Dave. Is there anything that you heard during your Event which you didn't already believe? I've heard you say many of those same things in the past. In fact, I know you've said some of those very things to console families when a loved one had died."

"I guess you're right. It's just easier to talk about religion in the abstract than it is to practice it when crunch time comes, but if something is true in good times, I guess it's no less true when you've been crushed. You're right, I think I pretty much believe all of it. Except one part."

"What's that?"

"Where did all that about one act that would benefit all mankind come from?"

John laughed. "That's a scary thought. I hesitate to say it lest I hex myself. I think that most of the time we operate on a sort of automatic pilot. We give little thought to what we do, or say, or believe until we're in a real bind. Perhaps each of us is required to consider each of our daily choices and actions, no matter how seemingly small or insignificant, and then proceed in the most ethical and loving way we can. Do you think any of the teachers and mentors of Abraham Lincoln or Adolf Hitler had an inkling of how their influence might affect humanity fifty years down the road?"

"No, I guess not. So what you're saying is, it's important to do what you believe is right, even if you're not sure it really matters."

"I couldn't have said it so concisely, but yes."

Once alone, Dave played everything back in his mind several times. It made sense. Maybe he hadn't had a celestial visitation, but that didn't make what he had heard, or thought he heard, or just thought in his own mind, any less true. The frightening thing was that if it was true, he was compelled to act, and deep down he knew it was true.

Chapter 14

The next several weeks were uneventful. From time to time, he thought he was being followed on his way home from work, but then the suspicious vehicle would turn off, leaving him feeling foolish and paranoid. Mike had told him that the police were trying to keep an eye on Slade. He had the germ of an idea about what to do next concerning the arsenic contamination. Since the EPA report had confirmed International Chemicals findings on the test wells, and the settling ponds showed no sign of leakage, the arsenic must be coming from elsewhere. Before he could develop his plans any further, the sky fell in.

Only two patients remained when Millie stopped him.

"Dr. DeMarco, there's a registered letter for you. Do you have time to sign for it?"

"Sure, who's it from?"

"International Chemicals."

"Just put it on my desk," he said after scribbling his signature. "I'll take care of it when I'm finished."

He saw the last two patients as quickly as possible then walked to his office with studied nonchalance . After settling into his chair, he eyed the envelope warily before wiping his moist palms and ripping it open. The single sheet of paper began to shake as he read. When he had read the terse message three times, he slumped back, feeling a faint nausea rising in his belly as if he'd been slugged in the solar plexus. Well, big guy, you've really done it now. A phrase from the Marines popped into his head. You have fouled your mess kit. He didn't call Millie because he knew her curiosity would get the best of her in short order.

"Is everything all right?"

"No, Millie, everything's not all right."

"The letter?" she asked.

"Have a seat. This is going to affect us all."

"What is it?" she said, moving the charts from the side chair to clear a place to sit.

"International Chemical is dropping me from their panel of approved providers."

"They can't do that. It'll ruin your practice."

"I'm afraid they can."

"Why would they?"

He handed her the letter and waited for her to read it. "That's absurd." Her voice rose in both pitch and decibels. "You're the best family doctor in four counties. Who'd say that 'your judgment has been impaired?'"

"They're a powerful organization, and I'm sure they can coerce someone to say whatever they want. They can always bring up some of the crazy things I did last fall and winter."

"But Kelli had just died. You weren't crazy; you were just stressed out."

"I know. I'll fight it, but I have no inherent right to treat their patients. So on November first, we'd better plan for the paying half of our practice to disappear."

He sat for over an hour considering his options. It was dark when he left. How was he going to tell Betty? After her initial outburst, she'd said nothing about his decision to confront the plant, but he really hadn't done anything else since the meeting with Albritton. Immediately after turning onto the highway, a truck pulled in behind him, practically on his bumper. The lights were on high beam, almost blinding him. When he sped up, it stuck tight on his tail; when he slowed, it did likewise. This continued until he turned into his drive. The truck roared off before he could make out any details.

"Oh, Dave, no," Betty said when he told her about the letter. "I told you..." she cut herself off before saying more. "What are we going to do?"

"I've struggled with that all evening. First, I'll get Bob to recommend a good lawyer. I don't want to spend a bundle in legal fees, but I need to see if there's anything I can do. I'm not real optimistic. I don't recall the details, but this was discussed at a conference a year or so ago, and, in the end, the doctor usually loses."

"I suppose I could start working full time." She didn't sound enthusiastic at the prospect.

"I brought this on us, and I'm really sorry, but I guess that has to be an option. We're not bad off financially, and I'll start opening at eight and closing at seven. We have three months to build up a little cushion." He paused, not wanting to go on. "I know I told you I'd go to the Compassionate Friends conference, but there's no way I can now."

"Dave, I really wanted you to go. I think it would help us both."

"I know, but now I need to try and get us a rainy day fund."

She started to say something else, but just shook her head.

With the extended office hours, he finished after dark each night and each night the truck tailed him. After the third time, he called Mike.

"Just call us when you leave, and I'll see to it that a patrol car cruises by."

The truck didn't show again.

❧

It was only two o'clock, and Dave, having skipped lunch, was seeing his thirty-second patient.

"Dr. DeMarco, telephone," Karen said, stepping into the examining room.

"Get a number, I'll call them back," he said, still peering into the patient's ear.

"You really ought to answer. It sounds important."

Dave heaved a sigh, "All right. Would you excuse me Mrs. Bradford?" He shut the door. "Okay, Karen, what's so all fired important?"

"It's Mrs. DeMarco. She sounds terrible, almost hysterical, line three."

"Betty?" He could barely understand her. She was crying and screaming at the same time.

"Kelli...The cemetery...He's ...He's going to kill us...You just wouldn't let it go...Why did he do it? ...It's all your fault...You and your holy mission."

"What's all my fault? Betty, calm down, talk to me." The only sounds were deep hoarse sobs; then the line went dead.

Curious and concerned, Millie and Karen looked up when he rushed from his office.

"I've got to go. Cancel out the rest of the day," he said on the way out the door.

When he ran onto the porch ten minutes later, the door was locked. He raced through the house and found Betty lying on the floor beside the bed, curled in a fetal position. She cringed when she saw him.

"Get away from me. I told you to leave them alone, but you had to do your great deed."

He knelt and tried to hold her. "Betty, what is it?"

"The cemetery...the cemetery," she moaned, pushing him away.

"What about the cemetery?"

She turned away and curled into a tighter ball.

He tried to help her onto the bed, but she jerked away. Leaving her in place, he covered her with a blanket then grabbed the phone to call Sarah.

"Sarah, I need your help. Something's happened to Betty... I don't know, but she's fallen apart. I need you to stay with her while I try and find out. Please hurry."

He knelt beside Betty again, but she still refused to let him touch her, so he just sat on the edge of the bed and waited. What have I done, God, what have I done? The slam of a car door jerked him back.

"Dave?" It was Sarah.

"Back here in the bedroom."

"Oh, Betty," she knelt and took her in her arms. "Help me get her onto the bed."

Dave moved to help, but Betty again drew back.

"Come on, put your arms around my neck," Sarah said. Betty complied while Sarah strained and coaxed until she could roll her onto the bed where she returned to her fetal ball. The bed shook with her trembling as Sarah wrapped her in a blanket.

"What do you think is wrong? What happened?"

"Something about the cemetery. Can you stay with her while I try to find out?"

"Sure, go ahead."

She was stroking Betty's forehead and crooning to her when he left.

The cemetery was less than five minutes away. He dashed past Jesus to Kelli's grave.

"Oh, no," he gasped.

Her marker was covered with vulgar graffiti and lewd drawings: "BITCH" was spelled out in bright orange spray paint on her grave. To the left, in the same orange paint was, "DR. D…R.I.P". and on the right, "NURSE D…R.I.P". Fresh cut flowers spilled from the vase Betty had dropped.

Slade. They'll do anything to make me drop it.

He drove straight to the police station and was relieved to see Mike's patrol car parked by the door.

"Dave, you're getting in too deep. I told you these are bad characters," Mike snapped, an edge to his voice.

"All I did was talk with the people at the plant."

"Evidently that was too much."

"So what should we do?"

Mike pulled a pad from his desk. "Let me file a complaint. We can say we're investigating this as simple vandalism." When he finished the form, he looked up at Dave. "I don't want to kid you. Slade's smart in a slimy sort of way. I doubt we'll find anything implicating him. We'll step up our patrols in your area, but, in all honesty, Slade won't get caught by something that simple. If I were you, I'd install a good security system wired into the station here." He scribbled two names and phone numbers on a scratch pad. "The first person does good security work at a reasonable price. The second fellow raises and trains guard dogs. You might get one. These hill people are terrified of Dobermans—must have seen too many old Nazi movies."

Before he left, he called home. "How's she doing?" he asked when Sarah answered.

"She's much calmer, but, Dave, keep your distance when you get here. You're not her favorite person right now. I'm in the kitchen so I can talk freely," Sarah said. "She's scared to death of staying here. She's welcome to stay with us until the shock wears off—so are you for that matter."

Dave gave her a brief description of what had happened. "I'm on my way home. We'll talk about it when I get there."

"In here," Sarah called from the sunroom when she heard Dave open the door.

He started toward Betty, but Sarah gave him a warning glare, so he sat in a chair facing them. Betty stared at him with eyes that were both frightened and wary but held a flinty anger he had never seen before.

"I'm so sorry. What they did was terrible. Mike's already working to find them." No response. "I'm going to install an alarm system and get a watchdog." Silence. "Betty, say something to me."

"I'm going to Sarah's."

He shuffled and looked down at his feet. "If that's what you want."

Nobody said anything. Finally Sarah rose. "Dave, why don't you help me get some of Betty's things together." In the bedroom he selected the necessities and threw them into a duffel bag.

"Dave, I'm sorry, but getting her out of here is all I can think to do. I'm not sure I can understand all of what's going on in her. She's been through so much. She's frightened to death and really angry with you. She blames you for not dropping the problems with the plant. When she saw the desecration at Kelli's grave something just snapped."

"You're probably right," he replied unable to think of anything else to say.

Betty was staring out the window when they returned; she hadn't moved. Dave held the door for them as Betty walked past him without looking back.

Dave slumped onto the couch. Dear God, what have I done? What have you done? Is this how you operate? A person tries to do what's right, and you take it out on an innocent bystander? Well, mankind will just have to fend for itself. I've had it. I quit.

He fished the paper Mike had given him from his pocket and dialed the phone. The security system could be installed tomorrow. He could pick up the dog the next day.

This done, he went back to the office.

He called Sarah's twice a day but Betty wouldn't come to the phone. The fifth day there was a message on their home answering machine. It was Betty, her voice flat, emotionless.

"Come get me. I want to come home."

It was almost nine o'clock when Sarah answered his call. "I'm sorry it's so late. I just got home. Will it be all right if I come now?"

Her bag had been packed and ready for hours.

"The alarm system's installed. It's really easy to operate."

"Show me how." Cool, civil.

"Gretchen stays in the utility room during the day. I let her in at night."

"Gretchen?"

"The dog. Mike suggested I get a watchdog. She's beautiful and really gentle but looks ferocious. Nobody's going to fool with her. Jack Johnson, a handyman, will be over Tuesday to build her a pen and house for the daytime."

"I see."

He sat on the bed while she unpacked, but unable to initiate any conversation, he said nothing and just watched as she threw the clothes to be washed in a pile and put the rest away.

"What's that?" he gasped.

"It's a gun," she said and placed it into the drawer of her bedside table.

"Betty, what's gotten into you? You never wanted guns in our home."

"I've never needed one until now," she said in the same controlled monotone she had used since she'd called.

"Why do you need one now?"

Through clenched teeth, for the first time her voice showed emotion. "Why? If I'm going to turn my home into a fortress hiding from a mad man, I'm going to do all I can to protect it. You go on tilting at your windmills and saving the world, Dave. Do what you have to do, but don't act surprised when I do what I must. If it makes you feel any better, I've signed up for safety classes to learn how to use it." She closed the drawer. "I'm really tired. I'm going to shower and go to bed."

Betty pretended to sleep until Dave had left each morning. She kept the drapes drawn and didn't open the door except when she let Gretchen out and when she drove to the firing range.

Depression, fear, and hate were alien to Betty. Growing up in the fifties in a conservative small town, being raised by loving, God-fearing parents, coupled with an inherent optimistic nature had resulted in a rosy, trusting view of life . Even the death of her parents soon after she graduated from college hadn't altered that perspective. She had glimpses of the seamier side of life when she trained in the emergency room of the University hospital, but dismissed that as an aberration of big city life. Working in pediatrics and being married to a staunch traditionalist had reinforced this outlook.

Kelli's death had thrown her into deep grief from which she'd been just starting to emerge. Now, Dave and his cockamamie crusade had caused her to fear and hate for the first time in her life. Grief, fear and hate combined to form an amalgam, which churned within her to the point that she allowed herself to express no hint of emotion lest she lose all control.

After two weeks in the darkened house, she called Sarah.

"Could you come over tomorrow?"

"I'm sorry to dump on you like this, but you're the only person I can talk to right now," Betty said. "I tried to write it all down and come to a logical conclusion like Dave does, but everything just swirls around in my head. "

"Fire away," Sarah said.

"I'm terrified of that horrible Slade, and I don't even know what he looks like. Even more, I'm frightened of what this is doing to me, to us. Things were so much better between Dave and me; then he just had to pick a fight with the plant. Now, we're back where we were right after Kelli died. I'm so angry with him. Why didn't he just leave well enough alone."

"You wanted him to play it safe like Bob told him?"

"Yes. I mean I think so. Well, why does he have to be so noble? For once couldn't he let someone else do it."

Sarah sipped her tea.

"I want to kill him. God help me, I want to kill him."

"Dave?"

"No, Slade," Betty laughed despite herself. "I'm afraid to go outside. I just know he's watching me."

After another half-hour Betty found she was rambling and repeating herself so she stopped talking.

"So what are you going to do?" Sarah asked.

Betty took a piece of paper from the coffee table.

"This is how I worked it out. I know it sounds crazy, but I can't stay barricaded in here forever. I can't help grieving, but the group has helped me learn how to cope with that pretty well. It's the fear and hate that are eating me alive and aggravating the grief. I've got to do something about those."

"And that would be…?"

"I'm going to let my anger with Slade grow until I'm not afraid of him anymore. I've got a permit to carry my gun, and I'm learning how to use it. If he comes near me, I'll blow him away."

"I thought you didn't know what he looks like."

Betty gave a high-pitched giggle. "Well, when I find out, I'll blow him away."

"Just be sure it's him," Sarah said.

When Dave cut the engine, he was startled by a loud noise that he immediately recognized as a gunshot, followed in rapid succession by two more. He tore around to the rear of the house.

Betty stood between the saltlick and the Jump Off, feet apart and solidly planted, the pistol held in both hands just as they'd taught him in the marines. The recoil lifted the barrel with each shot, but she didn't flinch.

"What are you doing?" he shouted. She didn't look at him. Then he noticed the noise suppressing earmuffs she wore. "Hey!" he shouted. She continued to shoot. He walked to his right and started to wave his arms, trying to position himself in her peripheral vision.

"Watch out!" he screamed throwing himself flat on the ground as she spun and pointed the gun at him.

Recognizing him, she lowered the gun, removed the earmuffs and walked to him.

"What in the hell are you doing? You could've killed me," he yelled as he brushed himself off.

"I didn't, did I?" she replied calmly. "You should've warned me."

"I tried, but you couldn't hear me."

She ejected the clip. "Next time it'd be better if you just stayed inside until I'm finished," she said and walked to the house.

He followed her in.

"Betty, what's the matter? You're so different. I don't know how to read you anymore."

"I am different. You might as well get used to it. All I ever wanted to be was a wife, a mother and a grandmother, and now two of those are no longer possible. I've always stood back and let you lead, and it never bothered me much until now. When I think of myself cowering on the floor, shaking like a frightened puppy waiting for you to rescue me, it makes me sick. I love you and appreciate the home you've helped make for us, but I will never be totally dependent upon you or anyone else again. Never."

A few days later, Dave picked at his salad as Bob wolfed down a cheeseburger.

"She really frightens me, Bob," Dave said. "Now I know how she must have felt during my crazy time last year."

"What's she doing that's so alarming?"

"That gun for one thing. She's gotten a permit and is going to gun safety classes at the police station."

"That seems sensible."

"I guess. But when Jack came over to build the dog pen, she had him build her a firing range in those woods behind the house. She shoots for an hour or so every day. She's a crack shot. Mike says she's one of the best they've ever trained," he said, shaking his head in a mixture of disbelief and pride.

"Now that's scary," Bob said.

"She's taken a leave of absence from work and refuses to leave the house."

"I haven't been on pediatrics for a while, so I hadn't missed her."

Dave pushed his salad away. "She's so cold. I mean, she's civil, but she shows no emotion. She just exists."

"I don't know what to tell you, Dave. She's had a real shock. Sarah's been worried that she was dealing with Kelli a little too well. Maybe this just brought it all back."

"Yeah, compliments of yours truly."

"Don't beat yourself up too much. I don't think I would've had the balls to stand up to the plant, but you were right to do it." He finished the burger. "And I wouldn't worry too much about Betty. She's solid. When she sorts all this out, she'll do fine—probably before she shoots somebody.

Dave smiled despite himself. "Thanks a lot."

"I enjoyed that," Dave said as they drove up the driveway. "It's been a long time since we ate out. I just wish Bob wasn't so shy and retiring."

"He's a nut," Betty said, "and they've really stuck by us. I love them both."

She'd actually laughed at the restaurant, and she was more animated, more like the old normal Betty. Maybe she's coming around, or maybe she's just a good actress.

"Oh, Dave," she said, "I bought some mums today. They're on the patio. Do you think you could plant them tomorrow?"

"Not only that, I'll fix breakfast before I start digging. How does that sound?"

"Great," she said and kissed him, then withdrew quickly to discourage further contact.

After breakfast the next morning, he went to the storage shed to get the wheelbarrow and shovel. On the potting table was a pile of large sheets of paper. He lifted the top one, a life-sized target of a man with large ragged hole in the center of its chest. Of the numerous bullet holes, only one round had missed the center circle, and it by a mere half-inch.

ꕥ

Dave now let Karen return most of his evening call-backs, which allowed him to get home a bit earlier, but, like tonight, he seldom got home before eight o'clock. Betty still kept the alarm on at all times, so he had to remember to disarm it before opening the door. Gretchen greeted him in the foyer, something Betty hadn't done since returning from Sarah's house. Today she was reading in the living room, and tolerated a kiss on her cheek, but wouldn't meet his eyes.

"Would you set the table while I serve?" Some of the hardness was gone from her voice.

"Beef Stroganoff. This looks great."

She gave him a weak smile. "How are things at the office?"

"Busy for now," he said, eager for any scrap of communication. To his surprise she made light conversation during dinner. He helped clear the table and put away the dishes. When they had finished, she put her hand on his arm.

"Dave, I need to talk. Please don't try to help, just listen. I can't go on like this. I'm scared to death, and I blame you even though that's not entirely fair. I told you when Kelli was killed that I refused to let it ruin our marriage, and I meant it; like it or not, you're stuck with me."

"Thank you."

She continued as if he hadn't spoken. "When we came back from Aruba, I thought that we were out of the woods. You were so much better. I don't pretend to understand it or even believe it, but whatever it was that happened to you after your heart attack really helped you. I'm different. God's not going to visit me, but he's not going to demand for me to be a martyr like you either, so I guess it's a wash. Anyway, when I get back from the conference, I'm going to see a therapist, Dr. Lillian Jamerson, in Lexington. I can go early, before the group meets. I've got to do something. I need to do some personal growing, but I want us to be a couple again."

"I'm going to the conference with you," Dave said.

"I don't think that would be a good idea."

"But you said you wanted me to."

"That was before Slade. You needed six weeks alone to get your head on straight. Now I need some time without you."

"Betty, I'm really sorry."

"Don't beat yourself up too much. One of the things that attracted me to you was that there was always a consistency between what you said and what you did. If you didn't follow your conscience, you wouldn't be Dave DeMarco, and, like it or not, that's who I married. I'm still angry as the dickens, but I think I partly understand why you do the improbable things you do. I don't know what I would've done if I'd been in your place, probably taken the easy way out. But what's done is done, and we have to go on. I really want things to go back like they were a month ago, but that may take a while, and it may turn out differently than we can imagine."

"I can wait," he said. "I'll make it up to you, I promise. When is the conference?"

"We're leaving next Wednesday. Carolyn's going with me. She's going to visit with her family in Atlanta the week after the conference. I know we can't afford it, but I've rented a cabin at Calloway Gardens for the next week. We'll be coming home on Sunday."

For the first time in a month he laughed. "Money's no problem. I'll just see an extra two hundred Medicaid patients."

Before going to bed, Betty made her nightly rounds, bedding Gretchen by the door, checking every lock and window, closing all curtains and blinds. Lastly she made sure the alarm was on, and the drawer of the bedside table was open.

Dave slammed the trunk of the car then leaned through the window and kissed her. "I'm going to the conference with you next year, and I promise to start going to the group."

"Don't make any promises you can't keep. I love you, Dave. Be careful and please don't do anything foolish."

"I promise."

"See you a week from Sunday."

"I'll make sure she behaves," Carolyn called out from the passenger seat.

"You do that." He waved until they were out of sight.

With Gretchen curled at his feet, Dave tried to concentrate on the book in his lap, but thoughts of Tamika and the dead Hodges girl kept intruding. If someone doesn't do something, it's going to happen again. I know it. Well, I've done enough—got to think about Betty. He rose and stood at the window, staring up into the sky. All right, what am I supposed to do? No message came. Nothing. He sat back down and let random thoughts pinball through his head. Somewhere in the back of his mind fragments of a phrase he'd read or heard in a speech or sermon kept pushing to the forefront—maybe he'd used it in a term paper. He knew the gist of it. After five minutes of searching through Bartlett's Familiar Quotations, he found it. *"The only thing necessary for the triumph of evil is for good men to do nothing."* Edmund Burke. Setting the book down, he knew what he had to do.

Chapter 15

He called Mr. Peterson the next day. "Could I come over tomorrow night after work? I need to talk with you about some things."

"That's fine Dr. DeMarco. I want you to see Tamika. That child is on top of the world. She feels better, and would you believe it, she got a four-year scholarship to Kentucky, just out of the blue."

"That's wonderful," Dave said.

He forgot to call Mike when he left and had only driven a mile when the headlights appeared, right on his tail. His head snapped back as the truck rammed into his bumper. He pressed his foot to the floorboard, and when he reached eighty, he began to pull away almost losing control as he skidded into his drive and raced to the safety of his house. The truck hadn't followed up the driveway, but Dave called Mike anyway.

At lunch on Friday he moved his car to the visitor's parking lot. When he finished at the office, he changed into a dark T-shirt, jeans and jogging shoes, walked to the hospital, took the stairs to the basement and slipped out to his car through the loading dock door. No trucks were in sight. Checking and rechecking his mirror to be sure no one was following, he crept down back streets and reached Boone Street just before the cut-off to Buffalo Valley.

Tamika came to meet him when he drove up. She'd gained some needed weight and, except for a slight limp when she ran, once again moved with a lithe grace. She threw her arms around him. "Dr. DeMarco, I got a scholarship! I'm going to college, and I'm going to be a nurse just like Mrs. DeMarco, and I'm going to work right here in Hillsdale, and—"

Mr. Peterson opened the door. “Tamika, let the doctor alone, he’s here on business.”

“I’m really happy for you,” Dave said.

“Have you had supper, Doctor?”

He shook his head.

“Rosa’s fixed some fried chicken. You eat, then you can talk.”

He knew it was useless to argue, and he was hungry. After supper, he and Mr. Peterson sat on the porch gazing down the moon lit valley.

“What can I do for you?” Mr. Peterson finally asked.

Dave pointed to the ridge where he’d seen the large man with the rifle. “Do you know of any way up there other than the path from the barn?”

“Why you want to go up there, doctor?”

“Is there another way?”

“Well, there’s an old logging road through the woods around over yonder.” He pointed toward the left flank of the hill. “I ain’t been up there in a long time. It’s probably all grown up with bushes. There were “Posted” signs on nearly every tree.”

“Could you show me where it starts?”

“Dr. DeMarco, I don’t think it’s a good idea you go up there. Those people don’t like folks snooping around.”

“I’m going. I’ll be careful,” Dave said cutting off any further debate.

Mr. Peterson led him to the base of the hill. What had once been a road was now barely a path. “I don’t think you can get up there in the dark. Up on the top you might fall into the old strip mine.” When Mr. Peterson saw he couldn’t dissuade Dave, he added, “About halfway up you’ll come on a little creek. Might be dry this time of year, but you can follow it to the top.”

“Thanks. There’s a full moon, and I’ll go slow.”

Mr. Peterson shook his head but said nothing else.

Dave had brought a hiking stick and a flashlight which he wouldn’t use unless absolutely necessary. The general outline of the path was lit by splotches of moonlight that filtered through the thick canopy of trees. Picking his way up the flank of the ridge, he stumbled once or twice, but found, that by feeling his way with his stick, he could anticipate rocks and holes.

"Holy smoke!" Something bolted from the brush and crashed down the hill. He exhaled slowly when he saw the white flag of a deer's tail. Leaning against a tree, he let his rasping breath and pounding heart slow. Maybe this wasn't such a good idea. He looked at his dark shirt and pants and smiled. All I lack is grease paint on my face—James Bond I'm not. Taking a deep breath, he resumed climbing up the path.

Just as Mr. Peterson had said, he came to a small creek. There was a bare trickle of water, and by walking up the creek bed he avoided having to fight his way through the thick undergrowth. After going about five hundred yards up the creek, he began to hear the sounds of heavy machinery and slowed to a creep. An eerie yellowish glow lit the sky beyond a small rise. When the creek bed ended in a small spring, he lay flat on his belly and began to snake his way forward, something he hadn't done since the minimal combat training for physicians he'd received before deploying to Vietnam.

The thick brush gave way to scattered bushes beneath tall pine trees. The floor of pine needles made no noise as he slithered from one tree to another toward the top of the ridge just ahead. He stifled a cry when he crawled over a fallen log and fell a good six feet, landing with a thud. It took a few seconds for his head to clear enough to realize he'd fallen into a sinkhole about the size of a table that lay beneath the log. He tried to formulate some contingencies. If I'm seen, I can't go back to the Petersons. I can't bring any trouble on them. Then what? Just don't be seen, dummy.

He raised his head above the rim of the hole and could hear men's voices filtering through the trees. It was now clear that the mechanical noise was truck engines. A windowless metal building was just ahead and to the left of it, the ridge fell away in a near vertical, densely wooded slope. The area beyond the building was dimly lit by light that spilled over the crest. He dashed to the back of the building then scuttled to the top and crawled beneath a large rhododendron bush right on the edge of a steep drop-off. Over his left shoulder, about a mile away, the lights of the plant glowed at the base of the ridge. Immediately below, a dump truck was just dropping its load into a deep open pit that had obviously been a strip mine. Dave recognized the bulky man in the dirty T-shirt giving directions to the driver as the figure he had seen on top of the ridge with a rifle. Three empty trucks were parked to one side; lights from two more zigzagged up the winding road from the plant.

That's it! They're dumping their solid waste here. It must've leached out and was being washed down the front of the ridge into Boogertown. Of course the EPA hadn't found anything different because they had just checked the wells and the plant property. He leaned farther out to get a better view of the truck. Slade Mining Co. He smiled. So Slade's in cahoots with Albritton.

Without warning, the lip of the bank beneath him gave way. He grabbed a thick branch of the rhododendron to prevent tumbling into the pit himself, but several large rocks bounded down the bank. The huge man turned and looked directly at Dave struggling back onto the bank.

"There's somebody up there," he bellowed, pointing to the spot Dave had just vacated. "Get him. Don't let him get away."

The driver bolted from his truck and shouted for the other three drivers to follow. Dave scrambled back to the top of the bank and dashed around the building. Their pounding feet thundered toward him, beams from flashlights stabbed through the darkness. Running full tilt, he leapt into the sinkhole, turned his flashlight on and heaved it down the steep slope to his left, then pressed himself as far back under the log as he could.

"Over there, he's going down there!" The man pointed to the light bouncing down the precipitous grade. The large man grabbed one of the drivers. "Get your ass back to the plant as fast as you can and bring some more men and lights. We can't let him get away."

Dave raised up enough to see him running back toward the truck. When the others scrambled down the hill after the light, he exploded from the hole and ran toward the trucks. By some animal instinct, the large man looked back just in time to see Dave disappearing in the opposite direction. "Get back up here," he roared. "The sonofabitch is still up here."

Dave ran down the path toward the departing dump truck, which was gathering speed. Spurred by an overwhelming fear, he made a mad dash and grabbed the chain on the rear of the truck. The gravel tore at his feet as he heaved on the chain and hauled himself onto the bumper. The large man stood in the road waving and shouting, but the tailgate hid him from the driver who sped on. Dave could see them racing to the other trucks as his continued to pick up speed, skid around curves, and bounce on the rough gravel road. Dave smashed against the rear gate and almost fell from the bumper as the truck rebounded from a deep pothole. Entwining his arm in the chain and locking his legs around the bumper, he held on until the truck sailed through the open gate into the perimeter of the plant. When it slowed to make a sharp turn onto the main road, Dave jumped off.

He sprinted for a nearby shed as the truck, horn blaring, sped down the road toward a large building. Dave leaned against the shed and caught his breath. After what seemed only seconds, a siren blared, and four pickup trucks raced past on the way to the mine only to screech to a halt just beyond the gate as they met the three pursuing trucks. Lights began coming on all over the plant complex. The men clambered down, began to fan out, and slowly sweep toward the plant.

Dave ran to another shed and then to a small structure that remained in the shadow of a larger building. The line of men came nearer and nearer, their lights probing every dark corner. Dave frantically searched for somewhere to hide, then spied a large garbage dumpster, its lid open, standing about fifty feet away. He tensed, then sprang forward only to be jerked back and slammed against the shed. A large hand covered his mouth and nose cutting off his breath. He struggled to get loose.

"Stop it! If you want to get out of here, stop it," a voice whispered in his ear. "Do you understand?"

Dave quit fighting and nodded, trying to place the vaguely familiar voice.

"In here quick!" The dark figure of a man opened the door to the tiny building, shoved him in and shut the door behind them.

"Who are you?" Dave gasped.

"There's no time to talk. You just hunker down and don't make a sound. I'll try to lead them away and come back for you later."

Before Dave could say anything, the man stepped outside and shut the door behind him. Dave heard the ominous click of a padlock, then nothing. In a few minutes he heard muffled voices outside but couldn't understand what they were saying. He shrank back as the lock rattled.

When the voices completely faded, Dave slumped down onto the floor of the pitch-black shack. You idiot. What have you gotten yourself into? His heart pounded like a jackhammer, and he was soaked with sweat. If I don't have another heart attack now, Bob's work will hold forever. He played the events of the night over and over, but finally his adrenaline ebbed and, despite fighting it, he drifted in and out of a fitful sleep. His head snapped up when he heard the rattle of the lock. A beam of sunlight streamed through a small hole in the dark curtain. Grabbing the only thing he saw, a broom, he stood behind the door. He drew the broom back as the figure of a man slipped into the shack.

"Put that down, Dr. DeMarco. We don't have much time."

"Mr. Williams." It was Matt's dad. "How did you know it was me?"

"Mr. Peterson had Tamika call Matt, and he called me. We have to hurry and get you out of here. They've clamped everything down tight. Where's your car?"

"Boogertown, but don't go where we can be seen. I don't want to bring trouble down on those people."

"As soon as they finish searching the main building they'll start backtracking. We have to get out of there. My car's just outside. I'm going to open the trunk, and you jump in as quick as you can."

Dave nodded.

"Whatever happens, don't make a sound."

Williams stepped out of the shack and looked around. The searchers had moved into the plant; no one was in sight. He opened the trunk, and Dave scrambled inside. Williams slammed the lid and checked his watch, ten minutes after seven. When there was a long line of outgoing cars, he joined them. The line inched forward as one by one the guards searched each car then let it pass. His knuckles turned white on the steering wheel when the guard approached him. He rolled down the window.

"Hey, Walt. Some night," the guard said.

"You can say that again. Did they ever catch him?"

"Not that I know of. I don't even know who we were looking for. I'm sorry, but I have to search your car; they'll have my job if I don't."

Williams grasped the wheel tighter and hoped the guard didn't notice him sweating. "I know, go ahead," he said as the guard peered into the interior of the car.

"You gotta open the trunk," the guard ordered and turned toward the rear of the car. The cars behind began honking their horns. "Keep your shirt on," he shouted at them, but they continued to honk. The guard returned to the window. "Ah, the hell with it. You're security anyway. Go on home, Walt."

Williams drove as fast as he could without attracting attention. A mile past Boogertown he turned onto a dirt road that looped around to a clump of trees a few hundred yards below the settlement. He opened the trunk and pointed the way to Dave.

Dave shielded his eyes from the sun's glare. "Thank you, Mr. Williams, you most likely saved my life."

Williams said nothing for a moment. "I'd appreciate if you never told a soul about this. I'd be fired for sure." Without another word, Williams got in his car and drove off.

Dave hurried to his car and left before anyone saw him. What do I do now? I've got to get out of sight before they discover I'm not still at the plant. Home is the first place they'll look… Mike.

He rang Mike's doorbell knowing that at seven forty-five Saturday morning, they'd still be asleep. Come on, come on. He pressed the button three more times. Mary opened the door.

"Dave?"

She stepped back as he pushed his way into the house. "Mary, I don't have time to explain. Can you move your car and let me put mine into the garage?"

She rubbed her eyes and brushed the frizzled bird's nest of hair out of her face. "Sure, but what's going on?"

"I'll explain later, just move the car, please."

He drummed his fingers as she took two tries backing out. He pulled into the garage and motioned for her to close the door.

Back in the kitchen she appraised him. "Dave, what's going on? You look terrible."

"Look who's talking," he said with a smile. "Mary, I've really stepped in it."

She plugged in the coffeepot. "Sit down, I'll get Mike."

Snatches of conversation drifted from the bedroom. "I don't know…He was just there…almost eight."

"What's happening, Dave?" Mike said, his voice distorted by a yawn.

"It's a long story," Dave said. "I need your help and a lot of advice."

Mike poured each of them a cup of coffee. "Fire away."

"This is real big, Dave, really big, and very dangerous," Mike said after Dave's detailed account. "You and Betty both have to lay low until we get a handle on things. Slade and his crew aren't people you want to fool around with. We've been trying to find a reason to get up there on Slade's property, and now I'm sure this is enough for the judge to give us a search warrant. I'll call the state attorney for added clout."

"Yeah, good," Dave was nodding off despite the coffee and the excitement of the night.

"Look," Mike said, "you're so sleepy you can't think straight. Go grab a couple of hours of shut-eye while I get things going down at the department."

"I've got to call Betty."

"When is she coming back?"

"Next Sunday afternoon."

"Why don't you hold off until tonight when your head's clearer, and I know better how things are playing out."

Dave woke just before noon, splashed cold water on his face and looked in the mirror. Man, you're a mess. His clothes were covered with dirt and bits of twigs and leaves. Mary looked up from a growing stack of sandwiches when he walked into the kitchen and headed for the back door.

"Don't go out there," she said. "Mike said to stay inside until he gets back."

"I was just going to dust off. These clothes are filthy; I'll ruin your furniture." He sniffed. "Whew, I need a shower, too. You'll probably want to burn the bed linens."

"Come over here and sit down. You must be starved. While you eat I'll round up some of Mike's things for you to wear. Then you can clean up."

The aroma of the food made his mouth water. He wolfed down three sandwiches.

Half an hour later Dave found Mary in the living room. "I feel like a new man. I used some of your mouthwash. It'll have to do until I can get my toothbrush."

Mike's clothes hung from him. Though they were about the same height, Mike was a good thirty pounds heavier.

"Could I borrow a scratch pad and a pen? My mind's flying in four different directions. I need to get organized."

"Use Mike's study; there's plenty of writing material on his desk."

"One more thing," Dave said, "I need to make several long distance calls. Could you keep track of them, and I'll pay you later?"

Mary just nodded and waved him away.

Dave listed everything he could think of and then prioritized them. The first thing he did was call Sue.

"I can't believe it," she said when he finished telling her of last night's events. "What can I do to help?"

"Who should I call to get an investigation going?"

He heard papers rustling and drawers opening and closing. "Here it is. John Hotchkiss. He heads the EPA for this region. He might be hard to reach on a Saturday, so I'll give you his home number and a hot line. God, this is exciting. Keep me posted. If there's anything else I can do, just call, and, Dr. DeMarco, please be careful."

Next he called Jim Campbell, a former classmate at Eastern Kentucky and now a reporter for the Lexington Herald-Leader.

"Jim, a voice from your past. It's Dave DeMarco."

"Dave, how are you doing? I was really sorry to read about Kelli.

How's Betty?"

"We're muddling along," Dave said.

"What can I do for you?"

Dave gave him a summary of the past several months, beginning with Tamika's poisoning. "Do you think you might help? I could fax you the pertinent points."

"Help. Hell, Dave, you don't realize how big this is. Have you talked with any other media?"

"No."

"Well, don't. Where are you?"

Dave told him how to get to Mike's house.

"I'll be leaving in fifteen minutes and I'll be there in an hour. Let me be your media guide, and we'll nail those polluting jerks to the wall. Be right there." Before Dave could reply, he was gone.

True to his word, Jim arrived less than an hour later.

"You must have flown," Dave said.

"No, just me and my trusty radar detector."

"You might want to put a lid on that—Mike's a cop."

"Heard and noted," Jim said.

He scribbled notes as Dave went into more detail of the events. "Am I going too fast?"

"Just keep talking."

Dave smiled. Jim was a stereotype of every reporter he'd seen in those 1940's movies, lacking only the brimmed hat with a press card stuck in the band. Jim interrupted him every few minutes to prod for more cohesive details. When they stopped, his legal pad was almost full.

"That's about it. I guess we should wait until Mike gets back before doing anything else," Dave said.

"He can be the 'unnamed reliable source'." While they waited, Jim called his editor. "He's holding the front page of tomorrow's paper. I trust you, buddy, but I have to talk with the Petersons and those two kids at the university to verify everything."

"I don't want any of them to get in any trouble," Dave said.

"Do you think I'm a rookie? I won't even mention the university. I just need two sources to cover my ass. Wild horses couldn't pull it out of me. There might even be a raise in this for me," he added, just to loosen Dave up enough to smile.

Three quick phone calls, and Jim had his confirmation.

"Hey, Mary, you got a computer around here? I can start banging this story out while we're waiting on your husband. Got to have the whole thing there by eight tonight if it's going to be in the main edition, and by golly, it's going to be in the main edition. This is front page stuff."

Mary pointed to the study. "There's a typewriter in there. You can—"

"A typewriter? Oh, I forgot. We're out in the boondocks. That's okay, I'm good with antiques." Jim grabbed all of his notes from the kitchen table and brushed past her.

Dave smiled and shrugged.

"Do you think some Ritalin might calm him down?" Mary asked.

"I guess this is the journalistic equivalent of a cardiac arrest—barely controlled chaos," Dave said.

"Here's Mike," Mary said as the patrol car pulled up to the curb.

They waited anxiously for him to speak. His face was somber.

"Dave," he said, placing his hand on Dave's shoulder.

"Yes," Dave answered uncertainly.

"I have to tell you..." at this point a huge smile split his face, "you're going to be a hero, and," he burst out laughing, "you look like a clown in those baggy clothes."

"What happened?" Dave asked, relaxing a bit.

"Let's go sit down, and I'll tell you. I have to get back soon. The station's a madhouse."

The clattering from the study caused him to pause.

"Who's in there?"

Dave fetched Jim.

"Mike, this is Jim Campbell from the Lexington Herald-Leader. Jim, Mike Bolton."

"I'm not sure we're ready for the press just yet," Mike said.

"I understand," Jim said. "For now, just tell me what's off the record. There's plenty of time to fill in later. I'll be checking into a motel tomorrow, so you'll probably be sick of seeing me in the next few days."

"Okay," Mike said, "but you compromise this case, and you'll answer to me personally. Understand?"

Dave and Mary leaned forward, intent on what Mike said, while Jim scribbled notes, circling those Mike indicated were not for publication.

"This is the biggest thing I've ever been involved with. It took a court order to get us through the gates at the plant. That prick Albritton and his silver-haired shyster gave us fits until the state attorney showed up. At that point they just disappeared."

"You found the dump?" Dave asked.

"We found the dump, but that's just the tip of the iceberg. That building you mentioned was chock full of drugs: prescription drugs, LSD, marijuana, heroin, cocaine. You name it; it was there. They were even concocting their own crack cocaine and LSD in two other buildings tucked back in the woods. This is the biggest drug bust I've ever seen."

"Did you arrest anyone?"

"Jail's packed, two or three to a cell. Some of the boys are combing the woods with dogs for the others. They scattered like a covey of quail when we hit them. Really brazen. Just going on with business as usual."

"How about Slade?" Dave asked.

"That scumbag got away. It's like he has a sixth sense or something."

"And the big guy with the beard?"

"Randle, wannabe tough guy, California biker. As soon as the D.A. laid 30 years to life on him, he started singing like a bird. He gave us leads on Slade and more than twenty others in eastern Kentucky plus several suppliers out of Cincinnati and Knoxville."

"You go ahead and talk," Mary said. "If you're going to be up all night I want you to eat something more than Twinkies. I'll whip up some spaghetti; there's sauce in the freezer."

After a quick meal, Mike rose to leave. "Dave, I suspect Slade is somewhere between here and California by now. With us and the Feds after his butt, he'll make himself scarce. Just the same, I want you to tell Betty to stay in Atlanta. I'll have one of the boys drive you home to pack what you need. You'll be staying with us for the time being."

"I don't want to be a bother, and what about the dog?"

"Bring the dog. I just want to guarantee that you stay alive until we catch Slade, or at least until we make sure he's long gone."

Mike opened the door, then paused and turned to Jim. "I want to work with you, but you'd better be super careful about what you print."

Mike rolled his eyes as Jim gave him a wink and a thumbs-up.

"I've got to move, buddy," Jim said as soon as the door closed. Motioning for Dave to follow, he headed for the study. "Now sit and observe the power of the press," he said picking up the phone and dialing.

"Hello, this is Jim Campbell with the Lexington Herald Leader. I'd like to speak with Mr. Hotchkiss…It's concerning contamination by International Chemicals…I see. And to whom am I speaking?… Well, Mr. McElhaney, I'm running a banner headline in tomorrow's paper about a huge illegal hazardous waste dump. Shall I just say that according to you the regional head of the EPA was too busy to do anything? …That's fine, but if I haven't heard from him in fifteen minutes, that's how it's going to press. Here's the number…Thank you, too."

He gave Dave an impish smile. "The best way to get through a bureaucracy is to make someone take responsibility."

Ten minutes later the phone rang.

"Mr. Hotchkiss, thank you for returning my call." There was a long pause. "No, no, I wouldn't bully anyone. I just have a deadline to meet, and I didn't want to blindside you…This concerns arsenic pollution by International Chemicals…Yes, I know that you've already checked that out, but you missed the biggest illegal solid waste dumping in state history."

He held the phone where Dave could hear angry shouts through the receiver .

"Mr. Hotchkiss, excuse me for interrupting, but I'm leaving for Lexington in a few minutes. The headline will read 'Illegal Dumping Kills One and Injures Others.' Shall I follow this with a statement from you that the EPA had investigated and found no problems, or that you're launching a full-scale investigation Monday? I'm willing to go along with whichever you prefer…That's very nice of you Mr.

Hotchkiss, and I'm sure the community will be pleased…Yes, sir, thank you. Goodbye."

"That should keep Albritton and company occupied for a while," Jim said, gathering up his notes. "I can't wait to get a piece of him and Braxton."

When he'd loaded everything into his car, he came back once more.

"Dave, I can't thank you enough for letting me in on this."

"I didn't know I was stirring up such a hornet's nest," Dave said.

"I'm going to need an interview from you later," Jim said.

"No, no interviews," Dave said. "I just want to go back to being a family practitioner."

"Sorry, Dave, but like it or not, for the time being you're a celebrity. There'll be bigger dogs than me after you. If you want me to guide you through, call me at the Holiday Inn. Thanks, again."

It was after eleven when Dave called Betty the third time and finally got her.

"How's the conference?" he asked.

"Oh, Dave, I'm really glad I came. I've gotten so much out of the workshops, and the speaker tonight was wonderful. This has really given me a boost. Now, I wish I'd let you come."

"Next year for sure."

"How are things at the office?"

"Slowly withering, but I'm keeping fairly busy."

After a few minutes, the conversation lagged. Get on with it, Dave.

"There's been a little excitement today," he said.

"Excitement?" Is anything wrong? Are you all right?"

"I'm fine."

He gave her a brief summary, leaving out last night's events at the strip mine.

"You'll probably be seeing something about it on the news, and I wanted to forewarn you."

"You said you wouldn't do anything foolish." From the brittleness of her voice he knew she was angry. "Things were going so well here. Should I come home early?"

"No, Mike thinks it's a good idea for you to stay in Atlanta as you planned. I'll be staying with Mike and Mary for a few days."

"It's Slade, isn't it?"

"He got away. All of his buddies are in jail, and as far as Mike can determine, Slade's long gone. He just wants us to lay low until they're sure."

"This is never going to end, is it?"

"Hopefully, this is the end. There're a few loose ends to tie up, but the dumping will stop, the area will be cleaned up, no one else will be poisoned, and Slade is gone."

"I'm not so sure of that," she said, the fear and skepticism in her voice was obvious.

"I'll call you with a daily report," Dave said.

"Please, don't. I told you I needed some time to think, and this isn't what I had in mind. This just complicates matters. If there's something I really need to know, please call. Otherwise, I'll call you, if you're not out on some new crusade."

"I love you, darling."

"I know, that's what makes it so hard," she said, "Goodbye."

The next week was a blur. Dave saved the Herald- Leader for Betty to read when she got home. The headlines tracked the course of the investigation.

Sunday, July 17, 1988: "Illegal Dumping Kills One and Injures Others, EPA Begins Immediate Investigation"

Monday, July 18, 1988: "Drug Ring at Dump Site Smashed, Largest Haul in State History, Leader Escapes"

Tuesday, July 19, 1988: "Local Physician Instrumental in Uncovering Toxic Waste Dump and Drug Lab"

Wednesday, July 20, 1988: "International Chemicals Environmental Officer Agrees to Testify, Indictments Expected Soon"

Mary and Dave waited impatiently for Mike to get home for Friday dinner.

"Hey, Dave, that was a good interview with Gumbel. You've really gone big time," Mike said as he removed his coat.

"Yeah, great, I just want to get back to whatever's left of my practice. Celebrity's not for me."

"Don't worry, buddy, in another week you'll be old news, pushed off the front page by a rock star or some congressman banging an intern."

"The sooner, the better for me. Any new developments?" Dave asked.

"We're just trying to build an airtight case against Slade's gang. The government's handling the dumping. Word is, that since Wheeler's turned state's evidence, it's only a matter of time before Albritton and Braxton are indicted."

"What about Slade?"

"He's gone, but where to is anybody's guess. He may have been seen in Louisville or Cincinnati, but definitely not here."

"If that's the case, I'm going home tomorrow. Think it's okay for Betty to come home Sunday?"

Mike ran his hand through his hair. "Yeah, there's enough activity so that Slade won't be back anytime soon, but just to be safe, use that alarm system, and keep the dog inside at night."

Betty called the next night.

"I saw you on TV yesterday morning, you did really well. I was proud of you."

Dave was encouraged by her positive tone. He told her of the events of the past five days, assuring her that Slade had not been seen or heard of.

"How are you doing?" Dave asked.

"Better. The conference was a big help, and I've been able to think some things through. I'm going to start nurse practitioner training as soon as I can. I meant that about being less dependent on you. Also, I'm more convinced than ever that the therapist is a good idea. I think I understand why you've done the things you have, and, intellectually, I guess I agree with you, but I'm still resentful and angry. The problem is, I'm not sure at whom: you, Slade, the plant. God help me, sometimes I'm even angry with Kelli for leaving us in this shape, as if she had any choice in the matter. Someone who's emotionally detached might be able to help me unravel all of this."

"You may be right. If she thinks it would be useful to see the two of us together, or just to have me come in to beat on, I'm game. Lord knows I deserve it."

"We'll see. I'm anxious to see you."

"That's encouraging," Dave said with a laugh. "So when will you be coming home?"

"Late Sunday afternoon."

"Would you like me to fix ham, eggs and pancakes."

"That sounds good, but have you ever considered expanding your repertoire?"

"I cook one thing well, then devote the rest of my talents to being a great lover."

She laughed. "I'll take the ham and eggs."

Just as Mike had predicted, the splash of front-page headlines and stories of two weeks ago were replaced by follow up articles relegated to the inside pages. Things would pick up again when the trials began, but that wouldn't happen before next spring. International Chemicals was trying to cut its losses by cooperating with the EPA, and in an attempt to short circuit litigation with the residents of Boogertown, they had offered a settlement about which Mr. Peterson had asked Dave's advice. Dave called Jim Campbell.

"Dave, good to hear from you. You not only got me a raise, but also a promotion, thanks, what can I do for you?" This was all said in one rushed sentence, sounding for the world like a TV car salesman.

Before Dave could finish explaining Mr. Peterson's request, Jim cut in.

"Hold on just a minute…Here it is. Jack Thompson. He's got lots of experience with personal injury claims, and he's honest, if that's not an oxymoron when used in conjunction with lawyer. In my opinion, ninety-nine percent of lawyers give all the rest a bad name, but I digress. Peterson's going to need someone good. Rumor has it that it could take years to clean up all the contamination since it's leached so deep over such a large area. The EPA could condemn the whole area, including Boogertown."

"What will those people do? They've nowhere to go."

"That's why they need Jack."

Jim had been right. Each family received a lump sum of $100,000. In addition, Tamika and the two boys who had evidence of arsenic poisoning were provided with insurance for future medical care and full four-year scholarships to college. The family of the dead Hodges girl would pursue separate litigation.

A few days after the announcement of the settlement, Dave answered a knock at his door.

"Mr. Peterson, please come in. Betty, Mr. Peterson's here."

He ushered him into the living room while Betty prepared coffee.

"How's Tamika enjoying school?"

"She loves it, Doctor. She's only made one B since she got there, all the rest A's."

"That's wonderful; tell her to enjoy herself."

"Oh, she's doing that all right. She's working as a volunteer trainer for the basketball team, and she's set her eye on some pre-med student."

He stood when Betty brought the coffee.

"Mr. Peterson, it's so good to see you." She poured him coffee and served him a large piece of chocolate cake.

"Thank you, Mrs. DeMarco, I can only stay a minute."

"I heard you telling Dave about Tamika. She'll be a wonderful nurse."

"Yes, ma'am," he agreed and dug into the cake. "This is some fine cake, Mrs. DeMarco, it truly is." He paused and sipped his coffee. "The reason I came over is I need your help."

"What's that?" Dave asked.

"Do you know the people at the University?"

"Some of them, yes."

Mr. Peterson took another bite of cake. "Well, we made that lawyer get the children scholarships. Mr. Thompson said it was the least those people could do. Anyway, with the new scholarship, Tamika won't be needing the one she got last summer, and you knowing folks at the University and all, I wondered if you could talk to them, and see if they wouldn't give it to somebody else who really needs it, maybe somebody local."

"I'll sure try," Dave said.

" I would really appreciate it," Mr. Peterson said.

They chatted as they finished the cake and coffee. As Mr. Peterson rose to leave he paused and took Dave's hand.

"I appreciate all you people have done, Dr. DeMarco. You and Mrs. DeMarco are fine, good people making something good come from a tragic loss. Miss Kelli won't be forgotten, that's for sure."

Dave and Betty exchanged glances. He knew, somehow, he knew.

"Thank you, William," Dave said.

Mr. Peterson nodded and without another word left.

Chapter 16

Dave sat on the patio swing basking in the warmth of Indian summer and watching the leaves reluctantly disengage and drift from the trees. Most were bare except for the oaks, which clung tightly to their brown leaves until the last gasp of autumn, and the beeches which wouldn't lose theirs until they were pushed off by new growth next spring. The sky was crackling blue, and the November breeze had a bite to it. Betty set a thermos of hot spiced tea on the table and snuggled next to him as he put his arm around her and nuzzled the freshness of her hair. Neither spoke. This had been their routine every autumn, except that for seventeen years, three had snuggled instead of two.

"Do you think everything will be all right?" she said.

He didn't answer at once. There were only fifteen to twenty patients a day rather than the usual thirty. "I don't know why, but for some reason, I'm not worried. I really think God's looking out for us. I only hope he backs off for a while and just lets me practice medicine and keep what practice I have left."

"I know. I worry about finances," Betty said. "I don't mind working full time until the nurse practitioner course starts, but I was serious about getting my certification."

"We still have Kelli's college money since Tamika didn't need it."

Dave took a deep breath. "Care to listen to a crazy idea?"

"What." At least his craziness was usually well intentioned.

"When we set up Tamika's scholarship, you said you wanted to do something worthwhile in Kelli's memory."

"Yes."

"What would you think about using the money to do the same thing for Matt?" He rushed on before she could object. " Mr. Williams told me Matt made the Dean's List last semester even though he's working nights in a packing house. I don't know how he does it, but he's also giving talks in high schools trying to prevent teen-age drinking." He swallowed hard as he waited.

Her eyes became misty. "I've had the same idea, but I didn't know how you'd react and with you working so hard because of our finances I didn't say anything. I think it's a wonderful idea. I don't know why but somehow I feel the financial situation will work itself out." Before he could say anything, she put her arms around his neck and kissed him . "I love you so much." She fluttered her eyelashes and gave him a playful smile. "I'm really getting chilly. If we went inside, do you think you could warm me up?"

"I'd love to try."

"Well, come on." She grabbed his hand, and they ran into the house.

"I love making love in the afternoon," Betty said nestling into the crook of his arm.

"Hmmm."

She poked her elbow into his ribs. "Don't you go to sleep. Men!"

"I'm sorry, I think afterglow is a hypnotic that works specifically on males."

They lay talking in the growing darkness.

"I feel so good it's frightening," she whispered.

"In what way?"

"At first I wouldn't let myself feel anything positive. I worried that if I let myself stop hurting, I'd forget Kelli. This last year has been such a terrible roller coaster. I'd start making some progress, and then something would knock the props from under me."

"I'm afraid I'm responsible for a lot of that," Dave said.

She lay without talking for a while. "Do you think that horrible Slade will bother us? Is he really gone for good?"

"Mike said they haven't seen a trace of him since back in July. They pretty well smashed his operation, and if he's caught around here, he's gone for life. He's probably in California by now."

ꟗ

"How did we do, Millie?" Dave asked, scanning the end-of-the-month financials.

"Not so good." She spread the October worksheet on her desk for him to see.

"Collections still seem pretty good."

"Not as good as they look. Most of that is what was owed to us from before October. Our accounts receivable from the plant insurance are about to dry up. We still have several plant employees willing to pay the extra twenty-percent co-pay to come to us, but most of the others can't afford to, or they left because they blame you for the job uncertainty at the plant. The other patients are paying what they have; they just don't have very much."

"What can we do?"

"Dr. DeMarco, if things don't pick up by the first of the year we're going to have to let Kathy go. We don't need a dedicated insurance clerk if we don't have any insurance to file."

"Gosh, I'd hate to do that," Dave said.

"There's something else."

"What's that?"

"You had the largest practice in the area." He winced at the past tense "had" but was at the same time grateful for her frank honesty. "Because most of your plant patients are going to the other doctors, they're busier now and refuse to see poor and uninsured patients. All of those are coming here. That increases our expenses and doesn't add a dime to the bottom line."

"I know, but we can't just turn them away," he said.

She slammed the book shut. "It makes me so angry. If all of the doctors would just see their fair share of the poor, it wouldn't be a burden on anyone. You've always done more than you should, and now it's come back to bite you."

"We're going to do what's right regardless of what they do," he said with finality. "Something will come up. I just wish I knew what." He slipped on his jacket. "Maybe bankruptcy."

"Dr. DeMarco, don't even joke about that."

"Hey, I just remembered. Betty's gone to Lexington tonight to her support group. Why don't you let me take you to dinner while I can still afford it. The Embers okay?"

"I'd like that, just let me freshen up. Oh, I almost forgot. Dr. Wistrom called. He didn't want to disturb you; said you could call him tomorrow."

Dave lay in the recliner staring at the ceiling. Who am I kidding? There's no way out. Seeing more patients won't help if they can't pay. It's obvious the plant will never allow me back on their panel. God, I need some help from you. I don't know what to do. I know I'm to take care in my choices, but I don't even know what the choice is. Right now I'm not interested in benefitting all of mankind; all I want to do is benefit my family.

"Dave?" He hadn't heard Betty come in. "Is anything wrong?"

"No, I'm just sitting here in the dark feeling sorry for myself."

He told her about the finances. "You warned me about getting on the wrong side of the plant. I thought the bad publicity would force them to take me back, but I think they want to make me an example for any other uppity doctors."

"I talked with Mary Johnson in personnel on Wednesday. She said they might have a full time position available the first of the year. She's going to try to get me some extra shifts between now and then."

"I'd hate for you to do that."

"Actually, I'd sort of welcome it. I can't start in the nurse practitioner program until July, and I need something to keep me busy and occupy my mind. If things get bad enough, I can come back to the office. We did pretty well with that when we started out."

"We did, didn't we?"

The next day he saw only four new patients before noon, two unemployed and the other two working but uninsured. Until last week they all had other doctors. He was reading a journal in his office when Millie stuck her head in to remind him to call Dr. Wistrom.

"Fred, it's Dave DeMarco."

"Good to hear from you, Dave. How's our patient doing?"

"Fine," Dave said, "she started in pre-nursing this fall."

"That's great, but that's not why I called."

"What can I do for you?"

"Remember several years ago when the medical school approached you about coming on the university staff? I've been talking with John Burcham, the new Chairman of Family Practice. We've heard about the raw deal you got down there and would like to talk with you. I've been appointed the assistant dean for academics and training at the medical school, and I could help move things along."

"Thanks, Fred, but I have the same problem now as then. Despite all that's happened, this is still our home, and I don't know if I could bring myself to leave."

"I can appreciate that," Fred said, "but just hear us out. Could we come down, day after tomorrow, say around four."

"That would be fine. I'm not as busy as I used to be."

Fred laughed. "Maybe we can help with that."

ℵ

Millie and Karen pitched in to help Dave straighten his office, no easy task.

"It's been so long since I saw the floor I'd forgotten it was hardwood," Dave said. The office hadn't looked this good since the first week after he opened. It was almost like moving into new digs.

"I want you to make a good impression on the bigwigs from the medical school. They all seem to think we're backward hicks who don't wear shoes," Millie said.

Karen rushed back from discarding a box of out of date drug samples. "They're here."

"Okay, Millie, bring them on back, and, Millie…"

"Yes?"

"Why don't you spit out your tobacco before they come in?" We wouldn't want them to get the wrong idea." He ducked as she threw a cushion from the couch at him.

"You just behave yourself and act professional, if you can," she said tartly.

"Dave, Fred's told me about your recent problems, and I'm sorry about the actions of International Chemicals and the universtiy, and even sorrier about your daughter. I've talked with other physicians and have heard only glowing evaluations of you. You've scored in the top ten-percent each time you've taken your boards. We all feel you'd be a great addition to the staff of the Family Practice department, and I think you'd be the ideal teacher and mentor for our residents."

"I've already told Fred that, for a lot of reasons, we want to stay in Hillsdale."

"We don't want you to leave," Burcham said. "There's a great need for provision of quality medical care to the rural poor and uninsured. We'd like for you to head up a new branch of our department here in Hillsdale. It would be the pilot project of a program that the Governor is considering starting statewide. Should it prove feasible, we'd have residents work in the clinic for six-month rotations. Of course you'd be an employee of the medical school, but we'd rely on you to run a tight, efficient practice, preferably self-supporting." He paused to let this sink in. "What do you think?"

"I'm stunned. Several years ago Betty and I had talked about something like this, only we hadn't considered residents. This would be a great location for it. We'd even considered using volunteers who are bored with retirement—nurses, secretaries and such—and making it a training center for medical office personnel." Burcham and Wistrom leaned forward, caught up in Dave's growing enthusiasm. "We could take these kids from the hills and hollows who have little chance of ever getting ahead, train them, then place them with doctors' offices and hospitals. There's always a demand for good receptionists, insurance billing clerks, nursing assistants, and people with computer skills. The list goes on and on. Most offices don't really have the time or money to train these people."

"That's a dimension we'd never thought of," Burcham said, "sort of a regional training center and placement service."

"We wouldn't hang onto the new trainees," Dave continued. "When they're placed, we'd simply start training new ones. I run a pretty tight ship, and, given a few good volunteers, I'll bet I could make it break even on Medicaid alone."

"How about the other doctors?" Wistrom asked. "Would they object?"

"They're unloading these patients anyway."

"What about the workload?"

"I can see a good number, but with residents, I think we can handle as many patients as come. Have you thought about using this as part of your nurse practitioner training program? That would increase our capacity even more."

They brainstormed for two more hours.

Burcham rose and shook Dave's hand. "I think this has real possibilities. Let me run it by the administration, but I feel certain they'll approve, and if they do, I think we can be up and running by the first of the year."

ꟹ

On November first, Dave's old practice disappeared, but on November third Dr. Burcham informed him of the University's decision to go forward with the clinic for indigents and the working poor.

Betty found Dave hunched over the dining room table surrounded by papers and forms.

"Hmmm," he murmured as she began massaging his shoulders.

"How's it going?" she asked.

"Things are starting to fall in place. Expanding into the space next door more than doubled the size of the office, and it looks like we'll need it. It should be ready by the first of the year; they've done a lot in just one month."

"It was nice of the hospital to free up the space."

"That wasn't entirely altruistic. They're just like the other docs in town, unloading their non-paying clientele so they won't clutter up the emergency room and suck up the hospital's profit."

Betty pulled a chair next to his and sat down. "Let's see what you've got."

She studied the papers he'd been sweating over.

"How many patients do you expect to see a day?"

"We'll be pushing a hundred a day when we open on January third."

He watched with growing admiration as she scanned first one form and then another. She's so confident, more like before. I don't know what that therapist's doing, but it's sure helping.

"How much experience do the nurses have?"

"One's worked in an industrial medicine clinic for six months; the other two are right out of school."

"Inexperienced and green as grass. You have three residents? What year?"

"One from each class—a first, second and third year."

"The third year will do all right, maybe the second year, but the new guy will spend most of his time looking for his stethoscope and bumping into the furniture."

Dave burst out laughing. "I'll bet you said those same things about me."

"Not where you could hear it. Besides, I had a long time to train you, and…" she turned and kissed him, "special enticements for good behavior."

After jotting several lists of numbers, she looked up. "The residents and new nurses are going to be as slow as molasses and bottleneck the whole clinic. If you don't want patients spilling out into the parking lot, you need at least two more experienced nurses. You might be able scrape by with one if she could do X-rays. That would decrease your overhead and increase your productivity significantly."

He reviewed her numbers. Why didn't I think about that? I forgot what a good manager she is.

"You're right, but finding a good nurse is hard enough, and I have no idea where to get one who can take X-rays as well."

She smiled. "Tonight after you go to bed, roll over and look directly to your left."

"You? I thought you were going to work full time at the hospital until the nurse practitioner training started."

"I need a challenge. You'll be making less than in private practice, but it's enough to meet our needs. The nurse practitioner curriculum requires one year in a doctor's office. I checked and some of this time could apply toward my certification. Most importantly," she rose to leave, "this way I can keep an eye on you and all of those sweet young things who just might want to latch onto a rich, handsome doctor."

ꟸ

"I'm going to forget how to cook," Betty said, spooning up the last of the hot fudge from her sundae.

"How can you eat that and stay so curvaceous?" Dave asked.

"Sundaes are why I am so curvaceous," she said with a puckish smile.

"This month has been great. The residents and staff surprised me at how quickly they fit in. Millie says we may break even the first month. Of course a flu epidemic helps, and taking the best looking member of the staff home with me doesn't hurt either." He sipped his coffee. "I actually look forward to going to work. I wasn't sure I'd ever feel that again."

"Me, too. It's sort of like we're starting over again, as if we've had three lives: before Kelli, with her, and now after. Life will never be like I expected it, but sometimes, I actually find myself thinking about the future."

Neither spoke for a while.

"Thanks for going to the support group with me," she said.

"I just wish I hadn't been bull-headed for so long. I get a lot out of them. Being able to talk about Kelli without inhibitions and maybe to help someone else over some of the rough spots you've experienced really boosts my spirits." He gave a rueful laugh, " If nothing else maybe I can serve as a bad example for the others. I feel like such a dunce. I've practically dragged alcoholics to AA—never had one stay dry for any significant period of time outside of it. It's the same as The Compassionate Friends, just a different set of problems. Somehow, though, deep down I've always thought of people who went to support groups as a bunch of weenies who couldn't handle their own problems. So much for my great insight. Thanks for persisting."

"We'd better get home. Gretchen will think she's been abandoned."

"You're right," he said, sliding his hand along her thigh, "and I want to check out those sundae curves."

She shoved him out of the booth. "Let's get out of here, you lecher."

"What's that?" Betty asked the next morning as they neared the end of the driveway.

Dave set the brake and went to inspect a large hound that lay dead at the foot of the drive. Only after he grasped its hind legs and started dragging it toward the ditch did he notice that its throat had been slashed.

"Must have been hit by a car," he lied. "I'll bury it this afternoon."

He dropped Betty at the clinic and went to the hospital to make rounds but, before returning to the office, he called Mike.

"There may be some simple explanation, but I'll just bet Slade's back," Dave said.

"We haven't heard anything, but we'll be on the lookout. You guys get back into the security routine, you hear?"

"Yeah, I know. That's just what we need. Things have been going so well, and Betty's been doing great."

"If it is Slade, he's starting to really hack me off," Mike said. "Be careful, Dave."

He buried the dog and said nothing further, but the next morning a white cat dangled from the mailbox, a hangman's noose around its neck.

Betty clenched her fists. "He's back, isn't he?"

"I hope not, but he probably is."

That afternoon she resumed her target practice.

"Any word on Slade?" Dave asked.

"No, but I'm sure he's around," Mike replied.

"There haven't been any more dead animals."

"Yes, there have. One of the nightshift guys cleans it up each morning. He even left one at the cemetery."

"He's sick."

"Yeah, dangerous, crazy sick."

"Don't answer it," Betty said, "I know it's him."

Dave answered the phone anyway. "Hello." Nothing, the same as the other calls that had come nightly for the last two weeks. He slammed the receiver back on its cradle.

"I'll put on a recording and route our calls through the hospital operator. She can page me for any I should answer. We'll just turn the sound down here so we can't hear it ring."

"I've never hated anyone in my whole life, but I hate this beast. If I get the chance, I swear I'll kill him," Betty said, fists clenched, jaw set, but no trace of the trembling, near hysteric fear she'd shown before.

"I hope that won't be necessary," Dave said. You are one tough lady he thought. Ever since returning from Atlanta and starting to see the therapist, she'd been much more decisive, sure of herself, and more like the nurse who intimidated him as an intern, but could she really kill someone? Could I? He remembered wondering the same thing when he was in Vietnam where his unit had seen heavy action, once even being overrun. He'd kept an M-16 in the aid station as he tended the wounded, but had never needed to fire a shot, so he still didn't know.

As they left the office the next evening, dull gray clouds scudded over the ridge from the northwest, and the air hung damp and heavy—always a bad sign in January.

"Watch your step," Dave said taking her hand. "It's starting to get slick."

A mixture of sleet and rain pelted them as they dashed to the car. Although it was only six, it was already dark. He drove slowly since black ice often formed on the north side of the hills. The hot blast from the heater melted the ice pellets as they hit the windshield and soon the car was so warm that Betty loosened her coat.

"Nice and snug. Remember where we were this time last year?" she asked.

"Snorkeling in Aruba; not freezing our buns off sliding around in Caintookey."

"I loved the Christmas card Juan sent us. I'm going to write him this weekend. The clinic will be well set by next winter, so what do you think of going back?"

Instead of answering, he accelerated, staring intently in the rear-view mirror.

"What is it?" Betty asked. She turned and was blinded by two high beam lights looming on their bumper.

"Hold on," Dave warned, clenching the steering wheel tighter and accelerating even more.

The truck stayed close behind as they roared past the cemetery entrance. Just beyond, the road curved sharply to the left around a high cut in the ridge, always the first spot to ice over. Gravel flew as he swerved across the left lane onto the gravel shoulder, cutting the curve and gaining traction. Unable to compensate, the truck hit the glassy surface, spun twice, and disappeared into the ditch.

"I hope he broke his neck," Dave said and slowed to a safe speed.

Gretchen bounded out of her house and yelped a greeting when they drove up. Dave opened the gate, and she blasted across the yard trying to expend a day's worth of pent-up energy before going inside.

Dave called Mike immediately.

"We're on our way. Maybe we can nab him if he's still alive."

After letting a panting Gretchen in, they turned on the alarm and waited. An hour later her barks announced someone's arrival. The blinking blue strobe lights identified it as Mike.

"Did you get him?" Betty asked

"Sorry, no such luck," Mike answered. "He was long gone, but he'll be significantly hampered by the loss of his truck. He must have been shaken up because he was in such a hurry to get away that he left his gun. Some of the boys are still combing the woods. He must be holing up in some old cabin. Most of his cronies are in jail, and those still out know they're being watched. If he hangs around here, we'll get him; it's only a matter of time."

"During which, we have to live like fugitives," Dave said.

"Yeah, I guess so. We're doing all we can."

"I know," Dave said. "It's just so frustrating. Things were starting to calm down."

"Just hang in there a little longer. We'll get him," Mike said. "I promise."

Neither Dave nor Betty was convinced.

They drove to and from work together and never ventured outside the house without Gretchen. That there was no further sign of Slade was scant comfort.

"Tonight is staff meeting," Dave said. "It should be finished by seven."

"I'll drive my car. I've got to go to Kroger; the cupboard's almost bare," Betty said.

"I don't want you to come home alone, so meet me at the Bistro for dinner when you're finished."

"That's a poor reason for dining out, but you're right, and I really don't want to come home by myself." Small shrug, then a small—but not vulnerable—smile. "My hero."

"Hold on, Mrs. Watson," Dave said, punching the hold button as Betty stepped into his office.

She leaned down and kissed him. "I'm running a little late, but I'm off to stock the larder. See you at seven."

"It's a date." They briefly clasped hands then she was out the door.

The overcast sky made the parking lot even darker. A cold wind bit at her as she unlocked the door. Thank goodness the windows didn't need scraping. After exiting the parking lot, she took the short way to Kroger through a residential neighborhood, stopping at the next intersection.

"What..."

The back of her seat shifted as a figure heaved up behind her. Fingers grabbed her hair and jerked her back against the headrest. The long blade of a knife glinted in the faint light from the dashboard. She struggled for a moment, but ceased when the blade touched her throat.

"Be still, bitch," his voice rasped in her ear. "You do just like I say or, so help me God, I'll slit your throat. Understand?"

The sour smell of whiskey and unbrushed teeth almost gagged her.

"Yes." Her heart was pounding. I've got to stay calm. Don't startle him.

"Turn that heater off. I want the windows fogged up. Now you just keep going to Maple Street, then go to the highway. You and me are going to your house for a party."

She looked in the rear-view mirror trying to get a glimpse of him.

Again, he jerked her head back by her hair. "Keep your eyes on the road. You'll see more of me than you want before this night is over."

She drove slowly on the route he'd directed. Her hand crept across the steering wheel toward the horn when she saw the patrol car parked in the lot of the mini-mart at the intersection of Maple and the highway.

"Do it, and you're dead."

She moved her hand back and turned onto the highway. Stay calm, Betty. Act frightened, maybe he'll get careless.

"Why are you doing this?"

"Why? Your prick of a husband ruins my business, and you ask why?"

"He meant you no harm. He was just trying to help some sick people."

"Yeah, right, put me out of business for a bunch of niggers. Well, I'll show that nigger-loving bastard that you don't fool with Frank Slade and get away with it."

Wrong question. Don't make him angrier. Act helpless.

"Please, don't hurt me."

"Don't hurt me," he mocked her. "You uppity, high class bitches are all the same—think you're better'n everybody else; wouldn't be caught dead with scum like me." He gave a cackling laugh. "Well, you're one high class bitch that's going to be caught dead with me."

"Please, I'll do anything you want."

"Damned right you will." He leaned forward, slid his cold hand down her blouse and fondled her breast. "And you know just what I want."

Betty gritted her teeth and shuddered, but made no move to resist.

"Slow down. Nice and easy up the drive. I know your place, so don't try anything funny. I been watching every day."

She killed the motor at the front door, but the knife at her throat kept her immobile.

"Now, open your door but no funny stuff," he said. Opening his door, he clambered out. Betty lunged for the passenger door. "Damn you." He dove across the seat, jerked her out by the hair and, standing behind her, again put the blade to her throat.

"Try something like that again, and you're history. Just move slow," he said pressing her toward the door. "Shit fire!" he shouted as Gretchen lunged at him through the chain link fence. "Wish I had my gun, I'd kill it." Gretchen went wild—leaping until her nose was even with the top of the fence.

"Open the door."

Don't spook him. "I need to turn off the alarm," Betty said and pressed the numbers on the keypad.

"That's a good girl. You learn quick."

She unlocked the door and they stepped inside.

"Turn on the light."

He reached behind him, locked the door, then lowered the knife and pushed her to the center of the room. For the first time she saw him. He was much smaller than she had imagined—lean, wiry and only an inch or two taller than she. His hair was matted and he hadn't shaved for days. The most frightening thing about him was his piercing eyes—light hazel, almost yellow, exuding hate.

"All right, bitch, I don't know when hubby is coming home, so we need to move this right along. I going to stand right here and watch while you get nekkid."

She was deadly calm despite her pounding heart and studied, helpless demeanor. "Please, don't so this," she said, her mind racing.

He waggled the knife menacingly. "You want to do it, or you want me to cut 'em off?"

She slowly unbuttoned her blouse. His eyes glittered, and he actually licked his lips.

"Take off the coat," he said, "I want to see everything."

She shrugged off the heavy coat. Before he could react, she flung the coat at his face, flicked off the light, overturned a large wing chair and darted down the hallway toward the bedroom.

"I'll kill you, you bitch," Slade screamed as he tossed the coat aside and followed her footsteps disappearing down the darkened hallway. "Goddammit!"

Betty heard him crash over the chair as she slammed and locked the bedroom door. Almost as one continuous action, she turned on the lights, ran around the bed, snatched the gun from the bedside table and punched the panic button on the alarm pad. Her hands shook as she inserted the clip and chambered a round. The doorknob jiggled; then the entire door creaked against the weight of his body pressing against it. For a moment the only sound was Slade's heavy breathing from the hallway, then he kicked the latch viciously. On the third kick, the door burst open in a shower of splintered wood. He lunged into the room and pulled up short.

Betty stood on the far side of the bed, feet solidly apart, holding the gun in a practiced two-handed grip aimed squarely in the center of his chest.

"I've already alerted the police," she nodded toward the alarm pad without taking her eyes from him. "They'll be here in less than five minutes. Just stand still and you won't get hurt."

"Hell, baby, you ain't going to shoot me. You ain't got the guts." He waggled the long blade of the knife. "I guess I don't have time to party with you, and that's a shame. But I have plenty of time to chop you up and get away." He took a step toward the foot of the bed.

"Please, I don't want to hurt you," Betty said, "but if you come any closer, I will." The gun remained centered on his chest.

"Snotty bitch, you won't do nothing." Like a snake coiling to strike, he tensed to spring across the bed.

Betty knew he was coming. At the last instant she shifted her aim slightly to her left and squeezed the trigger.

Slade slammed back against the door frame, his right shoulder shattered and his arm hung limp at his side. His wide, disbelieving eyes darted from his shoulder to the knife on the floor and to the gun which was still trained, steady as a rock, on his chest.

"You crazy, bitch," he shouted, then turned and ran down the hall. Betty didn't follow. The sound of sirens pierced the darkness as he ripped the front door open with his good hand.

The sight of the intruder and the pungent scent of blood drove Gretchen into a frenzy. Slade had just reached the end of the walk when she leaped high enough to get her front paws on the top of the six-foot cyclone fence and scramble over. Panic-stricken at the sight of the dog coming over the fence and the flashing lights turning up the drive, he began running past the rear of the house toward the woods.

Mike and Josh Morgan, his partner, piled from the car and pursued the figure silhouetted in the headlights. Slade fell and screamed when Gretchen ripped a chunk from his left thigh, but he immediately jumped up and continued past the saltlick with Gretchen hard on his heels. Then he just disappeared. Gretchen slid to a halt and began running back and forth, barking.

"Oh, my gosh," Josh said, shining the high intensity light on the figure sprawled on the rocks a hundred feet below the Jump Off. "I don't think he'll be causing any more trouble," he said when a panting Mike caught up.

"I guess not," Mike said, then smiled. "I'd say his career just hit rock bottom. Call in some help and haul him up. There's a path down over there," he indicated with his flashlight.

Mike found Betty sitting on the edge of the bed, pistol on her lap, staring at the bloody smear on the shattered doorframe.

"Is he dead?" she asked, her voice calm and flat.

"Yeah, but I don't think you did it," Mike said. "He was running from Gretchen and ran right off of the Jump Off. He was so scared I guess he forgot it was there and didn't see it in the dark."

"Then it's over?"

"It's over."

Betty stood and handed him the gun. "Could you get rid of this?"

"Be glad to." Mike put his arm around her and led her from the room. "Come on into the living room. I have to get a statement for my report. This place is a wreck."

"Could you get word to Dave that I'm all right? He's probably running back and forth between Kroger and the Bistro. I'm sure he's frantic."

"Good idea," Mike said. "If he drives up here and sees all of the blue lights, he'll probably have another heart attack." He called Josh from the bedroom where he was gathering evidence. "Could you go into town and bring Dr. DeMarco home? Don't let him drive. He can get his car tomorrow."

so

"You've had quite a night," Mike said when she finished her story.

"It's just now starting to hit me," Betty said, trying to steady her hand to sign the statement.

She stood when Dave burst into the room.

"Are you all right?" he stammered, hugging her to him. "Josh told me what happened."

"I'm fine. Mike was just finishing up."

A rumpled, unofficial-looking man entered the living room and motioned to Mike. After a brief conversation, Mike returned to Betty and Dave.

"That was the coroner. Slade's dead, but," he said looking directly at Betty, "it was the fall, not the bullet, that did it."

"Thank you," she said softly.

"You guys are more than welcome to stay with us until you get things cleaned up," Mike said, his professional demeanor gone.

Dave looked at Betty who shook her head. "Thanks, Mike," Dave said . "I think we're okay here. We'll sleep in the guestroom until I can get the bedroom cleaned up. Just let me know when you're through in there."

"We've got all we need," Mike said and began herding everyone out. "You should sleep better now."

Perhaps tomorrow, but tonight. Unable to sleep, they lay entwined in each other's arms long after midnight. The full moon shone through the window, the drapes open for the first time in two months.

"Want to talk?" Dave asked.

"I want to tell you what happened this one time; then I don't think I ever want to discuss it again," Betty said.

He listened with growing admiration as she calmly told him every detail she could remember.

"I think you were a lot braver than I would've been," he said when she finished.

"He was the most evil person I've ever met. He'd made our lives hell, and I truly wanted to kill him, but I couldn't. I'm not sorry he's dead, but I'm glad I wasn't the one who did it."

He held her, letting her talk out whatever demons that remained, until she drifted off to sleep.

Chapter 17

"Come on, lazy bones, time to get up," Betty threw the covers from him.

"Hey, woman, are you trying to frighten me to death or just give me frostbite? What time is it?"

"A little after ten."

"What? I've got to get to the office." He leaped from the bed and began searching for his trousers.

"Calm down. I'm sure the mortality rate won't soar if you're a little late. I called Millie and told her you'd be in after lunch. After last night, we both deserve to sleep in, and since we missed dinner, I've cooked us a farmer's breakfast: biscuits and gravy, ham, eggs and grits."

After breakfast they sat in the sunroom sipping coffee.

"I feel as if we're turning a new page in our lives," Betty said, " and I'm not sure where we're heading. I need to get away and do some thinking. In fact, we both do. I'm going to rent the cabin for the next ten days. I'm going up this afternoon, and you can come on Saturday. Three days should be enough for me to get my head back on straight."

"Sounds good to me; we've earned a break."

"If you have any spare time, I'd like you to start converting that berm on my target practice range into a raised planting bed."

"Good idea," he said with a laugh, "I'd much rather dodge turnips than bullets."

ꟗ

Winter in the Smokies is unequaled when the higher elevations glisten with a thick glaze of hoarfrost. Hikers who venture out in such weather find every twig transformed into a sparkling frozen caterpillar. Less hearty souls, such as Dave and Betty, view it at a distance from the cozy warmth of the fireplace.

"This has been good," Dave said. "I hate to go back, but duty summons. I promised John I'd speak at the Sunday evening service."

"I didn't know that. What are you going to talk about?" Betty asked.

"About dealing with grief, and how it's changed me."

"And how has it?" she said snuggling against him.

"You said it's as if we were turning a new page in our lives, but to me it's almost as if we're starting a new book altogether. I think the most striking thing is that I have my priorities straight. I didn't realize how much my life was dominated by the importance of unimportant things. I'd give anything to have back the years I wasted making phone calls, going to meetings and doing things that I felt wouldn't get done if I didn't do them and to be able to spend them with Kelli and you."

"Don't be too hard on yourself. The very things that make you a good doctor—that sense of responsibility, duty and dedication—that's you and that's your life, but they do have a way of taking over. I think there's a fine line between dedication and obsession."

"Yeah, and I crossed that line big time. I don't know quite how to put it," he continued, "but in many ways now I'm a better person than I was. People are still important, but in a different way and at a different level. The world is so beautiful, but until recently I never gave it more than a passing glance. It's as if I lived most of my life on automatic pilot, doggedly plodding toward that next goal, but seldom even thinking about savoring the moment. As good as this new perspective is, at times I find it maddening, because if it would bring Kelli back, I'd go back to being an obsessive-compulsive jerk in a heartbeat."

"Maybe it's insight, or maybe just time, but I'm starting to accept her death," Betty said. "People ask if I'm 'over it.' I'll never get over it. There is no closure—God, how I hate that word—just an acceptance of what can't be changed. Ever since my parents died, I've had an inordinate fear of death . After Kelli died, I absolutely wanted to die, not enough to do anything about it, but I wanted to die. Now, life's important again. I'd like to live to a ripe old age, but I don't fear death."

They sat watching the play of the fire on the logs.

"So what are you going to write in your new book?" she asked.

He stared intently into the fire. "I wasn't as close to Kelli as you were, but I've come to know her better through her diary. She always seemed to be doing good things for other people. If her life is to have any meaning at all, it's up to us to give it that meaning, to continue doing good things in her memory, in some small way to do the things she won't be able to do." He gave a short laugh. "I don't intend to take on any more corporate giants, but even little actions might, somewhere down the road, have significant effects."

"It's strange that you say that. Remember what Juan said? I haven't told anyone, but for the last several months, except on days when someone was trying to kill me, I've consciously tried to do something good each day in remembrance of Kelli. It may not be monumental, but it sure does a lot for me."

He rose, retrieved the remainder of last night's wine from the refrigerator, poured two glasses and brought one to her.

"To Kelli, to us, and to our new lives."

Eyes misted, unable to speak, Betty smiled and raised her glass.

Chapter 18

To Dave it was like Murphy's Law working in reverse—everything that could go right, went right. The clinic opened without a hitch. After six weeks it was running smoothly and now, three months later, fairly hummed. Far from being controversial, the other doctors welcomed it as an opportunity to pare non-paying patients from their practices. Dr. Burcham had provided him with the best resident from each class, and, contrary to Betty's earlier prediction, even the first year resident was able to contribute.

With a quiet confidence and self-assurance that surprised him, Betty took over the clinical aspects of the practice, supervising the nurses, aides and lab personnel. As usual, Millie kept a tight rein on the front office and finances, leaving him almost totally free to attend patients and to oversee and teach the residents.

ꕥ

"I still say that if they wanted to work, they could," Jason Hubbard, the tall third year resident, said as Dave walked past the break room. Dave leaned against the wall and finished the chart out of their line of vision.

"Jason, you arrogant jerk, what do you know about work? Your daddy sends you to a private prep school, then Dartmouth, and you're an expert on poverty. I bet, outside of the wards and clinics, you've never had a conversation with anyone who doesn't have a college degree and makes over six figures." Dave recognized Pete Hatfield's somewhat high-pitched voice. Pete was a first year resident who had escaped the coal mines through part time jobs and scholarships—top of his class, very sharp.

"Cool it, Hatfield, I'm not a McCoy," Jason said. "You're the exception. Admit it. Most of the people in your home town have been on welfare for two or three generations."

Dave stepped into the room before the situation could escalate. On one side of the table, Jason pretended sudden interest in his sandwich while, Pete, stocky and red-faced, glared across at him. Whit Thomas, the second year resident, leaned against the wall watching them with a bemused smile. Whit was much older than they—around forty—and had left a successful engineering job to go to medical school.

"Sounds pretty intense, " Dave said. "What's it all about?" Neither Jason nor Pete spoke. "Whit?"

"We were just talking about the socio-economics of medicine, especially here in Appalachia."

"There are some real problems, for sure," Dave said. "But they're not a lot different here than in inner city Louisville, Lexington, or Cincinnati. With all the delericts and down-and-outers in teaching hospitals we get a skewed view in our training, which makes most of our opinions pretty uninformed. We're just getting started in the clinic here, but Millie has some early data, that pretty much coincide with what I found in my practice. You might find it interesting. Can you stick around for a while after hours today?"

"Sure, Dr. DeMarco," Pete said and looked at the other two who nodded agreement.

They drank coffee, munched cookies, and talked shop as they waited for Millie.

"Dr. DeMarco, your wife is so sharp," Jason said. "It's embarrassing. Kid's mothers know that she's better at pediatrics than I am. She picked up a case of measles before the kid had even developed a rash. I've never seen Koplick's spots before. Heck, I've never seen measles."

"It's not just pediatrics," Whit added. "She bailed me out big time today. This little old lady was wheezing up a storm, and I'm fixing to load her up with steroids and fluids when Mrs. DeMarco pointed out the lady had gained twelve pounds in five days. She had heart failure, not asthma, and I'm about to drown her."

"Welcome to the club," Dave said with a smile. "You should have seen her when I was a green intern on the wards at the university. When she corrected you, was she nice?"

"Sure, she always is." Whit said. "Why?"

"She's mellowed with age," Dave said. Before he could continue, Millie walked in with her customary pile of papers.

"Ask Millie anything you want to know. Just to get things started, Millie, what percentage of our practice are freeloaders?"

"It really hasn't changed much from our old practice," she said. "Somewhere between eight to ten percent of our patients try to milk the system. They try to stiff us, the government, or both."

"How many of your patients are on welfare or Medicaid?" Jason asked.

"About seventy percent. The rest are about evenly divided between Dr. DeMarco's previous patients, who pay a twenty percent co-pay that their insuror charges to go outside their system. The others are just too poor for us to bother with billing. It costs about three dollars to send a bill, and they don't have three dollars."

"So eighty percent of this practice is broke or on welfare," Jason persisted.

Millie struggled to remain civil. "Yes, but that's not the whole story." She laid out a large computer printout consisting of several columns of figures ranging from twenty-five cents to five dollars. "This is a list of those whom we don't bill. Do you know how many of these people haven't paid anything?"

"Uh, no," Jason stammered.

"Only five. You hear those ladies cleaning the office?" Jason nodded. "We had so many patients ask to work to help cover their treatment that the state granted us a waiver to let them do so." She pointed to the remains of the cookies. "Did you like the cookies?"

"Yeah, sure," he said

"They were compliments of Mrs. Brumby, the lady with arthritis you saw this morning. She's a widow who lives in a two-room shanty on three hundred dollars a month from the UMW. These are good people. Most are too proud to accept charity, so they pay whatever they can by whatever means they can. Why, back in December, one of those deadbeats slaughtered a hog and brought us a pork loin as payment for his hospitalization. To that man, a pork loin was more precious than your Porsche," she finished, not trying to hide the barb.

The room was quiet.

"Thank you, Millie," Dave said.

"I have a lot more," she said with a smirk.

"I think that's enough."

"Man, she reamed me a new one," Jason said after she gathered her papers and left.

"Millie's very intense," Dave said. "Listen to her, and you'll know how to run a practice before you leave here." He sipped his Coke pondering what to say next. "She's right, you know. By and large these are good hard working people. Sure, there are deadbeats, but I'll lay you odds, you'll find more jerks percentage-wise in your big uptown practices than you'll find here."

"I guess I ran off at the mouth," Jason said.

"That's not the point," Dave said. "Say anything you want back here, but your patients know what you think about them. Regardless of what you say to them, you can't hide it. I'm new at this teaching bit, but I want to do more than to teach you to diagnose measles. I want you to learn about people, and about yourselves."

"You interact with patients so easily," Whit said. "What's your secret?"

"I think it boils down to why you went into medicine. Deep down, we all want to help people, but somewhere in the maze of the sheer volume of what we have to learn, technology, poor role models, and finances a lot of us let that slip away.

"I think most physicians fall into one of three categories. To some, medicine is just a job. You go to work, do as much as you can in as short a time as you can, charge a bundle for it, and then try to find time for the things you really love. I guess that's okay, but for the same amount of time and effort you could have made a whole lot more money by going to law school. The only problem is, then you're a lawyer."

The three residents laughed, and the tension around the table dissipated.

"Most doctors are better than that. The second approach to medicine is to be a professional. I think this is the largest group. These keep up-to-date; they're highly competent; they learn from their mistakes, and they care about their patients as long as it doesn't interfere too much with their lifestyle. In short, they're professionals. This is good, and it's all many are emotionally able to do."

They were leaning forward, hanging on what he said.

"Some special few approach medicine as a ministry, a calling. This is professionalism carried one step further. You truly care for your patient and aren't afraid to show it. You're his advocate in the tangled confusion of the health care system. Don't get me wrong. Nice doesn't replace knowledge, and compassion can't trump competence, but if you can combine all of these, the rewards to your patients and to you personally are immeasurable." He smiled and shrugged. "End of sermon."

"Can you do that all of the time?" Pete asked.

"Goodness, no," Dave said, "but if you consciously try over and over, it starts to become natural. It becomes who you are."

As they rose to leave, Dave said, "I know Hillsdale's a rocking place, but if you're free, you're invited to our house for some light conversation, good wine and Betty's famous beef stroganoff. Any takers?"

"What did you say to those guys?" Betty asked as they drove home the next week.

"What do you mean?"

"They're different; they're respectful; they're nicer. The patients have even commented on it."

"Just a little gentle persuasion," Dave said.

"Well, it worked."

After dinner Dave gathered up the last three issues of The New England Journal of Medicine and headed for the sunroom.

"I've got to stay up on my reading. Those hotshot residents like nothing better than to one up their teacher."

"They're pretty good," Betty said as she opened the newspaper, "but they have a long way to go to catch you."

"Thank you, my dear."

Chapter 19

For the first time in his life Dave felt relatively free, but it was a contradictory freedom. He'd spent his entire life trying to please foster parents, professors, patients, and an angry God. The need to please others and to be liked by everyone had been replaced by a quiet assurance that he was loved and not alone . He still had a nagging notion that somehow his actions were of ultimate importance but had mollified himself with the idea that doing good for its own sake was good enough.

This warm June morning he sat at a picnic table by the river with John Rankin having one of their periodic lunch and discussions.

"How was your hike?" John asked.

"May sixteenth will never be a good day, but we did okay," Dave said.

"You're so much better; everyone comments on it. You're an inspiration to a lot of people."

Dave took a bite of his sandwich and stared at the river. "The price was too high."

John had learned when to keep silent.

"Better than what? Calmer, less anxious? I know what you mean," Dave said. "I like myself more than before; it's just that…" he shrugged and left the sentence dangling.

"I don't know quite how to put it," John said, "but you're different. We've talked a lot during this last year, but you've never again mentioned what happened to you after your heart attack. At the time it seemed to be such a turning point."

Dave smiled. "Oh, it was. I don't talk about it because I'm not sure what, if anything happened, or if it did happen, that I really understand it. There are studies where selective areas of the brain are stimulated and produce long forgotten melodies or memories. You said when I told you about it that you'd heard me say most of those things from time to time—and I had—although in all honesty, I never took them very seriously until then. Perhaps a bunch of oxygen-starved neurons just rekindled recollections of things I'd stated in the past. Whatever it was, if it was anything at all, it and Kelli's death were a turning point, the two sentinel events of my life. But whether it ever happened or not, the odd thing has been how compelled I've felt to live out what I heard, recollected or whatever. Perhaps truth is truth whatever the source."

"Or," John interrupted, "perhaps all truth comes from the same source, whatever the messenger."

"I like that," Dave said. "Keep that up, and I may just stay awake during your sermons."

John laughed, then washed down the last of his sandwich with a swallow of lemonade.

"To more mundane topics, how's the clinic going?"

"Surprisingly well," Dave said. "We're already in the black, and residents are standing in line to work here. Four are staying over the summer."

"A lot of good things have come as a result of Kelli's tragedy. Perhaps 'all things do work together for good'."

"Don't go there," Dave said sharply. "A lot of people have repeated that to me. Maybe it makes them feel more comfortable if God's pulling all the strings, but a funny thing, none of them has really experienced some horrible event that brings about all of this good. If I accept this in the way they mean it, I also have to accept that God killed Kelli for the purpose of making something good happen, and I can't do that. If any good ever comes from this, it will be because some of us have decided to make it so."

Sensing he was on thin ice, John changed the subject. "How's Betty?"

"She still has some really down days, but her old sparkle is coming back. She loves the work," Dave said as he cleaned the remains of lunch from the table. "When we decided to put a satellite clinic in Roaring Fork, she said that as soon as she got her nurse practitioner's degree, she was going to run it. Even though I'm the Medical Director, I'm afraid to tell her no." He laughed. "And that's just the beginning. She's becoming a reactionary activist. Don't mention it yet, but she's about to stand the movers and shakers of this town on their collective ear."

"What do you mean?"

"You know that Boogertown's been condemned, and everyone's having to move."

John nodded.

"They don't want to leave Hillsdale, but the money the plant gave them won't cover buying land and relocating unless they split up on isolated plots out from town. They really want to maintain their community. Well, Betty's decided to give them fifty acres of Uncle Jeb's place by the river to rebuild on."

"Why would anyone object to that?" John asked.

"Even though it will be behind the ridge and a quarter-mile away, the developers are afraid having even unseen African-Americans in the area will lower the property values in the golf course development. I tried to persuade her to go easy, especially considering my escapade with International Chemicals, but she's determined. Said I'm not the only one with wave-making privileges. The more I think about it, the more I'm convinced she's right. I offered to help, but she said that this was her project and my moral support was all she needed. She's really done her homework. I'd hate to be the ones who oppose her at the Planning Commission. She's already lined up Jim Campbell, the reporter from Lexington, to cover the meeting. I don't think they'll have the stomach to publicly fight building homes for dispossessed African-Americans, especially after the speech she's prepared."

"I thought Jeb's place was your retirement nest-egg."

"We've got all we need. Who're we going to leave it to?"

John seemed lost deep in thought. "Several churches, including ours, have been anxious to build Habitat for Humanity homes, but, as you said, the cost of land is prohibitive. Would you consider allowing us to build there? I know there are four projects that are ready to go."

"I'll send Betty to see you. She'll probably find some way to goad you into doing more than that. You know, three years ago this new found independence would've intimidated me no end, but now it's so neat just watching her blossom."

"You've both grown immensely, not just Betty. I predict there'll be more growth and blossoming in ways neither of you ever imagined."

හ

"Have you realized that in three weeks, we'll have been in business for a year?" Dave asked Millie and Betty as they gathered for the monthly planning meeting. "Millie, Betty and I will be back from Aruba on January third. Could you put together a little anniversary party the next week?"

Millie smiled smugly. "Already done. Drs. Wistrom and Burcham, most of the residents and nursing students and all of the volunteers will be there."

"I'll bet you knew about this, too," he said, turning to Betty who feigned ignorance. "Why am I always the last to know? …No, don't answer that," he said with a laugh. "Okay, Millie, how did we do in November?"

"Financially, we're fine," Millie said. "We're seeing over one hundred-fifty patients a day. I'm starting an evening class in office management for the residents. They seem to think that you just come in, leisurely see a few patients, spend a ton on tests while the office manager goes out back and shakes the money tree to cover all costs and a handsome salary."

"I seem to remember a similar course you gave me," Dave said with a laugh. "In fact, you still give me refresher courses. You just don't think I notice." She smiled and winked at him. "Anyway, they need to learn to be practical as well as competent, and it's better coming from you."

"Tamika called me from Lexington and wants to volunteer next summer," Betty said. "Do you think we could use her? I know she can't be much help clinically, but I'm sure we have some gofer work and it would be invaluable for her next year."

"We're looking for two aides," Millie said, "and with summer vacations, we could use an extra pair of hands." She thumbed through her notes. "Two other things. Dr. Maxwell announced he's coming over tomorrow afternoon. You're booked, but I can shift things around. Doesn't he ever ask?"

"Cardiologists don't ask. They proclaim," Dave said. "I wonder what he wants."

"Who knows?" Millie said and hesitated.

"You said there were two things," Dave said.

"Matt Williams called and asked to volunteer. He said he wants no pay. He just wants to see what doctors do. I didn't encourage him, and he said he'd understand if we couldn't use him."

There was a long uneasy silence. Dave looked at Betty who doodled on a scratchpad in her lap but didn't meet his gaze. Clasping his hands behind his head, he stared at the ceiling. Things are going so well . Forgiveness is fine at a distance, but will I be as understanding up close and personal? He inhaled deeply and took Betty's hand.

"I'm willing to try if it's all right with you."

She smiled, squeezed his hand and nodded.

"Dr. Maxwell's here," Millie said. "Should I play a fanfare, or would donuts and coffee suffice?"

Dave laughed. "Don't be too hard on him; he means well. The donuts will be fine."

Millie snorted, laid a box of donuts on his desk and turned to leave only to bump against Bob who burst unannounced through the door.

"Millie, you lovely, efficient hunk of woman," Bob boomed, grabbing her in a bear hug. "You brought donuts, so I love you even more. If you ever want to move uptown and make some real money, just call. I'll hire you in a minute."

"Turn me loose," she said, unable to suppress a smile. "Treat me with respect, or you'll get your own coffee and donuts in the future."

"You do have a way with women," Dave said as Millie scooted out.

"Just comes naturally," Bob said lifting three donuts from the box.

"Has Alice decided what she's going to do?" Dave asked.

"She got accepted for a pediatric residency in Boston. God, it's bad enough that I have a daughter old enough to finish medical school, but even harder to admit that she's going somewhere that rejected me. But," he paused to inhale half a donut, "at least she's off the payroll. Four in college and one in medical school is a real drain." Bob sighed and sipped his coffee. "My blood sugar's back to a functioning level. You're probably wondering if there was some reason other than refreshments that brought me here."

"It had crossed my mind."

"I want you to listen and don't interrupt. Being serious doesn't come easily to me." He gazed out the window as he spoke. "I've been doing some soul searching recently, and I've come to the conclusion that major changes are in order. Sarah said that some people seem destined to serve as role models, pointing the way for the rest of us. You've been that for me."

Dave started to speak. "No interrupting or I'll lose my train of thought," Bob said. "Being around you since Kelli died has made me realize three things. One, time flies. My kids have grown up, and I've barely noticed. In two years Julie will be in college, and then they'll all be gone. Second, nothing is certain. Kelli died, you had a heart attack, and there was no warning of either. Sarah and I aren't immune, and we know it. But most important, I've been amazed at how you've managed to bring new meaning to your life. I want to do that." He paused and looked expectantly at Dave.

"I'm not sure what I'm supposed to say. How do you intend to do this?"

Bob hesitated, seeming to search for words. "I want to spend some time with my kids before they're completely gone. This area has been good to me, and I want to give something back. I've found a good cardiology fellow who agreed to join me. What I'd like to do is give him a good portion of the workload, slow down, and get to know my family. I'd also like to spend a day or two a week working with your program. I'm sure we could work out a rotation for the cardiology residents here. A lot of folks you see here can't afford what they need, and maybe I could help. What do you think? Can you use another body?"

Dave said nothing for a few moments. "I'm dumbfounded. Dr.

Wistrom and I have talked about the need for affordable subspecialists but had hesitated to even float the possibility for fear of frightening the local docs with the threat of competition."

"It would take two to three months to get the new guy in and functioning. Why don't we aim for early April?"

"This is going to be great," Dave said as he split the last donut and handed half to Bob.

Three days later when he arrived home from work, Betty greeted him in the foyer as usual. After a prolonged kiss, he hugged her tightly against him, and nuzzled her hair.

"This is still my favorite time of day," he murmured.

Betty extracted herself from his grasp.

"Come into the sunroom. We've got a package from Tamika."

Betty shook the shirt box-sized package. "I wonder what it could be."

"Why not open it and see?"

"Thank you Mr. Practicality."

Betty tore off the paper. Inside were a smaller package and a Christmas card with a handwritten message.

Dear Dr. and Mrs. DeMarco,
I won't be home until after Christmas, and I wanted to give you a gift. I started needle- point as part of my physical therapy to try to regain the coordination in my hands, but the first two weren't very good. This is a poem Poppa wrote for me. He read this to me many times when I was worried about not being able to go to college because I couldn't play basketball. It really helped. I know how hard Christmas is for you. I hope this is as much help to you as it was to me.
Love,
Tamika

The gift was enclosed in fragile paper with dainty blue flowers.

Betty didn't rip it apart as was her custom, but carefully loosened the yellow ribbon and removed the wrapping, taking care not to tear it. She held up a framed, needle point sampler.

Dreams
Whatever may happen,
Hold onto your dreams.
No matter how hopeless
And futile life seems.
Dreams may seem dead,
But hold tight to them, then
There will come a time
To dream again.

They read and re-read the sampler without speaking.

"What timing," Dave said, clearing his throat. "I'm ready to dream again."

Betty clutched the sampler to her breast, her eyes moist. "They'll be new dreams, different dreams, but I'm ready, too."

Chapter 20

November, 1999

Dave jotted a final note in the chart, laid it on the counter, stretched and headed for his office. His hair was totally gray, and, although he still appeared slim and fit, his gait lacked some of its previous bounce.

"Dr. DeMarco, could I see you for a minute before you leave?" Matt said as Dave passed.

"Millie's going to give me the month end reports. Why don't you sit in? She'll probably teach us both something."

They took their places on either side of Millie, who sat at the head of the large table in the conference room, several neat stacks of computer printouts before her.

"Unless there're any alarming trends, why don't you just hit the highlights? I want to get home and help Betty get ready for tomorrow. You're going to be there, aren't you? Thanksgiving wouldn't be the same without you."

"I wouldn't miss it. Anything I can bring?" she smiled coyly.

"You're bringing your world famous pecan pie, aren't you?" he said in mock alarm.

"Of course. Now let's get down to business. All four clinics are doing well. The only one in the red is Clear Springs, but that's to be expected after just four months. The daily visits are already up to thirty."

"That's great," Dave said. "How's Roaring Fork doing?"

"You better stay on your toes, or it'll be more successful than your base clinic here. You know how well Betty and Tamika have done there. Since Dr. Painter started, and we were able to add residents, it's booming."

"I'd worried about how well the community would accept an African-American doctor. They're pretty insular and conservative out there."

"No problem. They all love Tamika, and I think they'd accept him for no other reason than he's her husband, but it's more than that. He's really good, and so personable. He reminds me a lot of you when you started out." She turned to Matt. "Pay attention to this guy; you can learn a lot."

Matt nodded. "I already have. I wish I didn't have to go back to University Hospital Monday, but my rotation's up."

"We'll miss you," Millie said. "All of the patients' comments about you have been good. You have great potential."

Matt blushed. "Thank you, ma'am."

Millie finished her report, gathered her papers and left, pausing momentarily to pat Matt on the shoulder. "Good luck," she said and left.

After she was gone, Dave turned to Matt. "You don't realize what just happened. Praise from Millie is a rare and precious commodity, but she's right. You've done exceptionally well here. What was it you wanted to talk about?"

Matt toyed with his pen and shifted uneasily. He cleared his throat, took a deep breath, and plowed ahead. "That makes this harder," he said. "I've been trying to screw up the courage to tell you for some time. Dr. DeMarco, I'm not cut out to be a family practitioner."

"Why do you say that? You're an exceptional person and have great potential. You're one of the three or four best residents I've worked with."

Matt wiped the perspiration from his forehead with the sleeve of his lab coat. "I know I've done well, but relating personally to patients is really hard for me. With you and Dr. Painter, it seems effortless; with me it's forced." He paused. "But there's more to it than that. I loved doing research in medical school and seriously considered research as a career, but I wanted to be like you, and I didn't want to disappoint you."

"Disappoint me?" Dave said, his brow furrowed. "How would you disappoint me?"

"I mean, with what I said when you came to see me after…after Kelli, and then the scholarship—Tamika told me what you'd done—I just felt sort of obligated to go into family practice."

Dave stood, walked to him, and put his hands on Matt's shoulders. "You don't owe me anything. If I've been a role model, I hope it's because of what I am, not what I may have done for you. You had an opportunity, and you made the best of it. That's all I asked. I always dreamed of being a family doc, and I was fortunate enough to achieve my dream. What's your dream? What is it you want to do more than anything in the world?"

"I want to do research."

"Can I help?"

"You already have. Knowing the clinical side of medicine will give me a leg on the others, and having been here will surely help me keep the patient's needs first. It's really strange, but for several months something's been pushing me in that direction. I knew that fellowships were extremely competitive, and family practice isn't the usual springboard, but I applied anyway. I thought some mid-level school might take me. Last week I was accepted by Duke… Duke, can you believe it?"

"That's fantastic. I have two requests: be the best darn researcher you can and stay in touch with Betty and me."

Matt stumbled to his feet and threw his arms around Dave. "Thank you, Dr. DeMarco, thank you."

"Poppa Dave, Poppa Dave, get up, get up."

The small black boy bounded onto the bed and threw his arms around Dave's neck.

"Is it daylight yet," Dave asked, hugging the wriggling bundle of energy.

"Yes, and Momma Betty said for you to get up and help fix the turkey."

A few minutes later, still bleary-eyed, he stumbled into the sunroom where Tamika was nursing a small baby.

"Don't look at me," she said. "That was Betty and William's idea. Martin got called to the emergency room about six and his stumbling around woke Elizabeth, and she woke Gretchen, and she woke William, just like a row of dominos. Martin said to tell you that since there were only twelve patients in the hospital, he'd finish rounds and then come on over to help get dinner ready."

"Now that's what I call a dutiful associate," Dave said, softly stroking the baby's cheek.

He walked into the kitchen where Betty kneaded dough on a counter covered with bowls, pans and piles of food. She paused and kissed him, holding her hands wide to avoid dusting him with flour.

"How can I help without getting in the way?"

"Baste the turkey and build a fire. Bob and Sarah will be here soon. Then the most helpful thing you can do is to entertain William and the other children. Just keep them out of here."

"That's a tall order, but I'll try." He grunted as he heaved the monstrous turkey from the oven onto the counter. Its aroma filled the room. "Are you sure this will be enough?" he said with a laugh, wielding the baster like an over-sized syringe.

"There'll be twenty counting Bob and Sarah's kids and grandchildren."

After replacing the turkey in the oven, he poured himself a cup of coffee.

"Elizabeth's a little doll," he said.

"She's living up to her namesake. She has the same temperament Kelli did at that age," Betty said, returning to her bread making.

"Tamika's a wonderful mother. She reminds me of you."

Betty looked up at him and smiled. Her eyes were misty . "Now go stoke the fire." He knew when to leave.

William danced around him as he brought in several armloads of firewood.

"Can I help build the fire, Poppa Dave, can I?"

Dave pulled several sheets from a newspaper.

"Okay, we need to crumple the paper to put on the bottom."

William wadded paper and then broke twigs for kindling. Finally the fire was laid.

"Tamika, do you know anybody who could light the fire?" Dave asked in a loud voice.

"Me, me," William shouted.

The little boy sat cross-legged just off the hearth, entranced by the flames.

"I wish Momma and Poppa could have lived to see them, but you and Betty are wonderful grandparents," Tamika said. "You don't know how much we appreciate your keeping the children while we go to Atlanta. Just the two of us for three days, I can't believe it. We haven't gone anywhere alone in over a year."

"They're wonderful kids. The pleasure's ours, believe me. We're looking forward to doing it more often when you finish your house down below. It'll be nice to be able to walk down to your place and have William climb up here."

The chimes from the door sounded. "Brace yourself," Dave said. "The storm's about to hit."

He opened the door and stepped back as four squealing children swirled past him. Sarah struggled with a large basket of food while Bob balanced a bundled baby in each arm. Dave took the heavy basket from Sarah, who gave him a quick kiss on the cheek.

"Hey, what about me?" Bob said. "I need help, too."

"Ignore him," Sarah said and started back out the door. "Give that to Betty and follow me. There's more food in the car."

"You didn't know what you were getting yourself into," she said when Dave rejoined her outside. "The kids went out to breakfast and will be over later, probably after all of the work's done. This is the first time they've all been home together in so long. I hope we survive it."

"There are three cribs in the downstairs bedroom," Dave said to Bob over the din. "Take Melissa and Jeremy on down. I'll grab the diaper bags, round up the other little critters and herd them to the rec room." He enjoyed being Poppa-in-charge more than he could have imagined.

An hour later, their initial excitement dissipated, the children sat engrossed with Legos and Roadrunner videos.

"Now I understand why only the young can bear children," Bob said.

"Yeah, but it's fun in small doses," Dave said.

"Are you guys going to the game Saturday?"

"No, we're keeping William and Elizabeth for the weekend. Who wants to watch Tennessee pummel the Wildcats, anyway."

"You've got a point, but you're still on for the Louisville game aren't you?"

"For sure," Dave said. "They're right when they say Kentucky football is a pastime, but basketball's a religion, and I wouldn't want to go against my religion."

The children erupted in another spasm of hyperactivity when their parents arrived and did so again later when Sarah came down the stairs and announced, "Dinner is served."

"Whoa, hold on," she shouted blocking their rush toward the stairwell. "Form a line and follow me up; we'll say grace, then you can go to your table in the sunroom. This is an important time, so be very quiet."

To Dave's surprise, they trailed behind her in a solemn procession.

"How does she do that?" he whispered to Bob, who smiled and shrugged.

Everyone formed a circle around the table. The children stared wide-eyed at the huge candlelit turkey surrounded by mounds of food and remained somberly quiet as Tamika took one of the candles, walked to the buffet, and lit two of three candles set in the center.

"I light these candles in memory of Momma and Poppa," she said, her voice catching, and then replaced the candle on the table.

Dave and Betty retrieved two candles from the table.

"We light this candle in memory of Kelli," they said as they lit the one remaining.

After replacing the candles they stepped back into the circle.

"Everyone hold hands and bow your heads while Dave says grace," Betty said.

They all complied except William, who peeked over his clasped hands at Dave. Dave winked at him and then began.

"Father, we around this table thank You: for Your gift of life, a life in which we have known neither hunger nor want, for friends who are with us in good times and bad, and for loved ones who, though no longer with us, live always in our hearts and whom we know we will see again. We give You our thanks for these blessings spread before us and for the happiness yet to come. Amen."

ꟹ

December 18, 1999

"Four together, center court, who needs tickets, I'll buy your tickets." A gauntlet of scalpers lined the sidewalk approaching Rupp Arena trying to determine who were the basketball fans and who were the Christmas shoppers. Downtown Lexington was packed.

They waited, while Bob went through his ritual of bargaining, just to find out what the going price was.

"Nothing like the Kentucky-Louisville game to bring out the big bucks," he said rejoining them. "A hundred-fifty apiece. Man, I'm glad we got ours back when they were cheap. They must think Tubby's a miracle man." He turned to Dave as they walked on, "I just hope Magloire can keep from fouling out."

"Yeah, and if Bogans and Prince can hit a few threes early, that should loosen them up and make it easier for him," Dave replied.

"Just like two little boys," Sarah said to Betty with a laugh as they watched them dissect the team's chances as they had done before each game for as long as they could remember.

"Sarah, Dave, look," Betty pointed to two small girls dressed in Kentucky cheerleader uniforms with blue cat whiskers radiating from blue painted noses. There was a time when this scene would have devastated her, but now it triggered warm, fuzzy memories of a similar night many years ago.

The girls skipped along, chattering and tossing a miniature blue and white basketball back and forth, oblivious to the crowd of towering adults.

"Get your tickets, two together. Hey, watch it, kid," the scalper shouted as the girl nearest the curb ploughed into his leg.

The ball bounced past her into the street and, scrambling back to her feet, she dashed after it. Betty and Sarah screamed simultaneously as a car bore down on her. Dave lunged after her, grabbed the neck of her uniform and flung her back toward the curb. Only then did the driver hit his brakes, but it was too late. The car smashed into him and tossed him like a rag doll into the path of another car going the opposite direction.

There was no pain. In fact he felt oddly calm as he watched Betty, Bob and Sarah rushing to him.

"Oh, Dave, no, please be okay," Betty knelt over him. A trickle of blood drained from his mouth. She could see he was trying to speak and knelt lower.

"How's the little girl?" he gasped.

"She's fine," Betty said as her tears dropped onto his face.

A faint smile. "Good." Her face began to fade, and he stared intently at her, trying to memorize every feature. "I love you. I'll meet you in the foyer."

He recognized the familiar floating sensation as, for a brief moment, he gazed down on the crowd gathering around his lifeless body. Then he turned to see the glowing tunnel of light he knew would be there. He understood no more than he had long ago, but he now waited with an almost welcome anticipation. A brilliant concentration of light drifted down the tunnel and stopped before him.

"I'm going this time?" he said, more a statement than a question.

"Yes."

The voice he perceived seemed familiar, but before he could say anything further he began to take on the same brilliant luminescence as the form. Rapturous joy flooded his entire being as the form clasped his hand and without looking, he knew it was smiling.

"This is only the beginning, Daddy. Come on, let me take you home." For a moment he hesitated.

"What is it?"

"I never did do 'one great act.'"

"Oh, Daddy, don't be silly. You did that years ago. Look," Kelli said.

In amazement, seeing the future with eyes no longer limited to the immediate present but seeing all time—past, present, and future—as part of the eternal now, he looked.

"Of course," he said with a smile and, hand-in-hand they floated along the tunnel to the shimmering radiance ahead.

Epilogue

The faint smell of roses and lilacs from nearby gardens wafted over the crowd seated in folding chairs before a raised platform. A tall man spoke from the podium, his patrician bearing enhanced by his flowing silver hair which gleamed in the warm May sun.

"...and last, but by no means least, the president of the great University of Kentucky, Dr. Maxwell Dorfmann."

A rotund man rose from the group of dignitaries on the platform, acknowledged a smattering of applause, and sat down. The crowd stirred restlessly, and a gaggle of reporters talked and joked among themselves as the speaker droned on, trying to wrap himself as much as possible in the significance of the event.

"This occasion brings me more pleasure than any other since I've been governor of the great Commonwealth of Kentucky. We are here today to break ground for the Kelli DeMarco Institute of Basic Research which will be one of the leading centers for immunological research in the country, and to honor the man who made it possible. Funding for this project was begun by the generous donation of over three million dollars by our guest of honor. This represents the entire amount he received for the 2019 Nobel Prize in medicine for his work in developing the first effective vaccine for malaria which the World Health Organization states will each year save the lives of over a million children below the age of five. The New York Times said, and I quote, 'His innovative discovery of immunologic enhancement is a paradigm shift in medical thought, a quantum leap in preventive medicine no less significant than the work of Louis Pasteur, and is the first real hope of finding a safe and effective vaccine for the HIV virus.' I don't pretend to begin to understand his work, so with no further ado I give you the first director of the institute, a native son, Kentucky's own, Dr. Walter M. Williams."

As the governor took his seat, a tall, slightly stooped man with thinning, prematurely gray hair walked to the podium. The crowd rose and welcomed him with thunderous applause. He smiled and gazed out at them until they quieted.

"Thank you so much for that kind greeting. I will be brief." The crowd laughed appreciatively. "As you know, I grew up not far from here, and it feels good to be home to stay. The governor would have you believe that this has been the work of a solitary genius on the order of Albert Einstein. I am most certainly not in that league. This accomplishment was the result of many things. Some of it was just plain hard work, which I learned from my father," he said motioning to a stocky, elderly man behind him who squirmed uncomfortably at the attention. "Isaac Newton once said, 'if I have seen further, it was by standing on the shoulders of giants.' Much of my work I owe to those giants who broke ground and labored before me. Part of my inspiration came from a childhood friend for whom this institute is named, but two events, more than any other things, made it possible for me to be here today. As the newspaper said, this is a radical new approach to the immune system. I wish I could claim it solely as my own, but its discovery did not spring totally from my knowledge or training alone. Instead, the core idea came to me in a flash from somewhere beyond myself. For some reason unknown to me, I was chosen to be the one who received the message. The second event was of even more significance. A senseless tragedy almost prevented me from entering medicine at all, but because of a simple act of forgiveness by two dear, kind people I was able to become a doctor."

As he said this, his voice broke. He removed his glasses, blotted his eyes with his handkerchief and took a deep breath.

"I've come to believe that through love and forgiveness God can work backward into time, transforming suffering and tears into something good, and, in the end, can bring beauty from ashes.

Thank you."

The crowd once again rose and applauded. He turned and motioned for a small woman whose gray hair still showed a glint of its previous auburn hue to come forward. He put his arm around her as they acknowledged the applause. Her eyes glistened as she stood on tiptoe and kissed him on the cheek.

"Thank you, Matt," Betty said.

The End

The Compassionate Friends

The Compassionate Friends (TCF) is a national nonprofit, self-help support organization offering friendship, understanding, and hope to families grieving the death of a child of any age, from any cause. There is no religious affiliation. No individual membership fees or dues are charged, and all bereaved family members are welcome. Founded in England in 1969, TCF was established in the United States in 1972. TCF has nearly 600 local chapters throughout the United States. There are separate TCF organizations in an estimated 30 countries around the world.

For further information, contact:
The Compassionate Friends, Inc.
P.O.Box 3696, Oak Brook, IL 60533-3696
Toll-free: (877) 969-0010
Fax: (630) 990-0246
E-mail: nationaloffice@compassionatefriends.org
Web site: www.compassionatefriends.org

Introducing another book by Richard Dew...

RACHEL'S CRY
A Journey through Grief

The idea for a book of poetry came to me in the aftermath of the murder of my son, Bradley. Having read poetry since I was a child, after Brad died, I searched for poems that might help me cope. I found very few.

As a therapeutic outlet for my erratic emotions, I began writing poems of my own. Not only did this help me, but also it helped other bereaved parents when I shared some of them.

I realized a collection of poems dealing with the many aspects of losing a child would be helpful to other parents in my position, when they have precious little energy or motivation for searching. With such a collection of poems, a bereaved parent could have something readily at hand that might strike just the chord needed for some consolation. *Rachel's Cry* is that collection of poems — to help process, help comfort, and help one get through the next day or even the next hour.

The response has been gratifying. I have received hundreds of letters from bereaved parents and siblings saying how helpful it had been. To my surprise, many people grieving the death of a spouse, parent, grandchild, or friend also wrote. I even received two letters telling me how it had belped the writers cope with a divorce.

I feel this book can be beneficial for anyone who has experienced the death of a child or knows someone who has. It is also an appropriate gift when you do not know what to do for such a person. The following are a few excerpts.

Excerpts from *Rachel's Cry* by Richard Dew ...

A cry is heard in Ramah,
Lamentation and bitter weeping,
Rachel, weeping for her children,
Refusing to be comforted
Because they are no more.

Jeremiah 31:15

Excerpts from *Rachel's Cry*
by Richard Dew ...

An Ordinary Day

It was just another day.
No one special came.
Nothing unusual happened.
The evening was the same.
Just an ordinary day
And then the telephone rang.
From that monemt on forever
Everything was changed.

They've Got Each Other

Quiet comes the dawn through curtained windows,
Quiet as their breathing, pretending sleep.
Carefully not touching, for fear stray
Spasms betray silent sadness and sobbing.
Or, even worse, be misconstrued as a
Prelude to intimacy and rejected.
Finally, stirring with elaborate
Stretching and yawning, they confront the day.
"How did you sleep?" "Fine, and you?" "Okay."
Quaickly completing the morning ritual,
Newly self-conscious they dress. At breakfast
They speak in simple questions and answers,
Avoiding sharing, lest control be lost.
With an automatic, chaste peck on the cheek
They part with a secret sigh of relief.

"How could you possibly
Think about that?
And with him barely
Six months gone from us?
You men are all alike.
You have no conception.
Don't you understand?
Nine long months in me,
I carried him there.
I nursed and nurtured,
Now nothing. I'm numb.
I can't just pick up
And get back into
Life and work and sex.

"Damn! Why'd I do that?
I knew she wasn't
In the mood for romance.
She never is anymore.
It's not enough
That I've lost a son,
I've lost my wife, too.
Doesn't she realize?
My future is gone.
I am so lonesome.
I need to hold her
And be held in return.
Am I now so repulsive
We can't even touch?

Why don't you talk
To me? You're like a lump.
Sullen and surly
You snap off my head
If I mention his name.
You don't even cry.
You haven't been back
To the grave. Not once!
I don't think you care.
You sit and mope or
You just work, work, work.
What's the matter with you?"

Why won't she stop talking?
It tears me apart
To constantly dwell on him.
It's all I can do
To not break down and cry.
Must she visit the grave?
I can't stand that place!
I need to be alone.
With some peace and quiet
I can make it through.
Thank God, I have my work.
What's the matter with her?"

"How was your day?" "Fine, and yours?" "Okay."
Stiffly the afternoon ritual is done.
After another question and answer meal
And an awkward, near wordless evening
Of vacantly reading and watching TV,
With reluctance they rise and retire to rest.
"Help me," she silently screams at him.
"Hold and console me," his soundless reply.
Suppressing the love they're desperate to keep,
The motionless lie and mutely weep.
Quiet comes the night through curtained windows,
Quiet as their breathing pretending to sleep.

Would You?

To love is to risk,
With risk may come loss,
And loss is full of pain.
In full knowledge of this,
Would I want to go back
And do it all over again?

That we ever had you
Was a gift undeserved,
Unexpected and unearned,
An answer to prayers,
A completeness and wholeness
For which we had yearned.

The time that we shared
Was the Spring of my life,
But I expected Summer and Fall.
Still, if forced to choose,
I'd take Springtime alone,
Than to never have known you at all.

TO ORDER

Rachel's Cry and more copies of *Tunnel of Light* may be purchased at Dewbooks.com or by check (include your name and address) mailed to P.O. Box 1457, Gatlinburg, TN 37738.

Rachel's Cry	$10.00, plus $3.95 Shipping and Handling
Tunnel of Light	$13.95, plus $3.95 Shipping and Handling

With the purchase of 2 or more books, shipping and handling is $3.95 for the entire order. For orders of 10 or more books, contact me rates at 1-866-839-2044 about bulk shipping rates.